HOW TO APPROACH THE CHINA MARKET

English Version of JAPAN-CHINA TRADE HANDBOOK

JAPAN EXTERNAL TRADE ORGANIZATION
JETRO

A HALSTED PRESS BOOK

JOHN WILEY & SONS
NEW YORK

HOW TO APPROACH THE CHINA MARKET

LIBRARY OF CONGRESS CATALOG CARD No. 72-3843

DISTRIBUTED IN THE WORLD EXCEPT JAPAN

by

HALSTED PRESS DIVISION, JOHN WILEY & SONS, INC.

NEW YORK

ISBN 0 470-44265-4

Printed in Japan

Published
by
PRESS INTERNATIONAL, LTD.

3—1—21 Kami-Osaki, Shinagawa-ku, Tokyo, Japan

Tel.: 441—8465

PREFACE

With the admission of the People's Republic of China to the United Nations, United States President Richard Nixon's visit to China and other international developments involving that country, the multi-faceted activities of China in the international community have been increasing.

China's foreign trade has been growing both in volume and value year after year. Trade has witnessed a high rate of growth since 1966, and is assumed to have reached a record high during the 1970 to 1971 period.

Trade between Japan and China since 1950 has registered an aggregate value of $5,876 million. Japan is now China's leading trade partner.

In order to further promote trade between the two countries, the Japan External Trade Organization (JETRO) published the "Japan-China Trade Handbook" in Japanese in order to facilitate Japan's trade with that country in response to the trends in China's political as well as economic affairs.

JETRO, in the belief that this handbook, a primer for China trade, will be of great benefit not only to Japanese enterprises but also overseas businessmen who are interested in trading with China, decided to publish an English language version of the "Japan-China Trade Handbook."

We hope that the English version, "HOW TO APPROACH THE CHINA MARKET," will be of great use to those who are planning to trade with China and contribute greatly to their establishment of friendly relations with that country.

Yours sincerely,

February 14, 1972

President, Kichihei Hara

Japan External Trade Organization

FOREWORD

This publication is intended to provide an authentic, timely, and informative description of the history, development and current state of China's foreign trade. Originally entitled the "Japan-China Trade Handbook" and written in Japanese, it was designed to aid Japanese enterprises in opening up and expanding trade with China. Evidence that it is serving its purpose, is the increasing number of Japanese firms initiating trade contacts with the Chinese for the first time and the fact that the book sold 7,000 copies in the space of a few weeks.

WRITTEN BY the Japan External Trade Organization (JETRO), a semi-governmental agency of the Japanese Ministry of International Trade and Industry, the book was compiled and published in Japanese to facilitate the initiation of trade contacts with Chinese officials by Japanese enterprises. JETRO, the trade promotion arm of the Japanese Government, with 25 local offices throughout Japan and 69 overseas branches, performs a broad range of trade promotion activities throughout the world. Publication of the China handbook has substantially contributed to the present mood in Japan calling for a wide range of trade activities including not only increased trade but the exchange of technological know-how through personnel exchanges with the Chinese.

TRANSLATED AND PUBLISHED in English by Press International Ltd., a leading Japanese press research organization located in Tokyo, and renamed "HOW TO APPROACH THE CHINA MARKET," the book provides a unique combination of historical, statistical, and authoritative up-to-date information about China's foreign trade activities. Press International undertook the translation and publication of this work in English with the hope that it would be of benefit to enterprises in other parts of the world whose interest in China trade is rapidly increasing. The ultimate aim of Press International in the translation of this work, has been to most closely duplicate the meaning in the Japanese text, and in such a way contribute to the library of authoritative works which have been written about the People's Republic of China.

Press International has also published several booklets containing translations of feature articles appearing in Japanese newspapers about various topics of the day such as "United States-China Relations," and the affect of the so-called dollar shocks on Japan-United States relations. Through these publications and its daily press translation, THE JAPAN BULLETIN, Press International attempts to provide in-depth information about the business practices, thinking, and general activities of Japanese enterprises and trade organizations.

During the 1950's, a period when the rest of the world enjoyed little contact with China, Japan succeeded in establishing a dialogue with the Chinese in the form of trade contacts. Recently, with the announcement and culmination of United States President Richard Nixon's visit to China, and the admission of China into the United Nations, the eyes of the world's trading nations have turned toward China. Boasting a population of 800 million and with the initiation of her fourth 5-year economic development program, China's market promises to be the single largest source of demands for industrial plants, transportation· equipment, machinery and other items too numerous to mention here for some time to come. As a result, numerous enterprises in various countries are eyeing possible trade contacts with China.

"HOW TO APPROACH THE CHINA MARKET" is intended to serve as a handbook for those enterprises desiring to establish contacts as well as friendly relations with the Chinese. Knowledge and an understanding of the successful systems of Japan's trade with China will be an invaluable aid to those enterprises which desire to initiate trade negotiations with the People's Republic of China.

THE EDITOR

March 7, 1972

HOW TO APPROACH THE CHINA MARKET

CONTENTS

TABLES

HOW TO
APPROACH
THE CHINA MARKET

I. INTRODUCTION

In the People's Republic of China such expressions as "dida," "wubo," and "renduo" are used frequently. Founded in 1949, the People's Republic of China has a total land area of 9,550,000 square kilometers, including Tibet and Sinkiang Province, representing seven percent of the world's entire land surface. The southern and northern portions of China extend into the tropical and sub-frigid zones respectively, to conform perfectly with the expression "dida," which means vastness of land.

"Wubo" means an abundance of untapped subterranean resource deposits, potential sources of electric power and farm products. It is estimated that China's coal deposits amount to 1,500,000 million tons, iron ore deposits 100,000 million tons, and petroleum several billion tons. China's sources of hydroelectric power alone are estimated to total 540 million kilowatts. In addition, the estimated deposits of nonferrous metals including antimony and tungsten are said to be the world's largest. Agricultural production, when modernized, will certainly increase greatly. As a result, the expression "wubo" has come to be used widely in China.

"Renduo" is an expression meaning large population, and it is frequently used to refer to China's huge population of approximately 800 million people, which accounts for about a quarter of the world's total population. This is "renduo," indeed.

Such rich deposits of natural resources are certainly of great advantage to China's economic development. Therefore, an effective integration of these factors is of the utmost necessity for the development of her national economy.

The founding father of China, Sun Yat-sen, once stated that China had long been subjected to semicolonial treatment and continued oppression by Britain and other European powers for many years. Under such circumstances and with the outbreak of revolutionary wars and foreign invasions into the country following the collapse of the Ching Dynasty, China witnessed constant warfare being staged throughout the country. In addition, the exploitation which took place under a system of feudal landownership, complete with fiefs and landowners, made it utterly impossible for China to build a national economy as a modern nation and left the country in a completely retarded semicolonial state. Consequently, the country had little accumulated capital and her industrial development was limited to light industries since there was no foundation for modern industrial development. As a result, the technology needed for industrialization of the country made no progress whatsoever, and the country had to depend upon primitive extremely Low-productivity agriculture which prevented the accumulation of capital necessary to initiate reproduction on a progressive scale.

Since the founding of the People's Republic of China, however, the country has made great steps forward toward modernization through reorganization of its social structure, which used to be the fundamental defect in the nation's economy, in addition to investments and the accumulation of capital.

Following the successful formation of the People's Republic of China, the government of China carried out the first, second and third 5-year programs and achieved considerable success. Through the Great Cultural Revolution which began in 1966, and the 9th National Convention of the Chinese Communist Party, the nation's economy was steered onto a path toward stabilization. The country started its fourth 5-year program in 1971. Throughout these programs the Chinese Government has promoted socialization of the national economy and in particular the development of heavy industries. Success in heavy industrial development contributed much to establishing the bases for the development of modern industries. On the other hand, modernization of agriculture through the formation of People's Communes is being carried out extensively. Since mid-1968 in particular, China's economy has made marked progress to reach an all-time high in 1970.

China has come to exert great influence on world politics. Recognition of the Chinese Government by major western nations including Britain, France, Italy, and Canada, and in particular China's admission into the United Nations in October 1971, are having far-reaching effects on the international political situation.

The key objectives of China's foreign trade were the establishment of an independent trade system by eliminating the undeveloped trade setups and unequal semicolonial conditions that existed prior to the founding of the People's Republic of China while building a planned trade to meet the demands of developing a socialist economy. In 1949, China declared that one of its general principles would be to restore and develop commerce and trade relations with foreign governments based on the principles of equality and reciprocity, with these two being the most important principles.

As a result the Chinese Government is directly responsible for foreign trade and the establishment of trade systems in response to the demands of an independent and planned economy. For this particular purpose, the foreign trade of China is completely controlled by the state, with trade corporations and the Bank of China, which are government organizations, in charge of actual business transactions. In so doing, the country has closely coordinated foreign trade with domestic economic development programs, thereby making the most of import trade in developing her economy.

Therefore, the actual operation of China's trade policy is carried out in accordance with governmental trade agreements. After these agreements are concluded, arrangements are made based on long-range agreements and the policy of maintaining a balance between exports and imports. In connection with this policy, the Government of the People's Republic of China issued the following statement:

> "We strongly urge development of well balanced trade among all countries involved in China trade. Only an equilibrium between imports and exports can successfully eliminate unilateral payment difficulties and contribute to the normal and stabilized development of trade."

Japan has no governmental trade agreement with China; as a result Japan has carried out trade with China in accordance with private trade agreements. Trade with China through pro-China friendly trading houses and enterprises as well as memorandum trade, sometimes dubbed the "two wheels of a cart," are all private, "friendly" transactions. Chinese organizations represented in these negotiations are the China Committee for the Promotion of International Trade and the China-Japan Memorandum Trade Office.

Japan's trade with China has grown favorably since trade relations between the two countries were reopened in 1961, to reach a total value of $625 million in 1969, $822 million in 1970, and $900 million in 1971. Japan ranks first among China's trading partners and holds a 20 percent share of China's foreign trade.

With United States President Richard Nixon's July 1971 announcement of his planned visit to Peking and China's admission to the United Nations, the United States eased a Treasury Department Export Control Act involving China trade, in order to prepare for an imminent opening of trade relations with China. This is having far-reaching effects on Japan and the policies of other nations of the world, greatly altering the situation which has prevailed since 1949, and paving the way for possible stabilization of trade relations between China and the free world.

II. ORGANIZATIONS AND SYSTEMS FOR FOREIGN TRADE

A. BASIC POLICIES

The basic policies of Chinese external trade can be boiled down to the establishment and development of an independent state-run trade structure, and the execution of planned trading in response to demands for socialistic development based on the principle of self-reliance while emerging from the binds of underdeveloped trade as well as the unequal, semicolonialistic relations with foreign countries that existed prior to the founding of the People's Republic of China.

Cited as specific policies which will be taken by China to achieve these particular objectives are:

1. The enforcement of planned trade.
2. The employment of a protectionist trade policy.
3. Endorsement of the principles of equality and reciprocity in trade with other countries.
4. Endorsement of a policy asserting the inseparability of politics and economics.

Let us begin first with a review of planned trade.

The People's Republic of China, since her founding, has been importing those types of goods necessary for socialistic development in accordance with prearranged import programs, while exporting goods according to similarly prearranged export programs mapped out in light of domestic needs in order to achieve the goals of her import programs.

China's trade controls, which entail a strict approval system, comprise the administrative controls of the Chinese Government on the quality, quantity and prices of goods to be imported or exported, socialization of trade corporations and the state monopoly on foreign exchange. Consequently, almost all of China's foreign trade is conducted by state-run trade corporations through governmental agreements concluded between China and other countries, all of which are long-term arrangements accompanied by planned trade.

In this manner, China's foreign trade is executed within the framework of allocations set by the government for each ministry involved in accordance with national programs; however, judging from the recent trend of China's import activities, top priority in economic policies has been given to the expansion of agricultural production, with the emphasis on imports of fertilizers, agricultural machinery and equipment capable of directly contributing to the expansion of agricultural production including pumps, motors, tractors and transport equipment, or textile products and raw materials to serve the needs of the farming population.

As a consequence of China's trade being a state-run business, enterprise profit is not considered important in terms of import and export prices as in capitalistic countries. And, if the necessity should arise, it is quite possible for the country to purchase import commodities at prices surpassing world standards, although such standard prices are taken into account as references. Likewise, there is also the possibility of exporting at prices lower than the international standard in order to obtain foreign currencies. However, since trade corporations can benefit from importing at the lowest possible price while exporting at the highest possible price, it is quite natural that they should make the utmost efforts along this line. As a result, price negotiations on occasion meet with difficulty.

The second point pertains to the nation's protectionist trade policy. Although priority is given to the import of critical material in China, restrictive measures including protective customs duties are imposed to protect and aid the growth of domestic industries. For this purpose, tariff rates which run from a minimum of 5 percent to a maximum of 500 percent, are set in line with industrial promotion, and important import and export commodities are designated for direct handling by state-run trade corporations.

Exports are valued as highly as imports since they enable China to obtain the necessary foreign exchange reserves with which to buy them. Consequently, whether or not China's economic programs are attained depends greatly on the success of export activities. For this very reason, China adopts a protectionist trade policy.

The third feature of China's external trade is that it is based on the principles of equality and reciprocity, to which China's principle of barter trade in transactions with foreign countries is also attributable. In actual business dealings however, China follows a realistic policy depending upon the situation. In fact, in trade with Soviet bloc countries, China has done business more on a government set price basis than in her trade with free world countries.

What cannot be disregarded as the fourth characteristic of China's foreign trade is her policy of asserting politics and economics to be inseparable in the execution of trade. China's trade policy with free world countries is to exert China's influence as strongly as possible in an effort to further the socialist cause. In that sense, as far as China is concerned, economic activities that come under the heading of trade are considered to involve political ideology, and the rule of politics and economics being indivisible can be thought of as a firmly established rule in that nation.

For specific examples, China was quick to conclude a contract with Egypt for the import of cotton when that country was attacked over the Suez Canal issue. Also, China immediately purchased sugar from Cuba at the time of that nation's confrontation with the United States. For yet another example, China, an importer of foodstuffs herself, continued to export rice for political reasons to food importing countries in Southeast Asia as well as on several occasions supplying Japan's small and medium size enterprises with goods that the Japanese enterprisers greatly desired.

B. IMPORT PROGRAMS AND TRADE SETTLEMENT FORMULAS

1. Formulation of Import Programs

China's import programs consist of annual, quarterly, and long-term plans, each of which are worked out in the latter half of the preceding year. These programs are produced through the following procedures:

a. The Ministry of Foreign Trade, in conjunction with related divisions, sets a target figure for each exporting country and each group of goods, in accordance with China's foreign exchange reserves and the possible supply of the respective goods from overseas countries. This target figure also serves as a temporary index of the annual volume for goods to be imported.

b. The target figure(s) is presented by the Ministry of Foreign Trade to national trade corporations, which in turn work out the details. The trade corporations, in accordance with the particulars provided by the Ministry of Foreign Trade, process orders for the import of goods from demanding organizations. Meanwhile, those placing orders draw up application forms denoting the import demand volume for commodities, keeping within the framework of the target figure set for each government ministry.

c. The Ministry of Foreign Trade adjusts the target figure(s) based on the import demand volume for commodities verified by the government, and then readjusts the annual import programs on a country-by-country, item-by-item basis.

The quarterly programs are formulated chiefly on the basis of annual import programs, the contracts concluded with each foreign country, and actual changes which might occur during the course of contract execution.

The quarterly programs also perform a vital role in materializing and completing annual import programs prior to their expiration date.

Long-term import programs are worked out by the Ministry of Foreign Trade after consultation with each ministry concerned with the respective programs, and are drafted on the basis of the long-term national economic program (5-year plan), taking into consideration the long-term supply capacity of each exporting country and China's foreign exchange reserves. These plans are executed with the approval of the State Planning Commission which is responsible for the drafting and execution of long-term economic programs, and the State Economic Commission which is responsible for the drafting and execution of short-term economic programs.

The most important procedures during the course of executing import programs are the formulation of, and study of application forms which indicate the demand volume of goods to be imported. Since these applications are closely related to the country's economic policy and the production programs of the demanding ministries, a clear-out system of sharing responsibilities is employed among the national organizations, with responsibilities being borne by concerned production organizations according to the type of goods ordered. Other related organizations also participate in reviewing applications; however, the final responsibility for overall evaluation and equalization rests with the economic planning bureau in charge.

The Ministry of Foreign Trade is also tasked with the responsibility of formulating a list of applications denoting the import demand volume of commodities. At present, in China, these applications are categorized as follows:

a. Estimated Commodity List (estimated cargos): Catalogues for commodities listing only the most important commodities and the amounts which must be purchased during that particular year.

b. Overall Commodity Catalogue: Produced on the basis of an overall listing of goods validated by the government which lists reference numbers, nomenclature of goods, quantity and value.

Table II-1 — Chinese Trade Programs and Working Mechanisms

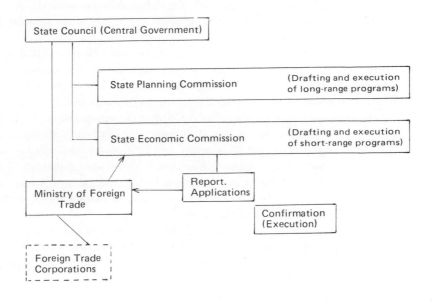

NOTE: The State Planning Commission and the State Economic Commission validate demands for goods by taking into consideration comprehensive programs, the balance between export resources and import demands, in addition to the status of foreign exchange reserves. The Ministry of Foreign Trade studies annual exports, supply programs, import programs and foreign exchange reserves in conjunction with production and the demanding ministries and organizations concerned with the drafting of import and export programs on the basis of data provided by the foreign trade corporations.

c. Import Commodity Demand Volume Cards: They contain the basic data concerning specific commodities to be imported, and are produced for use in conducting trade talks and concluding delivery contracts. A list of prices to be used as references is attached to the card when an order is placed with non-socialist countries.

The demanding organization which is tasked with placing an order fills in an import commodity demand volume card in accordance with its demands for commodities to be imported. This is in turn presented to the ministry in charge of production of the commodities concerned.

The ministry which receives the card, if after an appropriate study finds that the domestic industry can fully meet the demand, concludes a delivery contract with the demanding organization for the delivery of domestically produced products. When local production is incapable of meeting the demand and imports are required, the demanded volume is placed into a comprehensive annual catalogue of commodities to be imported for presentation to the planned economy organization, the State Planning Commission. The State Planning Commission, taking into account the economic outlook and supply and demand relations, presents its decision to the Ministry of Foreign Trade, while coordinating supply and demand in the light of data provided by that ministry.

The Ministry of Foreign Trade dictates that the foreign trade corporations under its jurisdiction make a detailed study of the technical data entered on the demand volume cards which includes nomenclature, specifications, quantity, use, delivery periods, consignee, the country with which the order is to be placed, or a country-by-country order allocation. This particular study is conducted on the basis of the demand volume cards verified by the government ministry, the target figure for allocation of foreign exchange provided by the Ministry of Foreign Trade and data on the domestic demand volume and the capability of overseas countries to supply the goods.

The foreign trade corporations then make a further detailed study on allocations for each exporting country and technical data, and send the results of the study to the Ministry of Foreign Trade where the study results are incorporated into a comprehensive catalogue of commodities for approval by the national organization.

2. Settlement Formulas

a. Settlement with Communist Countries

Payment for goods imported or exported between China and Communist bloc countries, and payments incidental to trade as well as economic and technological cooperation, are settled through the open account system based on the barter trade payment agreement between China and the country involved and the agreements between trade organizations of each country regarding delivery conditions.

Each country balances the volume of goods to be supplied during a one-year period, offsetting credits and debts with one another, and as far as possible negating the necessity of clearing the books with gold bullion or foreign currencies. Outstanding debts or accounts at the end of the settlement terms are balanced with additional orders for the supply of goods for the following year.

The currency used for settlement is the ruble; however, the Renminbi (RMB)* and Vietnamese currency are used in the case of limited frontier trade with North Vietnam. Payment temporarily made in the currencies of free world countries is to be settled in the currency agreed upon by the national banks of both countries.

The organizations in charge of effecting trade settlements are the national banks of the respective countries, with the People's Bank of China representing China. For the purpose of trade settlement, the national banks of both countries concerned mutually open a non-interest, non-commission ruble account. This particular account is termed, for example, the "1970" Trade Liquidation Account." Irrespective of whether or not an outstanding account remains on the books of the national bank of the partner country, payment is immediately entered into the debt side of the liquidation account.

When a contract is concluded for the sale or purchase of goods between the national trade organizations of the countries concerned, the seller presents documents on the goods shipped to the national bank of his country; the national bank then confirms the documents for immediate recording of payment amounts on the credit side of the seller's account, and, at the same time, also enters it on the debt side of the national bank account of the buyer's country. The bank then sends a payment notice and the documents to the national bank of the buyer's country, which, upon receipt, enters the payment on the credit side of the national bank of the seller's country based on the payment notice from the seller's national bank, and at the same time, collects the amount of payment specified in the notice from the trade organization of the buyer's country. In the case of transactions between China and the Soviet Union, it is specified that the buyer must make payment

---

* People's Note in English (Name for Chinese Currency)

within 10 days after its national bank receives this notice.

As far as liquidation methods at the end of settlement terms are concerned, the balance due on commodities is always settled within the shortest amount of time (usually 3 months); however, in case the balance is excessively large, it is cleared either by postponing the settlement term or through the issuance of import credits. As for individual agreements, there are of course some differences depending on the country involved. For instance, in the case of the China—USSR agreement concluded in April 1950, it is specified that the balance will be settled by "commodities, gold, the American dollar or the British pound sterling," while the agreement with Czechoslovakia reads: "The balance is to be settled in the currency agreed upon by the national banks of both countries."

In regard to pricing the commodities to be bartered, the China-Soviet agreement specifies, "The prices of commodities shall be based on international market prices," while the agreement with Poland concluded in April 1957, stipulates, "The price of commodities shall be based on the international market price at the time contracts are signed, and calculated in the ruble based on conversion rates promulgated by the national bank of the Soviet Union."

b. Settlement with Developing Countries

Settlement with those countries with which China has close trade relations is made in accordance with a governmental payment agreement concluded by both countries. Payment agreements are either independent agreements or contained in the trade agreement itself.

Among the developing countries with which China concludes independent payment agreements along with trade agreements are Burma, the United Arab Republic, Morocco and Brazil. China's trading partners which have a clause stipulating payment within the trade agreement include Ceylon, Guinea, Ghana and Mali. Some countries employ a liquidation account system in accordance with the payment agreement or payment clause stipulation. In some cases, Chinese banks open a deposit account with either one of the banks of the country involved, or that of a third country for the mutual settlement of liabilities and credits.

However, in any settlement formula (between banks), settlement is always made through letters of credit (L/C). The most widely used type of letter of credit is a payment against documents. Letters of credit for China are handled by the Bank of China, a sub-contracting bank that handles foreign exchange affairs for the People's Bank of China.

In the case of the liquidation of accounts system, China often agrees to use the currency of her trading partner as legal tender for trade payments. Some stipulations regarding the institution of liquidation accounts call for the use of "non-transferable booking currency" to be used in effecting payments. However, the pound sterling, the Swiss franc, the Hong Kong dollar and other convertible currencies of a third country are generally employed, and the dollar is not used. The agreements or clauses between China and Burma, the UAR, Afganistan and other countries stipulate that the pound sterling shall represent 2.48828 grams of gold per pound, and that should there be a change in the value of the pound sterling, the balance shall be readjusted according to the new gold standard. In trade with Guinea, in which the currency of that country is specified for use as payment, the pure gold backing one Guinea franc is set at 0.0036 grams, and, in the event the Guinea franc's value in terms of gold should decrease, or increase in excess of 2 percent, the balance shall be readjusted accordingly. The trade and payment agreements between China and Ghana stipulate that the pure gold backing per Ghana pound shall be 2.48828 grams, and, in case there is a fluctuation in the value of gold, the balance shall be readjusted. The commodity barter and payment agreement with Mali tentatively sets the required gold backing per Mali franc at 3.6 milligrams, with the balance being readjusted when there is a change in the value of the currency.

In the case of settlement via the liquidation accounts system, the maximum limit of swing is usually stipulated. The limit is £500,000 in trade with Burma, £2,600,000 with the UAR, £1,500,000 with Tunisia and 250 million Mali francs in trade with Mali.

c. Settlement with Capitalist Countries

China's trade settlements with major capitalist countries are made chiefly through letters of credit (rarely letters of guarantee). In most cases, the Bank of China, China's foreign exchange bank, handles the settlement of accounts in accordance with correspondence agreements concluded with the foreign exchange banks of the respective trading countries. In trade with the Scandinavian countries, Finland, Sweden, Denmark and Norway, China maintains a governmental trade agreement which contains a payment clause; however, the payment clause itself is an independent payment agreement for which China's national bank and those of her trading partner countries mutually open a non-interest, non-commission-type bank account to handle payments.

Under the China-Finland governmental payment clause, which is in the form of an independent payment agreement, the People's Bank of China opens a ruble account in the name of the Bank of Finland while Finland's bank opens a similar ruble account in the name of the People's Bank of China (both of the ruble accounts are of the non-interest, non-commission type). Further, it is stipulated that the pure gold value per ruble will be 0.987412 grams.

When either the People's Bank of China or the Bank of Finland make payment drawn on the amount entered in the ruble account of the respective national bank for juridical persons or natural persons of the respective countries, payment is made irrespective of whether or not the balance on the books of the bank which issued the payment is on the books of the paying bank. When either one of the ruble accounts opened with the People's Bank of China or the Bank of Finland, respectively, turns out to be an outstanding debt in relation to the other, and when the amount of outstanding debts exceeds 1.8 million rubles, the debtor country is requested to make the utmost efforts to bring this amount within a framework of 1.8 million rubles as soon as possible. In the event the debtor country is unable to do so within a period of four months, it must pay the sum that exceeded the stipulated amount within one month at the request of the creditor country. Whether such payment is made in the ruble or the currency of the country is left to the discretion of the creditor country.

The trade and payment agreement between China and Denmark stipulates that payment is to be made either in the Danish krone based on the "convertible krone account" of China's national bank opened with the Bank of Denmark, the convertible pound sterling or the currency of a third country which both countries agree to accept.

Settlement with Britain, West Germany, France, Belgium, the Netherlands, Switzerland, Italy, Australia, New Zealand and Japan, is made by means of a letter of credit or a letter of guarantee in accordance with the correspondence agreements which the Bank of China has concluded with the banks of the respective countries. The Bank of China has branch offices in London, Singapore, Karachi and Hong Kong.

The letter of credit, a major means of settlement for foreign trade, allows the bank which provides the letter of credit to make actual payment after ascertaining that there are no mistakes in the bill of exchange or the attached bill of lading forwarded by the seller himself or his bank. In short, a buyer of the country trading with China can import from China with the aid of his bank's guarantee, provided he forwards a letter of credit through his bank. Therefore, it is not necessary to remit cash to China beforehand, but payment can be made after the bills of exchange and other applicable documents are received from the Bank of China.

In the meantime, a seller can obtain loans necessary for the shipment of goods with his bank upon obtaining a letter of credit from China. When a bill of lading as specified in the bill of exchange and the letter of credit is prepared after shipment is made, the seller can forward them directly to the Bank of China through his bank for timely collection of payment. The seller's bank can accept these bills from the seller without risk thanks to a double guarantee — international confidence in the Bank of China, and possession of the cargo through acquisition of the shipping documents.

In dealings with major advanced industrial nations, the cash settlement system is generally employed between China and those countries with which she has concluded governmental trade agreements. However, China has been moving toward the employment of flexible settlement formulas, including partial adoption of a long-range comprehensive barter trade system, a deferred installment payment system for massive imports of wheat and the like, and a long-range deferred payment contract with western countries for the purchase of plants, machinery and equipment.

3. Foreign Trade Control Systems

China's trade controls, which comprise controls on quality, quantity and the price of goods to be exported and imported, socialization of trade corporations and the state monopoly on foreign exchange, is regulated by means of a rigid approval system.

According to the publication, the "External Trade of New China," published in 1955, the objectives of China's foreign trade appear to be:

a. Keeping China's economy and her industrial production free from the domination of the imperialists, thereby preventing imperialistic "dumping" and head off influences from crises in the economies of capitalistic countries.

b. The elimination of reckless speculative management within the country which destroys national domestic economic programs and endangers the interests of the people, while putting trade controls into force and incorporating private enterprises into the national economic programs in order to promote socialistic development.

c. Planned usage of foreign exchange by restricting imports of non-essential goods, thereby accelerating economic development, preventing an excessive outflow of national resources by exporting and assisting domestic production.

All the trade corporations, agencies and schools engaged in foreign trade are subject to government controls. At present, China's import and export activities are handled by the import and export corporations on a commodity-by-commodity basis; for example, the imports and exports of iron and steel are handled by the National Metals and Minerals Import and Export Corporation of China.

The trade corporations are under the jurisdiction of the Ministry of Foreign Trade. Special corporations under the jurisdiction of the Ministry of Commerce perform the same function as the trade corporations and handle domestic distribution of goods. However, each corporation under the jurisdiction of the Ministry of Commerce does not handle all of the domestic distribution. The Headquarters of Supply and Sales, the Sales Bureau and the Supply Bureau under the control of each industrial ministry concerned, the General Bureau of Supply and Sales linked with the Cooperatives and Sales and Supply Department of the People's Communes perform their respective business in the domestic aspect of distribution. At any rate, state-run organizations are involved in any of these activities.

Domestic distribution programs for commodities were prepared prior to 1960 and are executed systematically through a Goods Balance Table System, which maintains a coordinated balance between imports and exports. For instance, the distribution, procurement and supply of iron and steel, a major production factor, are balanced by the state. Prior to 1958, the State Planning Commission of the central government handled matters relating to systematic distribution and supply; however, this distribution system was replaced in 1958 by a new system of "systematic balancing, concentrated distribution and classified controls." In short, distribution and supply plans for iron and steel were changed from an item-by-item basis, although steel materials continued to be balanced and distributed by the State Planning Commission as one of the materials of general importance (e.g., coal, lumber, machinery and the like), while secondary products (nails, wire rods, electric welding machines, screws, tin products, copper products and the like) are systematically controlled and supplied by the Ministry of Commerce. Domestically-produced goods in the provinces are supplied with an eye to balance by the respective organizations and the authorities in charge of the respective provinces. All of this means a major transfer or diffusion of administrative authority. As another means of distribution, the Goods Balance Tables System is employed. This particular system was created in 1959, with priority being given to iron and steel, colored metals, ores, coking coals, machinery, petroleum, equipment for producing electric power, cement and lumber.

4. Tariff System

China employs a protectionist trade policy and therefore has a number of customs regulations. Included among them are "The People's Republic of China's Provisional Customs Law and Rules for the Operation thereof," "Import and Export Customs Duties Regulations and Rules for Operation" (publicly announced on May 4, 1951), and a detailed "Export and Import Tariff Rate Table." In addition to these, there are regulations concerning ports-of-call for ships, tourist baggage, preferential treatment for Chinese baggage returning from overseas, international shipping and freight, rail and air freight as well as cargo in transit.

a. Tariff Assessment

Import goods are assessed on the basis of CIF prices (including normal wholesale prices on spot purchases, export duties, packaging costs, shipping charges, insurance premiums and a commission, decided by the customshouse after appropriate evaluation, for handling charges until the goods are unloaded at their destination), while export goods are assessed on the basis of FOB prices. Particularly, goods that are imported, with the exception of bonded imports, must undergo customs clearance procedures or a customs duty must be paid within 3 months from the date a transportation organization reports the importation of the goods. In the event these procedures are not followed, the imported goods are subject to forfeiture.

b. Import Tariffs

Imports are classified into 17 groups, 89 types and 939 items. There are two types of tariff rates for each commodity, which is to say, the minimum rate of 5 to 150 percent, and the normal rate of 7.5 to 400 percent. Minimum tariff rates are applied to the goods of those countries with which China has a reciprocal trade agreement, and the regular rates are applied to the commodities of all others. In general, construction materials, raw manufacturing materials and machinery are subject to lower tariff rates while higher ones are levied on silk fabrics, high-quality watches and cigarettes. Educational films and platinum are tax free.

c. Export Tariffs

All but 96 items including peanuts (15%), peanut oil (19%), tung oil (19%), peppermint and its oil (55%) and pig hair (30%) are exempt from export duties.

5. Trade Control Organizations

The key organs of China's trade control organization are the Ministry of Foreign Trade and the foreign trade corporations. The Ministry of Foreign Trade, one of the organizations composing the State Council, works out export-import programs and foreign exchange balance of payment programs. It is also responsible for directing the foreign trade corporations in their execution of these programs. The foreign trade corporations are under the control of the Ministry of Foreign Trade which is the mainstay for the actual transaction of foreign trade.

As organizations that assist the Ministry of Foreign Trade and the foreign trade corporations in securing uniformity in trade activities, there are the Merchandise Survey Inspection Bureau and the General Customs Office, which is in charge of customs clearance procedures and issues export and import permits. In the provinces there are Regional Trade Control Offices, which are substructures of the Ministry of Foreign Trade. Meanwhile, the customs authorities have branch offices in the regional control offices and the Merchandise Survey Inspection Bureau is with the Regional Merchandise Survey Inspection Offices in the provinces.

a. The Ministry of Foreign Trade

In September, 1952, the Ministry of Foreign Trade separated from the Ministry of Commerce to become an independent ministry for China's foreign trade activities, and is now the supreme administrative organization that coordinates the foreign trade corporations.

The major activities of the Ministry of Foreign Trade include:

(1) The formation and execution of import and export programs as well as foreign exchange balance of payment programs through the authority vested in it by the State Council.

(2) Administration of the General Customs Office and the Merchandise Survey and Inspection Bureau (a nationwide organization for the inspection of import and export goods), and issuance of permits for exports and imports as well as in-transit cargos.

(3) The development of trade relations with foreign governments and peoples based on the principles of equality, reciprocity, mutual assistance and cooperation; conduct of trade negotiations with foreign countries on trade and technological cooperation with authorization granted by the State Council and the conclusion of contracts on behalf of the government.

(4) The direction of the foreign trade corporations in developing decisions pertaining to business operations, approval of fiscal programs, operations and controls on trade commodities, pricing of import and export goods, and domestic marketing.

As regional agencies for the Ministry of Foreign Trade, there are the Foreign Trade Control Bureau (or the Foreign Trade Bureau), the Customshouses and the Merchandise Survey and Inspection Bureau.

The Foreign Trade Control Bureau is an organization of the People's Committee (Provincial Government) in each province, under the jurisdiction of the regional government and also under the direction of the Ministry of Foreign Trade. Included in its major activities are:

(1) Guidance and control over the regional foreign trade control organizations and enterprises, and presentation/administrative control over the annual and quarterly programs for provinces, cities and communes under its jurisdiction.

(2) Improvement of the economic activities of the trade corporations, and guidance on such matters as cost reduction and quality improvement of commodities to be exported.

(3) Survey of the situation surrounding import and export goods at home and abroad.

(4) The collection and study of informational material regarding marketing situations.

(5) Research on new goods to be exported.

b. Overseas Branch Offices

As trade organizations of the Chinese Government posted in overseas countries, there are the Commercial Committee Member Offices, Commercial Councillors at Chinese Embassies, and Trade Representative Offices which are created on the basis of the agreement signed with each particular foreign country involved in trade with China, and the overseas branch offices or overseas agents of the state-run foreign trade corporations.

The functions of the overseas trade organizations are as follows:

(1) Promotion of economic exchanges with China and the country

in which they are located on behalf of the Chinese Government.

(2) Coordination of trade with China and the countries where they are located.

(3) Conclusion of trade negotiations and contracts in the countries where they are located.

At present, China has such offices in all the Socialist countries in addition to many other countries including Afganistan, Britain, France, Denmark, Finland, Norway, Sweden, Switzerland, Burma, Ceylon, Pakistan, Nigeria, the United Arab Republic, Ghana, Guinea and Cuba.

c. General Customs Office

Under the jurisdiction of the General Customs Office which is located in the Ministry of Foreign Trade, are the customshouses at each port-of-call that have branch offices located at points of entry into and exit out of the country including Tientsin, Shanghai, Tsingtao, Canton, and Chanchiang.

The customshouses handle the overall operation of external trade controls including customs affairs and administrative functions related to foreign trade. Among the specific functions of the customshouses prescribed under the Provisional Maritime Customs Laws of the People's Republic of China are:

(1) Controls on cargos and currencies entering or leaving the country.

(2) Assessment and collection of customs duties.

(3) Policing of illegal export or import traffic.

(4) Enforcement of the foreign trade permit system as well as price assessment.

(5) Administrative control over the registration of trade organizations.

(6) Formulation of import and export schedules at each seaport.

(7) Formulation of customs clearance statistics on external trade.

d. Merchandise Survey and Inspection Bureau

The Merchandise Survey and Inspection Bureau which is located at each of the principal ports and harbors, is an organization responsible for inspections of the quality, weight and specifications of export and import goods and the issuance of certificates of inspection and appraisal. In addition to cargo inspections usually conducted by the state, the Merchandise Survey and Inspection Bureau is somewhat different from the inspection offices of other countries in that it also handles the collection of special goods and other services for the export organizations.

e. The China Committee for the Promotion of International Trade

The China Committee for the Promotion of International Trade was founded on May 4, 1952 in Peking based on an agreement reached at an international economic conference held in April of the same year in Moscow for the purpose of promoting East-West trade. The committee is of a semi-governmental nature and is composed of government representatives connected with foreign trade affiliated ministries, representatives from the national trade corporations, legal experts, scholars and labor union representatives. Attached to the committee are the Administrative Office, the Trade Fair Department, the Liaison Department and the Arbitration Department. They are responsible for liaison with foreign trade organizations, presentation of informative material on Chinese trade, arbitration of claims, arbitration of maritime affairs, production of informative material on foreign economy and trade, inviting foreign trade representatives to China and dispatching of Chinese trade representatives to foreign countries, as well as arranging trade fairs.

In concluding trade agreements with foreign countries, the Ministry of Foreign Trade signs governmental agreements on behalf of the Chinese Government, while the China Committee for the Promotion of International Trade is responsible for initialling private trade agreements.

f. State-run Trade Corporations

The national trade corporations are organized on the basis of the commodities they handle and have branch offices in China's major trading cities and at the nation's seaports. Each corporation is a self-supporting institution that handles orders for specific commodities in accordance with programs drawn up by the State Economic Commission.

In line with an increase in merchandise and a clarification of the business to be handled, the export and import corporations, as organizations designed to handle business related to imports and exports, have been subjected to reorganization, integration and establishment of new divisions on several occasions. At present there are seven import and export corporations; namely, the China National

Trade Organizations of China

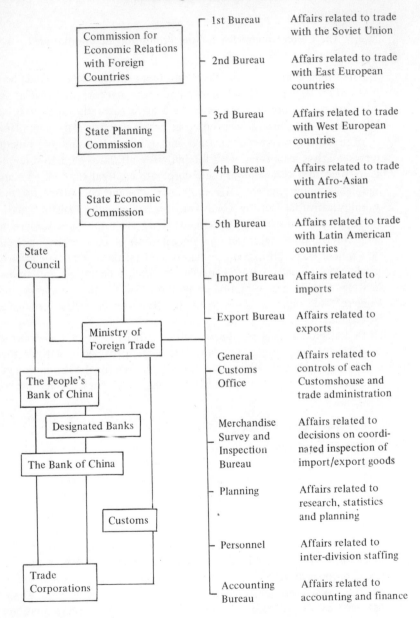

Organization	Affairs
1st Bureau	Affairs related to trade with the Soviet Union
2nd Bureau	Affairs related to trade with East European countries
3rd Bureau	Affairs related to trade with West European countries
4th Bureau	Affairs related to trade with Afro-Asian countries
5th Bureau	Affairs related to trade with Latin American countries
Import Bureau	Affairs related to imports
Export Bureau	Affairs related to exports
General Customs Office	Affairs related to controls of each Customshouse and trade administration
Merchandise Survey and Inspection Bureau	Affairs related to decisions on coordinated inspection of import/export goods
Planning	Affairs related to research, statistics and planning
Personnel	Affairs related to inter-division staffing
Accounting Bureau	Affairs related to accounting and finance

Commission for Economic Relations with Foreign Countries

State Planning Commission

State Economic Commission

State Council

Ministry of Foreign Trade

The People's Bank of China

Designated Banks

The Bank of China

Customs

Trade Corporations

Cereals, Oils and Foodstuffs Import and Export Corporation; the China National Native Produce and Animal By-Products Import and Export Corporation; the China National Textile Import and Export Corporation; the China National Light Industrial Products Import and Export Corporation; the China National Chemicals Import and Export Corporation; the China National Metals and Minerals Import and Export Corporation; and the China National Machinery Import and Export Corporation. As related organizations, there are the China Ocean Shipping Company and China Ocean Shipping Agency.

6. Foreign Exchange Control Organizations

Prior to the founding of the People's Republic of China, neither a stable currency nor monetary system existed in China, and the currency to be used in trade settlements was left up to the discretion of the foreign countries with which she traded. Foreign currencies were circulated throughout the country. Of course there was no foreign exchange control. However, the People's Republic of China, after it was founded, standardized currencies on a regional basis, prohibited the circulation of foreign currency, established the People's Bank of China as the central bank of the country, and issued the Renminbi notes. The state monopolizes foreign exchanges and the use thereof, and foreign exchanges including those for non-trade purposes are all controlled by the People's Bank of China. At present, the Renminbi notes are not used in trade settlements; however, such currencies as the Russian ruble, the British pound sterling and the Swiss franc, in addition to the currency of China's trading partners, are used in effecting payment settlements. The US dollar is not used as a result of a United States measure in 1950 which froze the dollar for use in trade with China. This measure was set aside by the United States Government in April 1971, again permitting use of the dollar in trade with China.

The objectives of China's foreign exchange controls are to effectively and advantageously meet the demands of socialistic development through trade with foreign countries and handles the remittance of funds from Chinese trading firms abroad as well as surmounting the historical barriers of a monetary system that has long been neglected. Accumulated foreign reserves are placed under the control of the State Economic Commission for distribution in accordance with China's economic programs.

A government regulation entitled "Temporary Measures on the Allocation and Use of Foreign Reserves," published in October of 1950, stipulates the major function of the foreign exchange controls to be as follows:

The State Economic Commission shall be the organization in overall control of foreign exchange reserves and foreign exchanges shall not be used without its authorization. The People's Bank of China will make scheduled reports to the State Economic Commission on the amounts of accumulated foreign reserves, and the commission will in turn regularly inform the bank of the manner in which foreign exchanges are to be allocated.

Foreign reserves are to be used for the import of production materials necessary for the execution of economic programs as well as the purchase of consumer goods, and used as sparingly as possible for goods which are not essential.

The national trade corporations are to apply through the designated organizations for the allocation of foreign reserves. A similar application is also to be made for non-trade use.

The General Customs Office shall issue an import permit when an application for the allocation of foreign reserves has been made through the above procedure.

a. Foreign Exchange Banks

China's foreign exchange controls are administered through the People's Bank of China and its designated foreign exchange banks under the control of the State Economic Commission. The designated foreign exchange banks which are made up of 15 semi-government banks and their branch offices including the Bank of China, are banks authorized to handle foreign exchanges. Selling and buying of foreign exchanges, foreign banknotes and gold or silver bullion, are monopolized by the state-run banks.

(1) The People's Bank of China

The People's Bank of China, founded on December 1, 1947 through the integration of four commercial banks which existed at the time, is the central bank and incorporated into the Government Organizations Law as one of the official organs of the Chinese Government. With headquarters in Peking, the bank had a total of 23,000 branch offices throughout the country and 330,000 employees as of 1957. Following the conversion of the agricultural villages across the nation into People's Communes, the smallest units of the bank in the rural districts were integrated into credit departments of the People's Communes and placed under the systematic control of both the People's Bank of China and the People's Communes. The major business functions of the

People's Bank of China include the following:

(a) Printing, issuance and control of all currency in circulation.

(b) Savings and loans.

(c) Control and management of currency, transfer operations and financial matters of state organizations and the People's Communes.

(d) Payment agreements with foreign national banks and control of foreign exchange reserves.

(e) Management of monetary affairs and the monetary market.

(f) Accounting for the national treasury (state budgets, revenue and expenditures).

(g) Flotation of national bonds.

(h) Management of the Bank of China and other banking institutions.

(2) The Bank of China

The Bank of China, which handles most of China's foreign exchange activities, is a specialized foreign exchange bank of China founded in accordance with "Regulations for the Foundation of the Bank of China" set down in 1950. Of a total of 600,000 shares amounting to 189,000 million yuan upon which the bank is capitalized, 400,000 shares are held by the Chinese Government, representing a strong shade of government influence in it's operation. Although the bank is on the same standing as other foreign exchange banks, it does not have the authority to control or direct other banks.

The Bank of China has branch offices in principal cities across the country, with a network of branch offices located in various parts of the world. Its major overseas branch offices are located in London, Singapore, Karachi and Hong Kong.

The Bank of China's major business functions include buying and selling foreign exchanges, extension of short-term loans for exports and imports and the remittance of funds from Chinese firms overseas.

b.   Foreign Exchange Quotations

The People's Bank of China in September 1949, began publishing two different kinds of quotations, rates for exchange (trade), and those for remittances (non-trade). A year later, in September 1950, the bank announced a single standard nationwide exchange rate. In March of the same year, a denomination was carried out to reduce the old Renminbi note of 10,000 yuan to the new Renminbi note of 1 yuan; however, the rates created at that time have undergone almost no change since then.

Exchange quotations are made on single rates, with no distinction between telegraphic transfers or payable on-sight quotations; buying and selling quotations are set within a fluctuation margin of 0.5 percent on either side of the basic rate.

Buying and selling quotations are non-existant in Socialist countries. The Soviet Union, Poland, East Germany, Czechoslovakia, Hungary and Bulgaria have exchange rates for non-trade purposes, in addition to the basic rates. The exchange rate for non-trade matters with the USSR is set at 100 rubles to 166.67 yuan, while trade exchange rates are set at 100 rubles to 222.22 yuan.

Trading Partners	Unit		Yuan
Canada	1	Canadian dollar	0.43666
Switzerland	100	Swiss francs	56.30
West Germany	100	DM	67.26
Britain	1	pound	5.908
France	1	franc	44.30

NOTE: These figures are the same as those used at the Canton Trade Fair in October, 1971.

All rates are based on the yuan-pound sterling exchange rate.

III. CURRENT STATE OF CHINA'S FOREIGN TRADE

A. OUTLINE

1. Particularities in China Trade

The foreign trade of China is, as is naturally assumed in terms of its nature as a socialist country, controlled by the state. It is a protectionist trade designed to develop domestic industries in order to build a socialist society as well as being a trade based on the principles of equality and reciprocity irrespective of whether its trading partner is a communist country or a free country. These characteristics have not changed even to the present day, more than 20 years after the founding of the country.

China's foreign trade is systematically controlled and executed as a means of serving socialistic industrialization. Consequently, priority is given to those imports which will aid in rapidly building China into an industrialized nation.

Therefore, as to particularities in China trade, in the case of exporting goods to China, export efforts, no matter how hard they may be, frequently end in failure for those goods which are not incorporated into the import programs of China. Since China's foreign trade is a totally state-controlled trade, which is not always conducted based on economic principles and is placed under highly centralized power, almost no trade contracts through China's overseas branch agencies or trade agents are successfully concluded. Trade contracts must be negotiated with the organization concerned in the China mainland itself.

Furthermore, China adheres to a trade policy that asserts politics and economics to be inseparable, and political affairs exert a strong influence on trade relations. For instance, political factors such as the "Flag Incident" in Nagasaki, Japan, or ideological disputes with the Soviet Union are likely to cause China to unilaterally sever trade relations with the

Table III-1 — Chinese Trade with the Communist and Non-Communist Blocs (1950 – 1969)

(Unit: $1 Million)

Year	Total Area Trade			Communist Bloc Trade				Non-Communist Bloc Trade			
	Export	Import	Total (A)	Export	Import	Total (B)	B/A (%)	Export	Import	Total (C)	C/A (%)
1950	620	590	1,210	210	140	350	28.9	410	450	860	71.1
51	780	1,115	1,895	465	510	975	51.5	315	605	920	48.5
52	875	1,015	1,890	605	710	1,315	69.6	270	305	575	30.4
53	1,040	1,255	2,295	670	885	1,555	67.8	370	370	740	32.2
54	1,060	1,290	2,350	765	970	1,735	73.8	295	320	615	26.2
55	1,375	1,660	3,035	950	1,300	2,250	74.1	425	360	785	25.9
56	1,635	1,485	3,120	1,045	1,010	2,055	65.9	590	475	1,065	34.1
57	1,595	1,430	3,025	1,065	870	1,935	64.0	530	560	1,090	36.0
58	1,910	1,825	3,735	1,250	1,100	2,350	63.0	660	725	1,385	37.0
59	2,205	2,060	4,265	1,595	1,365	2,960	69.4	615	695	1,310	30.7
1960	1,945	2,030	3,975	1,320	1,285	2,605	65.5	625	745	1,370	34.5
61	1,525	1,495	3,015	965	715	1,680	55.7	560	775	1,335	44.3
62	1,525	1,150	2,675	920	490	1,410	52.7	605	660	1,265	47.3
63	1,560	1,200	2,755	820	425	1,245	45.2	740	770	1,510	54.8

Year	Total Area Trade			Communist Bloc Trade				Non-Communist Bloc Trade			
	Export	Import	Total (A)	Export	Import	Total (B)	B/A (%)	Export	Import	Total (C)	C/A (%)
1964	1,770	1,475	3,245	730	395	1,125	34.7	1,040	1,080	2,120	65.3
65	1,955	1,740	3,695	645	480	1,125	30.5	1,310	1,260	2,570	69.5
66	2,170	2,035	4,205	595	505	1,100	26.2	1,575	1,530	3,105	73.8
67	1,915	1,945	3,860	460	340	800	20.7	1,455	1,605	3,060	79.3
68	1,890	1,820	3,170	460	340	800	21.6	1,430	1,480	2,910	78.4
69	2,060	1,825	3,885	460	325	785	20.2	1,600	1,500	3,100	79.8
Total	31,410	30,440	61,840	15,995	14,160	30,155	48.7	15,420	16,270	31,690	51.3

NOTE: (1)   Figures in the original table for the 1950 – 1965 period were calculated by rounding off to the nearest million. Therefore, the total figures added together may not exactly agree with the total.

(2)   Trade reported by Free World countries has been adjusted for time leads and lags in shipping, shipping costs, double counting, and unrecorded transactions.

SOURCES: (1)   For 1950 – 1965, *"An Economic Profile of Mainland China"* Vol. 2, P. 584.

(2)   For 1966 – 1969, compiled on the basis of *"Current Scene"* October 7, 1970.

country involved.; however, political influence on trade became somewhat less apparent in the 1960's.

In addition, since China promotes trade based on the principles of equality and reciprocity and depends on barter trade for trade transactions with foreign countries, they may be forced to import non-essential goods at higher prices than the international standard in order to expand Chinese exports.

With respect to actual dealings, no international commercial practices have been established, especially for the protection of patents, technical know-how, industrial designs, or procedures for inspection and the lodging of claims. Moreover, entry into and exit out of China, as well as the permissible period of stay and travel throughout the country are all rigidly restricted. As a result, it is impossible to satisfactorily conduct commercial or market research activities within China. Next, let us observe the characteristics of China's recent foreign trade.

One item to be noted is a change in the trading pattern. Countries in the communist bloc have made it a rule to handle three-quarters of their trade within the bloc, and China is no exception. However, as a result of a series of natural disasters for three consecutive years beginning in 1959, and a continuing decline in China-USSR trade, which was at its peak in 1959 but dropped off afterwards due to Chinese criticism of the "big-power chauvinism" of the Soviet Union, China's trading pattern has turned from sole dependency upon the communist bloc toward expanded trade with free world countries.

The second is the failure of China's economic development to proceed as planned as the result of a sharp increase in emergency imports of foodstuffs. This was due to a substantial shortage of foods and raw materials caused by a decrease in agricultural output because of the series of natural disasters which began in 1959, thereby reducing the nation's status from that of a food exporter to an importer. Consequently, a massive outflow of China's foreign exchange reserves for the purchase of foodstuffs put the brakes on production and impeded imports of capital goods necessary for socialistic industrialization.

2. Development of China's Foreign Trade

If the developments in Chinese foreign trade are examined carefully, a general increase and decline is observed in proportion to the growth in the country's national income in real terms. China's external trade began to level off during the period from 1955 to 1957; however, it began climbing again in 1958 to register a postwar high of $4,265 million including both imports and exports. This, however, started declining again in 1960 to record a decline of 7 percent for the year, 24 percent for 1961 and 11 percent for 1962, when it fell to $2,675 million, a decline of roughly less than 70 percent compared with 1959.

The stagnation in China's foreign trade during the 1956 to 1957 period was attributed directly to a decline in agricultural production due to natural disasters and an economic readjustment policy adopted during that period which included a cutback in investments. In the meantime, the decline in trade after 1960 was due in part to a decline in the national economy of China and also partly to suspension of Soviet economic and technological assistance to China as a result of a confrontation between the two countries.

However, in line with the recovery of China's domestic economy, in 1963 China's external trade showings took a turn upward, with exports recording an increase of 2 percent and imports 4 percent respectively over the preceding year. Total trade amounts for 1963 chalked up a rise of 2.9 percent over the preceding year. In addition, China's domestic economy recovered further in 1964 and surplus production permitting a resumption of exports was achieved. Shipments to Southeast Asia, Japan and West European countries increased, while imports of capital goods started going upward gradually, boosting China's total trade volume to $3,200 million in 1964, a 17.9 percent increase over the previous year.

China, after having achieved a complete recovery from its economic recession, decided to go ahead with its third 5-year program beginning in 1966. As the country started massive imports of machinery, iron and steel, and chemical fertilizers in preparation for increased industrial and farm production as well as implementation of the new long-range program, trade amounts for 1966, the initial year of the 5-year program, reached almost the same level as the all-time record of 1959. However, due to the Great Cultural Revolution which began in 1966, a number of problems including transportation difficulties emerged to present a number of adverse factors that restrained the expansion of China's foreign trade for a brief period.

In 1969, deteriorating relations between China and the Soviet Union began to exert a decisive influence and as a result two-way trade between the two countries registered only $56.8 million. In striking contrast with this, however, China's trade with advanced industrial nations (West European countries and Japan) gradually spiralled upward and trade with the Soviet Union began to mean less as China came to place overwhelming importance on her trade with non-communist bloc countries.

The composition of import goods gradually took shape in the latter half of the economic readjustment period which took place from 1956 to 1957. Among them, grains, materials for industrial construction including iron, steel and machinery, as well as agriculture-supporting goods such as chemical fertilizers became the three main items. This could be attributed to a policy switchover by Chinese authorities placing priority on agriculture as opposed to the emphasis on heavy industries. Although this pattern of imports has been basically maintained up to the present day, machinery and iron and steel have once again come to hold major importance in line with the progress of China's industrialization during the third 5-year program.

As agricultural production recovered, the exports of farm products and the processed goods thereof increased. Meanwhile, importance is gradually being attached to goods using a higher degree of processing technology in line with the industrialization of the country.

B. DEVELOPMENT OF AREA-WISE TRADE

China's international trade, at a peak in 1966 when it totaled $4,205 million, reverted to a downhill trend for two consecutive years in 1967 and 1968. However, thanks to a favorable increase in agricultural and industrial production, China's total amount of trade turned upward in 1969 registering $3,885 million, a 4.7 percent increase over the previous year. China's domestic economy began expanding in 1969 and the upward trend of her foreign trade activities became even more marked in 1970. Trade with major countries in the first half of 1970 showed a drastic increase of 18 percent compared with the corresponding period of the preceding year.

China's trade volume in 1969, as shown in Table III-1, was $2,060 million for exports and $1,825 million for imports, revealing an export surplus of $235 million; total trade amounted to $3,885 million, a decrease of 7.6 percent in comparison with 1966, but a 4.7 percent increase over 1968. Since imports were on almost the same level as the previous year, the increase in overall trade volume was due to China's increase in exports which resulted from positive efforts to expand export activities supported by import controls and a high level of agricultural and industrial productivity.

Observing trade trends in terms of area, Chinese trade with western industrialized countries in 1969 (13 countries in Table III-2) reached $1,499.6 million. This consisted of $652 million for exports and $847.6 million for imports, a 10.9 and 2.8 percent increase respectively over the previous year. These figures fell short of the $1,544 million recorded in 1967, but showed a 6.1 percent increase over 1968; however, the rate of increase in exports surpassed those of imports, and exports to Japan, West Germany, Britain, France, Italy and Switzerland exceeded those of the previous year. Another factor worthy of note is that imports from Japan and Britain drastically increased over the preceding year by 20.9 and 78.5 percent respectively. The increase in imports from Japan was caused by a sharp increase in imports of iron and steel (which account for 41.8 percent of all Chinese imports from Japan) and machinery (12.4 percent) by 19.9 percent and 46.7 percent respectively over the preceding year. As far as Britain is concerned, the increase in imports from that country was due to a rapid increase in the imports of industrial diamonds (which constitute 18.3 percent of the imports from Britain), and nonferrous metal (54.0 percent) by 84.9 and 189.5 percent respectively over the previous year. The increase in exports to Italy and France was caused by an increase in the exports of raw silk and textiles to those countries. Raw silk occupied 41.9 percent of total exports to Italy in 1969, showing a 54.4 percent increase over the preceding year. In trade with western industrial nations in 1969, China overimported by some $195.6 million, but this margin was considerably smaller in comparison with the $252 million and $236.7 million overimported in 1967 and 1968, respectively.

In trade with wheat exporting countries (4 countries in Table III-2), China overimported by a margin exceeding $187 million during 1968 and 1969. Wheat accounted for over 90 percent of China's imports from these countries, Canada in particular, from which 97 percent or more of China's total imports consisted of wheat. A peculiar characteristic is the fact that China alternately imports wheat from Canada and Australia.

The trade volume with wheat exporting countries in 1969 registered $302 million, showing a 0.7 percent decrease compared to the previous year, mainly influenced by a decrease in imports which is attributable to delays in signing wheat purchase agreements. On the other hand, exports such as peanuts, walnuts, low-grade textiles (cotton sheets, pillowcases, gloves, towels, and the like) are increasing slowly but steadily each year.

Trade with countries in Southeast Asia (Hong Kong Singapore, Malaysia, Ceylon and Pakistan) reached an unprecedented level of $890.3 million, consisting of $706.2 million in exports, a 3.6 percent increase over the previous year and $184.1 million in imports, a 5.8 percent increase. This resulted from an increase in the exports of livestock, fruits, vegetables, meat and meat processed goods, eggs, clothing and other foodstuffs to Hong Kong. The rapid increase in imports was due to an increased amount

Table III-2 — Trends in Chinese Trade with Major Countries (1966–1969)

Yearly Exports and Imports Countries	1966			1967		
	Export	Import	Total	Export	Import	Total
Japan	306.2	315.2	621.4	269.4	288.3	557.7
Britain	94.7	93.6	188.3	81.6	108.1	189.7
W. Germany	92.5	129.4	221.9	76.6	206.6	283.2
France	53.9	92.5	146.4	48.1	93.2	141.3
Italy	56.5	62.8	119.3	57.7	73.9	131.6
Belgium·Luxembourg	15.4	20.3	35.7	13.0	22.7	35.7
Switzerland	16.0	21.3	37.3	17.5	21.3	38.8
Denmark	6.9	2.5	9.4	8.9	6.0	14.9
Netherlands	30.2	16.1	46.3	27.8	12.2	40.0
Sweden	14.4	24.7	39.1	17.0	43.9	60.9
Norway	4.9	5.3	10.2	5.2	7.5	12.7
Austria	9.2	4.7	13.9	8.4	13.7	22.1
Yugoslavia	2.0	0.2	2.2	14.4	1.0	15.4
Total Western Industrialized Countries	702.8	788.6	1,491.4	645.6	898.4	1,544.0
Argentina	0.4	84.0	84.4	0.3	6.5	6.8
Canada	19.1	171.0	190.1	23.2	84.5	107.7
Australia	26.4	83.5	109.9	27.8	194.4	222.2
New Zealand	4.1	7.1	11.2	4.0	10.6	14.6
Total Wheat Exporting Countries and Others	50.0	345.6	395.6	55.3	296.0	351.3
Hong Kong	484.6	12.1	496.7	397.2	8.4	405.6
Singapore	88.8	44.8	133.6	128.6	31.9	160.5
Ceylon	45.6	37.1	82.7	38.4	31.5	69.9
Pakistan	28.3	30.1	58.4	33.7	34.6	68.3
Malaysia	78.4	1.4	79.8	63.0	6.4	69.4
Total (S. E. Asian Countries)	725.7	125.5	851.2	660.9	112.8	773.7
(A) Grand Total	1,478.5	1,259.7	2,738.2	1,361.8	1,307.2	2,669.0
(B) Total Foreign Trade	2,170.0	2,035.0	4,205.0	1,915.0	1,945.0	3,860.0
(A)/(B) %	68.1	61.9	65.1	71.1	67.2	69.1

NOTE: 1. Figures are based on the statistics of the respective countries and have been converted into the US dollar.

2. The total amount of foreign trade in (A) was taken from an estimate published in the October 7, 1970 issue of *Current Scene.*

Unit: $1 Million)

1968			1969				
Export	Import	Total	Export	Import	Total	Balance	Increase/ Decrease Comp. to '68 (%)
224.2	325.4	549.0	234.5	390.8	625.3	−156.3	+13.8
82.2	69.8	152.6	90.6	124.6	215.2	− 34.0	+41.6
85.2	173.9	259.1	88.2	157.9	246.1	− 69.7	− 5.0
53.3	87.7	141.0	71.2	41.9	113.1	+ 29.3	−19.0
47.9	59.6	107.5	64.1	56.3	120.4	+ 7.8	+12.0
11.8	19.9	31.7	12.4	16.4	28.8	− 4.0	+ 9.1
16.0	19.5	35.5	19.0	14.4	33.4	+ 4.6	− 5.9
8.3	2.1	10.4	9.1	1.3	10.4	+ 7.8	± 0
27.2	28.9	56.1	27.9	23.0	50.9	+ 4.9	− 9.3
18.2	23.8	42.0	18.3	11.6	29.9	+ 6.7	−28.8
5.4	6.4	11.8	5.9	4.8	10.7	+ 1.1	− 9.4
8.2	6.8	15.0	9.9	4.0	13.9	+ 5.9	− 4.7
0.3	1.1	1.4	0.9	0.6	1.5	+ 0.3	+ 7.1
588.2	824.9	1,413.1	652.0	847.6	1,499.6	−195.6	+ 6.1
0.3	0.6	0.9	0.7	0.3	1.0	+ 0.4	+11.1
21.6	151.0	172.6	16.4	122.4	138.8	−106.0	−20.0
30.5	89.1	119.6	34.7	117.2	151.9	− 82.5	+26.3
5.0	5.8	10.8	5.7	4.6	10.3	− 1.1	− 5.6
57.4	246.5	303.9	57.5	244.5	302.0	−187.0	− 0.7
400.9	7.4	408.3	445.5	6.1	451.6	+439.4	+10.6
153.3	27.1	180.4	136.7	57.1	193.8	+ 79.6	+ 7.4
41.2	32.7	73.9	40.4	47.4	87.8	− 7.0	+18.8
29.3	25.5	54.8	26.4	28.9	55.3	− 2.5	+ 0.9
57.3	23.8	81.1	57.2	44.6	101.8	+ 12.6	+25.5
682.0	116.5	798.5	706.2	184.1	890.3	+522.1	+11.5
1,327.6	1,187.9	2,515.5	1,415.7	1,276.2	2,691.9	+139.5	+ 7.0
1,890.0	1,820.0	3,710.0	2,060.0	1,825.0	3,885.0	+135.0	+ 4.7
70.2	65.3	67.8	68.7	69.9	69.3		

3. Malaysia is construed to be only West Malaysia.

4. Wool accounts for 70% of New Zealand's exports to China. Although not a wheat exporting country, it is included in the group for statistical convenience.

of crude rubber being imported from Singapore, Ceylon and Malaysia, and also partly to a hike in import prices of the material.

China's balance of international payments by area in 1969 showed overimports from western industrial countries and wheat exporting countries by $195.6 million, and $187 million, respectively; $522.1 million was overexported to Southeast Asian countries. The pattern in China's external payments of balancing overimports from western industrial countries and wheat exporting countries by overexporting to Southeast Asian countries and Africa was particularly apparent in 1969.

According to fragmentary data on China's trade with communist bloc countries (the Soviet Union, East Europe and Cuba), the amount of trade with the Soviet Union further decreased from $96 million in 1968 to $56.8 million in 1969. Comparing the trade volume between China and Czechoslovakia in 1968 with that of 1967, Czechoslovakia showed a 33.3 percent increase from $33 million to $44 million. Hungary, Poland and Rumania also increased their trade by 6.3 percent, 18 percent, and 16.3 percent, respectively. Rumania in particular, has been increasing her trade yearly, $65.8 million in 1966, $72.6 million in 1967 and $84.4 million in 1968. The increase in the amount of trade with these countries, in contrast to the decrease in trade with the Soviet Union, is considered to be a mirror of China's trade policy which is based on the view that politics and economics are inseparable.

The amount of trade with Cuba and Albania in 1968 is unknown; however, assuming that it was the same as that of 1967, and China's trade with the communist bloc as a whole in 1968 and 1969 as well, it may be considered to have increased 3.7 percent over that of 1967.

Due to a delay in receiving statistics on China's trade with Africa and the Middle East, all-inclusive figures are not available. However, according to the October 1970 estimate of the Middle East Economic Digest (MEED), a British publication, China's exports to Africa and the Middle East in 1969 showed a 9.9 percent increase over that of 1968. The countries to which Chinese exports greatly increased include Algeria (56.2 percent), Iran (16.0 percent), Lebanon (58.5 percent), Aden (72.4 percent) and Syria (63.1 percent). The exports of these countries have been rising for the past several years. Increases in trade with Tanzania, Sudan and Aden are closely related to Chinese foreign aid to these countries. Although most of China's foreign aid is free of interest, since the aid recipient countries are subject to importing some Chinese merchandise in return, China's exports increase in proportion to increases in her foreign aid. A good example of this can be seen in the $330 million worth of

Chinese foreign aid for the construction of a railroad between Tanzania and Zambia.

The amount of China's total trade with major countries (60—70 percent of China's total foreign trade) during the first half of 1970 reached $1,502.4 million; it consisted of $804.4 million in imports, a 42.8 percent increase over the corresponding term of the previous year, and $698 million in exports, a 1.7 percent decrease, the total amount showing an 18 percent increase over the $1,273 million recorded in the corresponding term of the preceding year. During the first half of 1969, China overexported by $146.9 million in trade with these countries, while overimporting $106.4 million in the corresponding term of 1970, due to a sharp increase in the imports of western industrial nations, wheat exporting countries and others (61.1 percent and 34.2 percent respectively), although both exports and imports in trade with Southeast Asian countries decreased. China had until that time exported consistently to Southeast Asia.

In trade between China and 13 western industrialized countries during 1969, China imported $582.5 million, a 61.1 percent increase over the corresponding term of the previous year, and exported $331.5 million, a 2.9 percent increase compared to the same period. The $914 million in export/import trade reflects a drastic increase of 33.7 percent over the corresponding term of the previous year.

China's imports from major countries increased greatly, particularly those from Japan which accounted for 52.8 percent of all imports, more than a two-fold increase over the corresponding term of the previous year. Britain, France, Switzerland, Belgium, Luxembourg and Norway also increased their exports to China, though West Germany showed little change. However, imports from Italy, the Netherlands and Sweden decreased. Principal items among increased Japanese imports were iron and steel, 2.1 percent over the previous year; chemical products, up 3.1 percent; and equipment and machinery, up 2.9 percent. As for Britain, nonferrous metals including platinum, copper and lead, which accounted for 54.1 percent of that country's exports to China, showed a 28 percent increase over the corresponding term of the previous year, and industrial diamonds which accounted for 23.5 percent, also sharply increased by 37.2 percent, although Chinese exports to Britain showed only a slight increase of 2.9 percent.

Trade between China and five Southeast Asian countries in the first half of 1970 amounted to $410 million, showing a 6.9 percent decrease against a total of $440.4 million in trade for the same period of the previous year.

Table III-3 – Chinese Trade with Major Countries in the First Half of 1970

(Unit: $1 Million)

Countries (Yearly Exports and Imports)	Chinese Imports 1969 (Jan-Jun)	Chinese Imports 1970 (Jan-Jun)	Chinese Imports +/- (%)	Chinese Exports 1969 (Jan-Jun)	Chinese Exports 1970 (Jan-Jun)	Chinese Exports +/- (%)	Total Exports and Imports 1969 (Jan-Jun)	Total Exports and Imports 1970 (Jan-Jun)	Total Exports and Imports +/- (%)
Western Industrialized Countries	361.5	582.5	+ 61.1	322.2	331.5	+ 2.9	683.8	914.0	+ 33.7
Japan	124.6	307.3	+146.6	115.9	119.3	+ 2.9	240.5	426.6	+ 77.4
Britain	60.3	67.2	+ 11.4	43.9	43.9	± 0.0	104.2	111.1	+ 6.6
W. Germany	88.3	88.3	± 0.0	39.8	43.4	+ 9.1	128.1	131.7	+ 2.8
France	16.5	45.2	+173.9	39.5	37.1	− 6.1	56.0	82.3	+ 50.0
Italy	30.5	27.5	− 9.8	32.5	34.4	+ 5.9	63.0	61.9	− 1.7
Belgium.Luxembourg	(1~6) 6.9	(1~5) 8.4	+ 21.7	(1~5) 6.1	(1~5) 4.8	− 21.3	13.0	13.2	+ 1.5
Switzerland	5.7	9.9	+ 73.7	(1~5) 8.8	(1~5) 9.5	+ 8.0	14.5	19.4	+ 33.8
Denmark	0.5	0.6	+ 20.0	4.5	4.8	+ 6.7	5.0	5.4	+ 8.0
Netherlands	16.4	11.0	− 32.9	13.2	14.0	+ 6.1	29.6	25.0	− 15.5
Sweden	7.8	6.7	− 14.1	9.7	10.3	+ 6.2	17.5	17.0	− 2.9
Norway	2.1	7.1	+238.1	3.1	3.4	+ 9.7	5.2	10.5	+101.9
Austria	1.6	2.1	+ 31.3	4.7	6.1	+ 29.8	6.3	8.2	+ 30.2
Yugoslavia	0.3	1.2	+300.0	0.6	0.5	− 16.7	0.9	1.7	+ 88.9
Southeast Asian Countries	94.8	78.4	− 17.3	345.6	331.6	− 4.0	440.4	410.0	− 6.9
Hong Kong	3.0	4.8	+ 60.0	201.4	209.6	+ 4.1	204.4	214.4	+ 4.9
Singapore	31.4	17.6	− 43.9	72.6	60.7	− 16.4	104.0	78.3	− 24.7
Ceylon	19.7	21.1	+ 7.1	24.9	24.4	− 2.1	44.6	45.5	+ 2.0
Pakistan	17.2	17.3	+ 0.6	21.1	9.6	− 54.5	38.3	26.9	− 29.8
Malaysia	23.5	17.6	− 25.6	25.1	27.3	+ 6.6	49.1	44.9	− 8.5
Wheat Exporting Countries and Others	106.9	143.5	+ 34.2	42.2	34.9	− 17.3	149.1	178.4	+ 19.7
Canada	64.5	76.2	+ 18.1	15.1	8.6	− 40.3	79.6	84.8	+ 6.5
Australia	42.1	63.9	+ 51.8	16.5	17.6	+ 6.7	58.6	81.5	+ 39.1
Argentina	(1~5) 0.3	(1~5) 1.2	+300.0	(1~5) 0.4	(1~5) 0.5	+ 25.0	0.7	1.7	+142.9
Lebanon	...	...	...	6.8	4.8	− 29.4	6.8	4.8	− 29.1
New Zealand	...	2.2	...	3.4	3.4	± 0	3.4	5.6	+ 64.7
Total	563.2	804.4	+ 42.8	710.1	698.0	− 1.7	1,273.3	1,502.4	+ 18.0

NOTE: (1) Figures in parenthesis show the number of months.
(2) ... means figures below the unit, not zero.

SOURCES: Based on statistics of respective countries which have been converted into the US dollar.

(Imports — $98.45 million (17.3 percent decrease) — exports —$331.6 million (4 percent decrease)). The decrease in imports was due mainly to a decrease in the imports of crude rubber from Singapore and Malaysia, and the decrease in exports was due to a decrease in the amount of rice shipped to Pakistan.

In trade between China and wheat exporting countries, in the first half of 1970, imports reached a total of $143.5 million, a 34.2 percent increase over the corresponding term of the previous year, and $34.9 million in exports, a 17.3 percent decrease over the same period. The total trade volume reached $178.4 million, showing a 19.7 percent increase over the $149.1 million registered in the corresponding term of the previous year.

Judging from the status of China's domestic economy, which is now making steady progress aimed at bringing to completion her fourth 5-year plan which began in 1971, the scale of her foreign trade appears to be gradually expanding. In particular, China's trade with major countries during the first half of 1970 showed a drastic increase of 18 percent compared with the corresponding term of the previous year, though this is mainly attributed to large quantity purchases at the Canton Trade Fair during the fall of 1969. China's trade with major countries in the first half of 1970 showed a drastic overimport of $106.4 million, which suggests the possibility of her having overimported for the whole year.

C. COMPOSITION OF GOODS IMPORTED AND EXPORTED

The composition of goods imported and exported on the part of China — though the present state of the Chinese economy is now in the course of industrialization — is basically dictated to by the demands of economic development which places relatively great importance on agriculture.

China's basic economic policy with respect to imports aims at (1) self-sufficiency and (2) rapid economic development based on a high rate of capital accumulation.

Considering point number (1) above, import is conducted as a rule when a) materials wanted are either not domestically producible or when b) materials are not producible in accordance with required specifications or quality standards. Concerning number (2), as a rule consumer goods are not imported; capital goods as well as industrial materials are imported although there are of course some exceptions. For instance: a) the import of some specific items in order to cope with unforeseen circumstances; or, to correct discrepancies in estimated import plans (emergency food imports after 1951); b) the import of advantageous items based on monetary parities (importing low-priced wheat and barley and exporting expensive rice); c) the import of certain materials with the intention of reexporting them as a part of diversified trade transactions e.g., the reexport of Malaysian rubber to the USSR; and d) imports for solely political reasons (imports of Cuban sugar). China's exports are conducted in order to effect payment for imported goods and for political convenience.

The present composition of goods imported and exported is basically determined by the aforementioned principles, but it has been progressing in this direction incorporating various economic policies and trends during the respective periods. The composition of goods imported and exported for industrial development (the import of machinery, equipment and industrial materials and the export of agricultural and industrial products as well as textile products) was established and developed throughout the 1950's. According to official Chinese data, the composition of imported goods at the time the first 5-year program was implemented, consisted of machinery and equipment 60 percent; raw materials for industrial production and agricultural use (iron, steel, industrial and chemical raw materials, raw cotton, rubber, chemical fertilizers) and consumer goods (medical supplies, petroleum and sugar) 40 percent. The composition of exported goods consisted of agricultural products and the processed goods thereof (75 percent), and mineral products, textile fibers and other industrial products (25 percent).

The Chinese planning authorities decided to gradually change the composition of goods imported and exported following the second 5-year program and decided as follows:

Imports — To gradually bring the importance placed on machinery and equipment to bear upon an increase in the imports of raw materials required for industrial and agricultural production and consumer goods for everyday use; however, the stable composition of goods imported and exported in the 1950's and the intention of the planning authorities to change this composition were both frustrated by a drastic recession which resulted mainly from an agricultural slump in the early 1960's. With the mass import of grains beginning in 1961, the importance of foodstuffs which had been almost negligible until that time greatly increased, while on the contrary, machinery, equipment, iron and steel and nonferrous metals rapidly decreased.

Exports — The importance of foodstuffs and raw materials decreased while industrial exports took an upward turn. This was caused by a decline in the capacity to export resulting from the economic standstill caused mainly by an agricultural slump, a decrease in the demand for imports, discontinuance of aid exports of machinery and equipment from the USSR and emergency imports of foodstuffs. With the upturn of the economy following the second half of 1962, the imports of machinery and equipment, iron and steel increased, and the composition of import goods gradually returned to the traditional pattern it had followed in the past. The change in policy from neglecting agriculture to attaching importance to agriculture was stimulated by the economic recession which attached greater importance to the imports of chemical fertilizers and other products necessary for agricultural production. However, since foodstuffs amounting to around five million tons annually are still being imported, the present composition of import goods has changed little in comparison with the pattern set during the 1950's. On the contrary, the composition of goods exported, in proportion to economic recovery, has been returning to the traditional patterns of the past.

1. Change in the Composition of Goods Imported

Among goods imported during the 1950's, machinery and equipment ranked first (23 – 41% of all goods imported), followed by iron and steel and nonferrous metals (8 to 18%), textiles (around 10%), chemical products (5 to 9%), petroleum and petroleum products (4 to 9%), rubber (3 to 7%) and foodstuffs (2.6%). With regard to machinery and equipment, finished plants which formed the core of the first and second 5-year programs, held the greatest importance, and performed an important role in China's industrialization. With the industrial expansion in the 1950's, imports of industrial materials and fuels (iron and steel, nonferrous metals, rubber, chemical products, textile raw materials, petroleum and petroleum products) gradually increased. These items accounted for one-third the total amount of Chinese imports in the early 1950's, and gradually increased to one-half by the end of the period. This pattern of a steady increase in the imports of industrial raw materials continued until 1960, suddenly changing in 1961.

The composition of goods imported in the 1960's showed an overall decrease in machinery and equipment as well as industrial raw materials. In particular, a drastic decrease was noted in the importance and value of imports of machinery and equipment. These items accounted for 40 percent of the total amount of imports in 1959 or $670 million in value (nearly $1,000 million if trade with East Europe is included), but decreased to 5· percent or $43 million in 1962. On the other hand,

Table III-4 — Composition of Goods Imported

(Unit: $1,000, %)

Items	1960	Composition Rate	1966	Composition Rate
Food and Live Animals	38,385	2.6	436,696	26.1
Cereals	1,647	0.1	345,236	20.6
Rubber and Rubber Products	95,986	6.4	105,348	6.3
Crude Rubber (Synthetic Rubber included)	95,535	6.4	104,966	6.3
Lumber, Pulp, Paper and Products thereof	10,865	0.7	47,877	2.9
Paperboard and Products thereof	3,847	0.3	9,186	0.5
Non-metalliferous Ores	7,917	0.5	8,497	0.5
Metalliferous Ores	1,723	0.1	1,158	0.1
Mineral Fuels	115,901	7.7	2,911	0.2
Petroleum and Petroleum Products	115,847	7.7	2,892	0.2
Animal and Vegetable Oils and Fats	3,764	0.3	2,861	0.2
Chemicals	86,899	5.8	211,343	12.6
Chemical Fertilizer	37,922	2.5	139,392	8.3
Agricultural Chemicals	5,502	0.4	16,421	1.0
Plastic	8,623	0.6	10,000	0.6
Textile Materials and Products	166,870	11.1	149,905	8.9
Textile Materials (Half-finished Goods)	135,376	9.0	119,562	7.1
Textile Goods	31,407	2.1	30,279	1.8
Iron and Steel	183,622	12.2	206,343	12.3
Nonferrous Metals	81,838	5.4	57,749	3.4
Machinery	561,776	37.4	351,798	21.0
Total Amount of Goods	1,503,214	100.0	1,675,430	100.0

NOTE: The above statistics were arrived at by totaling the amount of trade between China and about 50 countries of the non-communist bloc and the USSR, accounting for over 80% of Chinese trade. The statistics excluded trade with E. Europe, the Asian Communist bloc (North Vietnam, North Korea, Mongolia), the breakdown of which was unknown. Trade with Cuba was partly included in the breakdown. Composition of goods traded with E. Europe was the same as that with the USSR. If included, the composition rate of machinery would increase to some extent.

SOURCE: Exports to/and Imports from Communist Areas in E. Europe and Asia by Free World Countries, 1960, the United States State Department. Compiled on the basis of USSR Foreign Trade Statistics, 1966.

industrial materials decreased in value, but showed only a slight decrease in the composition rate of total goods imported. Meanwhile, the imports of petroleum and petroleum products gradually decreased in line with the progress of domestic industrialization. Grain imports began in 1961, and during the same year exceeded one-third the amount of total exports, or $330 million in value. This commodity has been imported on the same scale during each consecutive year since then. Incidentally, the amount of foodstuffs imported in the 1950's occupied only 0.3 to 2.6 percent of total imports, or $5 to $38 million in value.

Accompanying the economic recovery observed in the second half of 1962, China's international trade began to take a favorable turn in 1963, and imports of machinery and equipment and raw materials for industry gradually increased. During 1966, the year in which China's third 5-year program began, the import scale recovered to the 1959 level, a peak year in the past. The composition of goods imported at this time suggests that a pattern typical of favorable periods for the Chinese economy developed once again. The major goods imported during 1959 were grain, machinery and equipment, each accounting for 20 percent of the total amount of imported goods, followed by iron, steel and nonferrous metals – 16 percent; chemical products – 13 percent; textile raw materials and products – 9 percent and rubber – 6 percent.

A comparison between the import patterns of 1950 and the second half of the 1960's reveals the following characteristics: (1) a decrease in imports of equipment and machinery; (2) an increase in imports of grain and chemical products, particularly chemical fertilizers; (3) a decrease in imports of petroleum and petroleum products; and (4) a return to imports of iron and steel, nonferrous metals, rubber and textiles to a composition rate similar to the 1950's. Although business was favorable in both the 1950's and the second half of the 1960's, the composition of goods imported during the two periods was different due to changes in economic policy, prolonged imports of grain and the achievement of self-supply capabilities for petroleum in 1965. Since the recession in the early 1960's which resulted mainly because of an agricaltural slump, China's planning authorities have abandoned the "industrial (particularly heavy industrial) priority formula" adopted during the 1950's and established the "agriculture priority formula" which has been executed since the early 1960's. This policy was reflected in the increased imports of chemical fertilizers and agricultural chemicals, materials which support agriculture. Further, a chronic food shortage due to a population increase necessitated long-range importing of grain in large quantities.

2. Change in the Composition of Goods Exported

The amount of food China exports during a certain year is easily influenced by the success or failure of agricultural production of the preceding year. And, during a year with an average crop or better, the amount of food exported usually accounts for 20 to 30 percent of her total exports. The overall amount of food imported in the 1950's was rather small, and corresponded to only 10 percent of those goods exported, however, the amounts of grain imported drastically increased after 1961, while the net exports of food have become relatively smaller.

Major items among food exported were livestock (pigs and cattle), meat (processed products, pork, beef, poultry meat and canned meat) and grain, usually totaling around 8 percent of total annual exports and valued at $150 to 200 million. Livestock was exported to the USSR during the 1950's, but recently has been exported mostly to Southeast Asian countries.

Recently, grain (mainly rice and corn) has increased to become second to meat in terms of export amounts, and has come to hold a position as a staple article for export in the years which follow good harvests. The amount of grain exported in 1959 totaled 1.86 million tons valued at $200 million, while that of an average year is only 1.1 to 1.5 million tons, actually some $110 to $180 million in value. Rice, the key export item, registered a record export in 1959 amounting to 1.57 million tons valued at $180 million. Incidently, the amount of rice exported in 1966 totaled 1.1 million tons valued at $140 million; on the other hand, this item is also being imported from Ceylon and Burma in quantities ranging from 50 to 100 thousand tons per year.

The exports of corn did not increase, perhaps because it was useful in meeting domestic demands for feed. In 1962, under the effects of an agricultural failure, 490,000 tons of corn were imported. Recently, imports of this item have decreased and exports have risen, but nevertheless, the 240,000 tons exported in 1965 was the highest amount ever recorded.

Other major food items exported include — fruit, vegetables, fish and shellfish, dairy products, sugar, tea and feed; the exports of the first three items mentioned above have been increasing.

The principal items roughly grouped in Table III-4 include the following: fruit and vegetables — apples, mandarin oranges, bananas, chestnuts, canned fruit, red beans, broad beans and their canned products and canned vegetables; seafood — fish, lobster, jellyfish and canned seafood; dairy products – bird's eggs; sugar – sugar, honey; feed – wheat beans, linseed oil stained lees, peanut stained lees, fish meal and others.

These items are exported mainly to the Middle East and Hong Kong, countries in Southeast Asia and Africa, and also to advanced industrialized countries in Europe and Japan, creating an important source for the acquisition of foreign exchange.

Textile materials and their products (raw materials and clothes) are another principal export item in addition to food, and account for 20 to 30 percent and sometimes even nearly 40 percent of the total amount of exports, bringing in $400 to $600 million in foreign exchange annually.

About half of the above mentioned exports consist of textiles and clothing products which come second in export amounts because China is making increased efforts to export processed products. Raw silk and wool make up the majority of textile materials. Their exports total 6,000 and 20,000 tons respectively. Raw cotton amounting to as much as 90,000 tons was exported in 1959, but has not been exported much of late. Flax, jute and hemp are also exported, though in limited quantities.

Textiles as a single product, is the most important item among China's export merchandise totaling $200 to $300 million in value annually. Cotton fabric ranks first, followed by wool, silk and bastfiber fabrics, matting and blankets. In addition, ready-made suits and knitted goods are also exported in large quantity.

The actual state of China's iron and steel industry is reflected in the dominant position of pig iron exports which account for 60 to 80 percent of the iron and steel exported annually. The export of steel material which started in 1955 showed peak records of 139,000 tons in 1958 and 247,000 tons in 1965 following economic recoveries in China.

Staple items include bar steel, section steel, iron wire, cast iron pipe and wire rod. Exports of metal products including secondary products such as bolts, nuts and wire netting are increasing considerably. Pig iron exports registered 1.16 million tons in 1964 but have shown little increase recently.

Major countries to which iron and steel (pig iron included) were exported in 1965 included Japan, Hong Kong, Singapore and the United Arab Republic. Exports to Asia, the Middle East and Africa, centering around Southeast Asia, are gradually increasing.

The export of oil bearing seeds registered its highest total a record $200 million in 1959, but has been decreasing since then, and barely recovered to a level of $100 million in 1966. Besides soybeans and peanuts, castor-oil, sesame and sunflower seeds are also exported. A record export

Table III-5 — Composition of Goods Exported (Unit: $1,000 %)

Items	1960	Composition Rate	1966	Composition Rate
Food and Live Animals	351,494	21.9	590,225	30.1
Animals	27,428	1.7	73,307	3.7
Meat and Meat Preparations	35,571	2.2	85,244	4.4
Dairy Products	17,439	1.1	33,260	1.7
Fish and Fish Preparations	18,156	1.1	60,610	3.1
Cereals	129,463	8.0	136,061	6.9
Rice	114,359	7.1	119,251	6.1
Corn	3,629	0.2	9,543	0.5
Fruit and Vegetables	69,612	4.3	120,633	6.2
Sugars	1,926	0.1	30,541	1.6
Tea	35,016	2.2	22,831	1.2
Feed	2,226	0.1	11,474	0.6
Beverages and Tobacco	15,296	1.0	10,053	0.5
Tobacco	13,862	0.9	2,767	0.1
Hides and Skins (undressed) and Leather Products	10,152	0.6	34,083	1.7
Seeds and Oil Bearing Seeds for Oil Extraction Use	113,598	7.1	102,165	5.2
Textile Materials and Their Products	609,546	37.9	400,481	20.4
Textile Materials and Half-finished Goods	101,346	6.3	90,855	4.6
Textile Goods	305,694	19.0	222,343	11.4
Clothing	202,453	12.6	87,283	4.6
Non-metalliferous Ores	12,091	0.8	22,734	1.2
Metalliferous Ores	64,238	4.0	34,284	1.8
Animal Materials (others)	44,212	2.7	58,571	3.0
Vegetable Materials (others)	22,213	1.4	31,595	1.6
Mineral Fuels	6,315	0.4	18,216	0.9
Coal and Coke	5,962	0.4	14,706	0.8
Animal and Vegetable Oils and Fats	36,476	2.3	36,987	1.9
Chemicals	34,519	2.1	63,324	3.2
Paper, Paperboard and Products thereof	13,604	0.8	21,960	1.1
Building Materials	20,071	1.2	16,143	0.8
Glassware, Earthenware and Porcelain	9,221	0.6	17,556	0.9
Iron and Steel	22,844	1.4	50,769	2.6
Nonferrous Metals	74,202	4.6	22,635	1.2
Total Amount of Exports	1,608,521	100.0	1,958,892	100.0

NOTE: Same as in Table III-1.   SOURCE: Same as in Table III-1.

of 1.34 million tons worth of soybeans was recorded in 1959, but the amount has decreased to around 550,000 tons recently.

D. INTERNATIONAL BALANCE OF PAYMENTS AND FOREIGN EXCHANGE RESERVES

The balance of international payments and the amount of foreign exchange holdings are important materials when judging the solvency of a foreign country. For want of this data on China, a conclusion with respect to the subject is made here based on fragmentary materials obtained on the outside.

Trade balance is a major item in China's balance of international payments in the sphere of current accounts. The items involved include current accounts, trade balances, balances of invisible trade, expenditures for trade missions, diplomatic officials, and Chinese technicians dispatched overseas; laborers' remittances from overseas, pay for foreign technicians sent to China, and others. Those items that come under the balance of capitals account are remittances from overseas Chinese, special sales, loans from the USSR and their repayment, loan interest payments and economic aid to developing countries. Loans accepted or granted and their repayment occupy the largest portion of the balance of capitals account. Nevertheless, they are, in principle, registered as import and export materials in ordinary trade, one of the characteristics of China's balance of international payments accounts.

In China's balance of international payments, principal revenue items are trade profits resulting from overexports to Southeast Asia, remittances from Chinese merchants overseas ($30 million annually), and loans from the USSR. Principal payment items are imports, foreign economic aid and repayment of loans from the USSR. However, the situation has changed considerably. Loans from the USSR have been discontinued and the repayment of previous loans from that country was completed in 1965.

It was inevitable that China's balance of international payments would change in content after being subjected to considerable fluctuation due to the fact that there was a poor agricultural harvest for three consecutive years after 1959, and economic aid from the USSR was discontinued. Evidence to support this is found in the fact that China has come to import food on a deferred payment basis, the fact that Japan was requested by China to export on a deferred payment basis during Japan-China trade negotiations, and the fact that she is trying to import industrial plants on the same payment basis from other free world countries.

Table III-6 — Chinese Balance of International Payments (1950 – 1961) (Unit: $1 Million)

	Total Amount 1950—54	Total Amount 1955—59	Total Amount 1960—64	Total Amount 1950—64
A. Total Amount of Chinese Expenditures	5,919	10,449	9,111	25,480
(1) Total Goods Imported (f.o.b.)	5,367	8,057	6,902	20,326
(2) Freight Insurance	245	424	466	1,135
(3) Expenditures for Soviet Specialists	45	50	5	100
(4) Expenditures for Chinese Students Studying in the USSR	20	25	25	70
(5) Expenditures for Overseas Chinese	50	50	50	150
(6) Repayment of Debts to USSR	65	1,045	1,133	2,244
(7) Foreign Aid	127	798	530	1,455
(7)/(A)	(2.1%)	(7.6%)	(5.8%)	(5.7%)
B. Total Chinese Revenue	6,732	10,142	9,106	25,981
(1) Total Goods Exported (f.o.b.)	4,867	8,993	8,546	22,406
(2) Expenditures by Foreigners in China	40	25	25	90
(3) Remittances by Overseas Chinese	350	350	350	350
(4) Food Packages	—	2	139	141
(5) Loans from the USSR	1,475	772	46	2,294
(5)/(B)	(21.9%)	(7.6%)	(0.5%)	(8.8%)
C. Balance	(+)813	(–)307	(–)5	(+)501

NOTE: Promised Chinese aid to developing countries during 1954 – June 1968 amounted to $998.8 million, and that to Socialist countries during the 1953 – 1969 period $2,128.5 million (loan to Tanzania for Tanzanian Railroad Construction, about $400 million, not included).

SOURCE: "Economic Trends in Communist China" edited by A. Eckstein, W. Galenson, and T. C. Liu.

However, due to a drastic reduction in imports and the introduction of short-term credit from abroad during 1961 and 1962, a further deterioration in China's balance of international payments was prevented. At the same time, with increased exports aided by a recovery of the domestic economy in 1963, and a succession of restrictions on imports, China's balance of international payments began to take a favorable turn. Gold and foreign exchange reserves also began to increase, foreign debts were completely repaid in 1965, and China's international balance of payments once again began taking a turn for the better. Incidentally, some West European reports estimated that China's gold and foreign exchange reserves amounted to $400 million at the end of 1964 and $600 million at the end of 1968.

E.   CHINA'S FOREIGN AID

Concerning the basic principle, purpose and form of China's economic aid, Premier Chou En-lai, during his visit to Africa from December 1963 to February 1964, announced the "Eight points of Chinese Foreign Economic and Technical Aid." They are described below:

The Chinese Government offers aid to foreign countries based on the principles of equality and reciprocity; China has never regarded such aid as a unilateral gift, but deems it of a reciprocal nature.

In offering aid to a foreign country, the Chinese Government will strictly respect the sovereign power of the aid recipient country, will make no incidental conditions, and will never request any special privileges from that country.

The Chinese Government will offer economic aid on an interest-free basis or in the form of low interest loans, and will also extend the term of repayment when necessary to ease the burden on aid recipient countries.

The purpose of Chinese foreign aid is not to induce aid recipient countries to rely upon China, but to help them win their way to the development of a self-supporting economy through their own efforts.

When aiding recipient countries in construction work, the Chinese Government will carefully select industries which will become profitable with as small an investment as possible, in order to enable aid recipient countries to increase revenue and accumulate funds.

The Chinese Government will offer domestically produced equipment and materials of the highest quality, setting prices in accordance with standard international levels. In the event there should be any discrepancy in the standards or quality of the equipment and materials provided by the

Table III-7 — Aid Promised to Socialist Countries

(Unit: $1 Million)

Year	Total	Albania	Cuba	Hungary	North Korea	North Vietnam	Mongolia
1953	200				200		
54							
55	204	4				200	
56	49.5	2		7.5			40
57	54	4		50			
58	55	5			25		25
59	119	19				100	
1960	220	5	60		105		50
61	282	125				157	
62	(1)	(1)(2)					
63	40		40				
64							
65	(1)	(1)				110	
66	(1)					170	
67	(1)					225	
68	(1)					200	
69	(1)					200	
Total	2,128.5	164	100	57.5	330	1,362	115

NOTE: (1) Unknown.

        (2) Aid promised was reported in Albanian newspapers, but the true figures are unknown.

SOURCE: *"An Economic Profile of Mainland China"* New York Times; compiled by the Joint Economic Committee of the United States Congress and from other materials.

Chinese Government and those agreed upon, the Chinese Government will guarantee replacement of those items.

In any case in which the Chinese Government offers aid to a foreign country, the Chinese Government will ensure that the recipient country sufficiently masters any techniques that may be required.

Chinese technicians sent by the Chinese Government to aid recipient countries in construction work are to be accorded the same treatment as the experts of the recipient countries. No special requests or treatment will be demanded or permitted.

No data published by the Chinese Government on expenditures for foreign aid or amounts received are available. However, the promised amounts of economic and technical aid to socialist nations or developing countries have been disclosed fragmentarily by the Chinese Government or the aid recipient countries each time agreements were concluded. Table III-7 and 8 show the amounts systematically arranged.

1. Development of Economic Aid

a. While offering economic aid in the first half of the 1950's, China had many accounts receivable from the USSR which covered her shortage of foreign reserves and contributed to her economic development.

b. China began to expand her foreign aid around 1954. The total promised amount of foreign aid from 1953 to June 1968 totaled $2,927.3 million. Of this, $1,928.5 million went to socialist countries, 65.9 percent of the total amount, and $998.8 million to developing countries ($502.7 million to Asia, $332 million to Africa and $164.1 million to the Middle East).

c. Aid to socialist nations by 1964 rose to 90 percent, while that to developing countries was 14.7 percent. The principal reason for this low rate was the change of governments in partner countries.

d. Aid recipient countries in Asia and the Middle East during the 1950's were limited to Ceylon, Indonesia Egypt, Syria, and Yemen, and the promised amount of aid was on the average below $30 million per year. Aid amounts to African countries such as Tanzania, Guinea and Zambia showed an increase after the Great Cultural Revolution.

2. Characteristics of Economic Aid

a. In comparison to foreign technical aid, donations make up the major portion of China's economic aid. However, priority on the type of aid has been shifting to the granting of loans recently.

b. Chinese foreign aid conditions are much easier than those of the

Table III-8 — Aid Commitments to Developing Countries

	1956	1957	1958	1959	1960	1961
Africa	—	—	—	0.5	26.0	39.2
Algeria	—	—	—	—	—	—
Central Africa	—	—	—	—	—	—
Congo (Brazzaville)	—	—	—	—	—	—
Ghana	—	—	—	—	—	19.6
Guinea	—	—	—	0.5	—	—
Kenya	—	—	—	—	—	—
Mali	—	—	—	—	—	19.6
Mauritania	—	—	—	—	—	—
Somalia	—	—	—	—	—	—
Tanzania	—	—	—	—	—	—
Uganda	—	—	—	—	—	—
Zambia	—	—	—	—	—	—
Asia	51.7	15.8	21.7	—	47.5	123.8
Afganistan	—	—	—	—	—	—
Burma	—	—	—	—	—	84.0
Cambodia	22.9	—	—	—	26.5	—
Ceylon	—	15.8	10.5	—	—	—
Indonesia	16.2	—	11.2	—	—	30.0
Laos	—	—	—	—	—	—
Nepal	12.6	—	—	—	21.0	9.8
Pakistan	—	—	—	—	—	—
Middle East	4.7	—	12.7	0.7	—	—
Syria	—	—	—	—	—	—
UAR	4.7	—	—	—	—	—
Yemen	—	—	12.7	0.7	—	—
Total	56.4	15.8	34.4	1.2	73.5	163.0

SOURCES: "An Economic Profile of Mainland China" by the Joint Economic Committee of the United States Congress.

(Unit: $1 Million)

1962	1963	1964	1965	Cumulative Total (1956—65)	Cumulative Total (1954—Jun. 1968)	DECP Report (1954—68)
1.8	71.6	115.1	15.0	269.2	332.0	296.0
1.8	50.0	—	—	51.8	51.8	50.0
—	—	4.0	—	4.0	4.0	4.0
—	—	25.2	—	25.2	25.2	25.0
—	—	22.4	—	42.0	42.0	40.0
—	—	—	—	26.5	54.9	25.0
—	—	18.0	—	18.0	18.0	18.0
—	—	—	—	19.6	22.6	23.0
—	—	—	—	—	4.0	4.0
—	21.6	—	—	21.6	23.3	22.0
—	—	45.5	—	45.5	54.4	53.0
—	—	—	15.0	15.0	15.0	15.0
—	—	—	—	—	16.8	17.0
14.5	—	114.2	44.0	433.2	502.7	479.0
—	—	—	20.0	28.0	28.0	28.0
—	—	—	—	84.0	84.0	84.0
—	—	—	—	49.4	92.3	50.0
10.5	—	4.2	—	41.0	41.0	41.0
—	—	50.0	16.0	123.4	123.4	105.0
4.0	—	—	—	4.0	4.3	—
—	—	—	—	43.4	63.0	62.0
—	—	60.0	—	60.0	67.0	109.0
—	16.5	108.5	—	143.1	164.1	174.0
—	16.3	—	—	16.3	16.3	16.0
—	—	80.0	—	84.5	105.7	106.0
—	0.2	28.5	—	42.1	42.1	52.0
16.3	88.1	337.8	59.0	845.5	998.8	949.0

DECP Report is from "Resources for the Developing World."

USSR and East European countries both in terms of interest as well as repayment periods. In most cases, aid is offered without interest or at a low interest rate of 0.5 percent to 2.5 percent with the repayment period usually set at twenty years with payment for the first 10 years deferred.

c. Since China's economic aid is spread over a wide sphere of developing countries, the accumulated promised amount of aid per country is on the average below $50 million, the amount offered to eighty percent of aid recipient countries.

d. Most of China's aid projects are integrated and include preliminary investigations, execution programs, equipment and machinery, raw materials and technical aid, and include such industries as paper, textile, food processing, cement, match plants and others in addition to the construction of roads, bridges and railroads.

e. Technical aid encompasses a large share of overall Chinese aid since many aid projects involve agricultural development, the construction of roads, dams and railroads. Technical aid involves planning and supervision of construction projects in addition to training the technicians of the aid recipient countries in China. The number of Chinese technicians sent to aid recipient countries is on the increase and has reportedly reached around 5,000.

3. Future Outlook

China's economic and technical aid is offered with a competitive awareness of the USSR, and there is the strong likelihood that aid competition between the two countries will intensify in the future. As seen in the aid for railroad construction in Tanzania, Chinese aid (loan) terms will probably become easier in the future. It is anticipated that with the expansion of foreign trade, China's foreign reserves will take a turn for the better and the amount of her foreign aid will increase.

Ⅳ. ECONOMIC DEVELOPMENT AND FOREIGN TRADE

A. DEVELOPMENT OF ECONOMIC POLICY

According to an official Chinese announcement, the economic growth rate during the first 5-year program was 4.5 percent in agricultural earnings, 18 percent in industrial income and 8.9 percent in the national income. In the second 5-year program, influenced by an economic policy aiming at a "simultaneous development of agriculture and industry," the planned economic growth index was set at 14.8 percent in industry, 6 percent in agriculture and 8.4 percent in the national income. However, these goals were not reached due to discontinuance of the second 5-year program in January of 1961. No data was disclosed on the third 5-year program; judging from the discontinuance of the second 5-year program due to the agricultural slump, the planned growth index is not considered to have been as high as that achieved during the period in which drastic economic growth was brought about through the execution of a heavy industry-first policy and simultaneous development of agriculture and industry. The growth index in the agricultural department is purported to have been within 4.5 percent, the actual index of the first 5-year program. However, since it was necessary for China to make her industries of a more agriculture-supporting nature in order to bring about agricultural development, industrial growth presumably set a lower level than that of the second program.

Chinese economic policy during the third 5-year program was clearly described in a thesis entitled "The Way to China's Socialistic Industrialization" in the "Red Flag" (10th period, 1969). It said in effect that China would continue to follow the economic policy established in the early 1960's — a policy "based on agriculture led by industry." The article stressed that the purpose of industrial construction was "to make pro-

Table IV-1 – China's Gross National Product

GNP Year	Gross National Product (Western Formula)			Per Capita Gross National Product	
	Renminbi Term Billion Yuan	US Dollar Term Billion Dollar	Growth Rate 1957 = 100	Renminbi Term Yuan	Growth Rate 1957 = 100
1957	1,196	486	100	185	100
58	1,459	593	122	220	119
59	1,447	588	121	215	116
1960	1,471	598	123	213	115
61	1,304	530	109	191	103
62	1,208	491	101	174	94
63	1,268	515	106	179	97
64	1,411	574	118	196	106
1965	1,507	613	126	205	111
66	1,662	676	139	224	121
67	1,579	642	132	207	112
68	1,459	593	122	191	103
69	1,674	680	140	(Estimated) 213	115

SOURCES: The U.S. Department of State *"Issues."*
"1970 Annual World Report" prepared by the Japanese Economic Planning Agency.

visions for war and natural calamities and to serve the people," and that this would also be the basic policy by which the future course of economic development would be decided, particularly that of the location of industrial plants and factories. Specific examples of such basic economic policy are seen in the development of small-scale industries after the Great Cultural Revolution. Concerning the significance of the local small-scale industry, first, it may be said to be a revival of the minor and household industries which existed at the time of the "great step forward" in 1958. These industries seemed to have disappeared during the economic recession in the early 1960's, but made a comeback under the agriculture-based policy established during the economic adjustment period of 1964 to 1965. They have been actively developed and built up since the latter half of 1969 after experiencing a period of confrontation over policies of economic development during the Great Cultural Revolution; one stressing decentralization of the economy placing heavy emphasis on agriculture and the other centralization of the economy attaching importance to economic efficiency and giving priority to heavy industries. Secondly, another significant factor is the combination of agriculture and industry. Almost all examples of reported development of local small-scale industry are those of an agriculture-supporting nature. Major types of industry include — a) chemical fertilizer, b) cement, c) iron and steel, d) electric power plants, e) machinery and f) coal mining. In particular, those from a) to e) are industries which directly support agriculture. An increase in the amount used and self-supply capabilities of chemical fertilizers are reported by each province; the increased production of cement due to the development of irrigation facilities, increased iron and steel production due to the manufacture and repair of agricultural machinery, the expansion of irrigatable areas through electric power and the establishment of machine factories all indicate favorable results for the policy of promoting agriculture supporting small-scale industries.

Economic development during the third 5-year program could be summarized in the expression "to develop heavy industry simultaneously with the development of a certain sphere of industry and agriculture" ("Red Flag" — 10th period, 1969). Specific examples of this may be said to be the development of agriculture-supporting local small-scale industry with an eye toward economizing national financial resources.

Now let's have a glance at the productivity status of agriculture and industry under such an economic policy. According to an official Chinese announcement, China has enjoyed a succession of bumper agricultural crops since 1962; in 1966, raw cotton and food crops showed the highest amount harvested in the 17 years since the founding of the People's Republic of China. According to an estimate disclosed by the Food and Agricultural Organization (FAO), crop production was 206 million tons in 1966, 214 million tons in 1968 and 222 million tons in 1969. China apparently suffered little damage from natural calamities in 1970; the nation's estimated agricultural production, when considered in connection with the development of an agriculture supporting small-scale industry, was on the same level as, or a little above, that of 1969.

B. DOMESTIC ECONOMIC DEVELOPMENT AND TRADE VOLUME

The scale of Chinese foreign trade, after having established a peak record in 1966, declined for two consecutive years in 1967 and 1968. However, this was not because of a change in the basic economic policy or failure of the economic programs, but due to temporary factors resulting from the Great Cultural Revolution. With the Ninth Chinese Nationwide Communist Party Conference held in April, 1969, the Great Cultural Revolution performed its mission for the time being by motivating economic activities as the trade volume in 1969 rose to $3,885 million, surpassing the 1967 level. Foodstuffs and livestock, textile materials and their products accounted for 50 to 60 percent of total exports. Although the trade volume of a certain year is usually closely related to the agricultural production of the preceding year, trade amounts decreased in 1967 and 1968. This was wholly attributable to the confusion which arose during the procurement and transportation of materials during the Great Cultural Revolution. However, owing to a favorable tone in agricultural and industrial production, China's foreign trade during the period of the third 5-year program may be said to have been basically in a state of expansion; the same can also be said of trade in 1970, the final year of the third 5-year program.

China's trade accounts in 1966 and 1969 registered an overexport of $135 million, an overimport of $30 million in 1967, and an overexport of $70 million in 1968. The overimport in 1967 was caused by a decrease in the exports of food and textiles, and an increase in the imports of iron and steel from western industrialized countries.

In terms of areas, China overimported from western industrialized countries (Japan and West Europe), wheat exporting countries (Canada and Australia), and overexported to countries in Southeast Asia and Africa. This has been the pattern of China's trade balance since she changed her trade partners during the economic adjustment period in the 1950's, and this did not change during the third 5-year program. The margin of excess exports to Southeast Asia, particularly Hong Kong and Singapore during the 1966–1969 period amounted to an annual average of $500 million. The trade balance during the same period is indicated to be an overexport to Southeast Asian countries of $2,135.9 million, and an over-import from western industrialized countries and wheat exporting countries of $1,673.3 million, showing an accumulated credit balance of $462.6 million.

China's major trade partners have always been Japan, West Germany, Britain, Canada, Australia, Hong Kong and Singapore. Japan's position in Chinese foreign trade in particular, is becoming increasingly more favorable by the year. Japan's share in Chinese trade was 12 percent in 1965 and almost 16 percent in 1969. Judging from these and other factors, Japan-China trade has been and probably will continue to be influenced by the trends in China's domestic economy.

China's foreign trade is in a mutually dependent relationship with her domestic economic development, clearly influenced by changes in domestic investment as well as agricultural and industrial production levels. Furthermore, exports determine the scale of imports as well as overall trade. Since agricultural production is the mainstay of exports, the scale of export and composition of goods exported depends upon the results of agricultural production during a certain time period, with the size of domestic investment and the increase rate of industrial production controlling the import demand volume in foreign trade Since China adheres to the principle of a balanced export-import trade, import demands can only be satisfied in so far as they do not exceed the scale of exports. Therefore, based on this, it is evident that the possibilities for an expansion of China's trade scale are wholly dependent upon the level of agricultural production. However, if the mainstay of exports shifts from agricultural products which at present account for 50 to 60 percent of total exports, to industrial products, the trade scale will not necessarily be so extensively controlled by the level of agricultural production. Nevertheless, the composition of China's export goods showed little change throughout the third 5-year program. It is inconceivable that the pattern in which the trade scale is controlled by agricultural production will change in the near future. Next let us take up the basic characteristics of the composition of goods exported and imported by China.

China's rapid industrialization policy was reflected in the composition of goods imported during the first and second 5-year programs. The principal items imported were machinery and equipment, consisting

Table IV-2 — Chinese Imports

(Unit: $1 Million)

Year / Commodities	1966 Value	1966 %	1967 Value	1967 %	1968 Value	1968 %	1969 Value	1969 %
Foodstuffs and Animals	510	25.1	380	19.5	410	22.5	360	19.7
Wheat	330	16.2	260	13.4	260	14.3	295	16.2
Chemicals	250	12.3	285	14.7	315	17.3	295	16.2
Chemical Fertilizers	150	7.4	200	10.3	200	11.0	180	9.9
Industrial Products	910	44.7	940	48.3	775	42.6	810	44.4
Iron and Steel	225	11.1	325	16.7	265	14.6	310	17.0
Machinery and Equipment	490	24.1	380	19.5	275	15.1	250	13.7
Nonferrous Metals (including Platinum)	55	2.7	85	4.4	125	6.9	160	8.8
Textile Yarn and Fabrics	35	1.7	45	2.3	40	2.2	30	1.6
Crude Materials, Fuel and Edible Oils	340	16.7	320	16.5	300	16.5	330	18.1
Rubber	85	4.2	70	3.6	80	4.4	120	6.6
Textile Fibers	150	7.4	150	7.7	100	5.5	90	4.9
Others	25	1.2	20	1.0	20	1.1	30	1.6
Non-Communist	1,530	75.2	1,605	82.5	1,480	81.3	1,500	82.2
Communist	505	24.8	340	17.5	340	18.7	325	17.8
Total	2,035	100.0	1,945	100.0	1,820	100.0	1,825	100.0

NOTE: The 1966-68 totals are from official U.S. Government sources and are adjusted for shipping and lead and lag time. The 1969 totals for non-Communist trade are based upon data from the PRC's 12 major non-Communist trading partners. These totals are adjusted for shipping costs, but not for lead and lag time.

SOURCE: October 7, 1970 Edition of the "Current Scene."

Table IV-3 – Chinese Exports

(Unit: $1 Million)

Commodities	1966 Value	1966 %	1967 Value	1967 %	1968 Value	1968 %	1969 Value	1969 %
Foodstuffs and Animals	595	27.4	505	26.4	525	27.8	580	28.2
Animals, Meat and Fish	225	10.4	170	8.9	175	9.3	210	10.2
Grains	150	6.9	140	7.3	125	6.6	90	4.4
Fruit and Vegetables	115	5.3	125	6.5	140	7.4	155	7.5
Industrial Products	900	41.5	830	43.3	815	43.1	835	40.5
Textile Yarn and Fabrics	280	12.9	245	12.8	260	13.8	280	13.6
Clothing	190	8.8	160	8.4	170	9.0	185	9.0
Iron and Steel	90	4.2	70	3.6	25	1.3	15	0.7
Nonferrous Metals	40	1.8	35	1.8	25	1.3	10	0.5
Crude Materials, Fuels, and Edible Oils	480	22.1	435	22.7	405	21.4	470	22.8
Textile Fibers	105	4.8	100	5.2	90	4.8	130	6.3
Crude Animal Materials	90	4.2	75	3.9	95	5.0	110	5.3
Oil Seeds	90	4.2	90	4.7	85	4.5	90	4.4
Chemicals	90	4.2	85	4.4	85	4.5	90	4.4
Others	105	4.8	60	3.2	60	3.2	85	4.1
Non-Communist	1,575	72.6	1,455	76.0	1,430	75.7	1,600	77.7
Communist	595	27.4	460	24.0	460	24.3	460	22.3
Total	2,170	100.0	1,915	100.0	1,890	100.0	2,060	100.0

NOTE: Commodity figures for 1969 are estimates based upon the most recent data and upon previous patterns. For 1966 through 1968, figures are drawn from the U.S. Department of Commerce Country-by-Commodity Series, and other Government sources.

SOURCE: October 7, 1970 Edition of the *"Current Scene."*

Table IV-4 — China's Commodity Imports from

	Year	(1) Japan	(2) OECD European Total	Belgium/ Luxembourg
Total Imports	1966	315.2	473.4	20.3
	67	288.3	610.1	22.7
	68	325.4	499.5	19.9
	69	390.8	456.8	16.4
Iron and Steel (67)	1966	107.1	82.4	6.1
	67	102.7	156.9	4.7
	68	136.2	81.8	2.3
	69	163.4	72.8	1.9
Machinery and Equipment (7, 86, 8911)	1966	54.1	210.0	1.1
	67	44.1	181.6	0.4
	68	32.9	91.9	0.5
	69	48.4	67.5	. . .
Chemicals (5)	1966	115.7	89.0	7.9
	67	98.7	124.1	10.1
	68	111.7	142.3	11.0
	69	122.4	121.7	6.9
Nonferrous Metals (68)	1966	2.2	47.6	3.4
	67	6.4	57.8	3.5
	68	11.6	87.9	2.8
	69	22.5	120.7	2.8
Chemical Fibers Crude Textile Materials (26, 65)	1966	25.3	17.6	0.9
	67	25.0	28.1	1.4
	68	28.2	23.4	0.5
	69	17.6	21.2	. . .

NOTE:

(1) Included in major European nations are Britain, West Germany, France, Italy, Belgium/Luxembourg, The Netherlands, Switzerland, Denmark, Sweden, Norway, Austria and Yugoslavia.

(2) OECD European Total represents total imports from the 12 European countries listed in (1).

(3) Figures in parenthesis below the name of commodities show SITC Commodity Classification Numbers. Although some difference was noted in part between OECD figures for Chinese imports from Japan and those compiled based on Japanese customs clearance basis, the OECD statistics were used.

Major European Countries and Japan (Unit: $1 Million)

The Netherlands	West Germany	France	Italy	Britain	(1) + (2)
16.1	129.4	92.5	62.8	93.6	788.6
12.2	206.6	93.2	73.9	108.1	898.4
28.9	173.9	87.7	59.6	69.8	824.9
23.0	157.9	41.9	56.3	124.6	847.6
1.1	24.9	9.0	20.2	14.4	189.5
0.4	88.3	12.9	19.2	17.4	259.6
. . .	49.6	5.0	8.1	9.2	218.0
. . .	46.5	6.3	6.9	5.2	236.2
5.4	54.7	49.9	15.2	49.7	264.1
0.8	49.7	35.8	15.8	34.0	225.7
0.5	31.9	16.6	7.4	9.6	124.8
. . .	16.0	11.9	10.3	8.1	115.9
8.9	20.4	13.0	22.8	7.3	204.7
10.4	37.1	16.8	27.5	10.9	222.8
25.8	36.0	13.4	34.0	8.4	254.0
22.1	38.5	6.6	31.6	9.3	244.1
0.1	26.5	8.5	0.3	8.1	49.8
0.3	13.9	18.1	1.2	18.1	64.2
2.1	39.5	18,1	1.1	23.2	99.5
0.4	45.2	4.2	. . .	67.9	143.2
0.3	. . .	4.1	3.6	7.8	42.9
0.1	2.3	6.0	8.8	8.4	53.1
0.1	3.0	5.1	9.5	2.7	51.6
. . .	3.7	0.8	6.8	8.7	38.8

(4) . . . represents figures not more than the unit figure of 1 million.

SOURCES: Statistics prepared by the OECD and various countries of the world.

mainly of finished industrial plants. Imports during 1959, in which economic development reached its peak, consisted of machinery and equipment (two-thirds of which consisted of finished industrial plants) 40.5 percent, metals (iron and steel) 12.2 percent and chemical products (1/2 of which consisted of chemical fertilizers) 7.8 percent. On the other hand, goods exported consisted of agricultural goods and their processed products 75 percent, mining products and textiles 25 percent. The trade pattern in the 1950's consisted of the imports of machinery, equipment and materials for industrialization, and the export of agricultural items, mining products and textiles. However, during the economic recession brought on by the agricultural slump in the early 1960's, a change in imports was observed in that machinery and equipment became less important while increasing emphasis was placed on the import of grains. Food ranked first in imports during 1961, accounting for 32.5 percent of total imports or $303.3 million in value. The amount of food imported in the 1950's ranged from $5 to 38 million, occupying only 0.3 to 2.6 percent of the total amount of imports. Influenced by an "agriculture-first" policy, the imports of chemical fertilizers and agricultural chemicals rapidly increased. Of total exports in 1956, foodstuffs (grain, livestock, tea and tobacco) and textiles occupied 40.6 percent, and 20.5 percent, respectively. During the period of the second 5-year program, these items increased in value and percentage to reach 36.3 percent respectively of total exports in 1959. In the early 1960's, the percentage of food exports decreased due to an agricultural slump while exports of textiles increased to 40.7 percent in 1962.

During the latter half (1964–1965) of the economic readjustment period however, agricultural and industrial production recovered remarkably. The rate of food imported decreased from 39.4 percent in 1962 to 25.1 percent in 1966. On the contrary, the exports of food and textiles increased in 1966 totaling 27.4 percent, and 21.7 percent respectively. No change was observed in this composition during the third 5-year program (1966–1970). Food, textiles (yarn for use in clothing) and raw materials (fabric fiber and oil seeds) accounted for 22 to 28 percent of the composition of exports. Goods to be imported have been divided into 4 classifications, namely, food, iron and steel, machinery and raw materials (rubber and fabric fibers).

Concerning China's principal goods for import classified by items, a brief explanation follows:

1. Machinery

Throughout the 1950's, machinery accounted for 20 to 40 percent of total imports, but this rate gradually decreased from 24.1 percent in 1966 to 13.7 percent or $250 million in value in 1969. The import of machinery in the 1950's consisted mainly of industrial plants, but was replaced by fertilizers, textiles and oil refinery plants during the period from 1963 to 1965. In and after 1966, no sizable industrial plants were imported and it is believed that no plants have been imported at all since 1968. The decrease in plant imports may be regarded as evidence that China has increased her self-supporting capability with regard to machinery. The imports of machinery have also been decreasing in the past few years. Imports from Western European countries in particular have registered a marked decline. On the contrary, imports from Japan have been increasing since 1969, and set a new record high of $119.16 million in 1970, which sharply surpassed the previous record of $61.8 million in 1965. The main items which resulted in the increase of Japanese exports to China were machine tools and automobiles, which might be attributed to China's evaluation of the quality of Japanese-made machinery. China changed her import trade partner from the Soviet Union to West European countries in the early 1960's but this actually meant nothing more than a change in import markets. After 1967, however, imports switched from industrial plant-centered imports to individual unit-centered imports such as that of machine tools and machines for transportation, mining, public works and construction. The increase in Chinese imports from Japan is considered to have been caused by — a) Japan's holding a more advantageous position than western countries regarding prices and delivery dates and b) a change in China's import policy reducing import difficulties including a deferred payment system.

Major Chinese imports cover a wide range including metal cutting machines, pumps, centrifugal separators, heating and cooling equipment, loading and unloading machines, minerals, lumber, machines for processing hard plastic and other similar materials, ball bearings, roller bearings, generators, electromotors, transformers, electronic measuring instruments, buses, trucks, automobiles for special use, aircraft and optical instruments. Imported items that have decreased in number in recent years are motors, agricultural machines, paper manufacturing machines, printing machines, passenger cars, buses, optical instruments and ships. The amount of machinery and equipment imported has gradually been decreasing, while aircraft, office machines, power transmissions and distribution equipment have increased to some extent. Japan ranked first among China's import partners in 1969 and exported $48.4 million in goods to China, followed by West Germany, France and Italy.

Judging from the decrease in imports from western industrialized countries and the increase in the exports of machine tools to Southeast Asia, it appears that China's self-supporting capabilities in the field of machinery are rapidly increasing. Therefore, it is predicted that the machinery China will desire to import in the future will be limited to those requiring high level manufacturing techniques or parts that will require special machining to produce. The items that China needs most seriously now are machinery and equipment for use in transportation and communication. From recent information about truck and tractor production and frequent news concerning shipbuilding, it is evident that China is giving positive support to industries in these fields. In exporting trucks to China, Japan will be at a continuous advantage over West European countries from a geographical viewpoint especially in supplying the required parts.

2. Chemical Products

The amount of chemical products imported in the 1950's was at its highest in 1958 totaling $130 million, reaching roughly $300 million in the 1960's, and accounted for 16.2 percent of the total amount of goods imported in 1969. Chemical fertilizers ranked first among imported chemical products, making up two-thirds of the total, followed by agricultural chemicals ($10 to $20 million annually since 1965) and plastic products reflecting China's agriculture-first policy. The amount of chemical fertilizers imported in the past few years has leveled off to about $190 million including those on a contract basis not yet delivered, showing little change, although the amount of chemical products imported has increased slightly. Japan has been increasing her share in the exports of chemical fertilizers to China since 1968, due to her more advantageous position with regard to prices, freight costs and delivery dates. Characteristics of China's trade in chemical products are: a) a decrease in the amount of petroleum and its products imported due to an increase in the self-supporting capability on the part of China, although priority is still given to imports rather than exports viewed from the point of chemical products as a whole; b) an inclination to select trading partners from western industrialized countries; c) agriculture-supporting chemical products such as fertilizers and agricultural chemicals account for two-thirds of the whole because of the emphasis placed on the "agriculture-first" policy and d) through the establishment of a self-supporting structure, the production of chemical and industrial processed goods increased, and with the change in the import composition from that of finished to intermediary stage organic and inorganic products, these items have considerably increased in quality. This trend will apparently continue for the time being. Agriculture-supporting small-scale factories are engaged in producing fertilizers, centering around nitrogeneous fertilizer. Since the quantity of fertilizer actually applied in China is small – the amount of nitrogenous fertilizer applied per hectare during 1965–1966 was 12.59 kg, corresponding to 90 percent of the world's average of 13.26 kg, and 9.8 percent of Japan's 129.08 kg – it will be a considerably long time before China is able to sufficiently supply herself with fertilizer. In view of the present execution of the "agriculture first" policy, it is not likely that there will be a sudden decrease in the amount of chemical fertilizer imported by China.

3. Iron and Steel

The amount of iron and steel imported in the past as shown in Table IV-2, varies each year; however, it is clear that the amounts imported from respective countries have changed. The amount imported from Western Europe has decreased since 1968, and Japan has become one of China's new trading partners. This can also be attributed to the fact that western countries had only limited amounts to export due to active domestic demands for the respective items, and to Japan's advantage over West European countries in the aspects of price, freight costs and delivery dates. Another reason for the increase in Japanese exports to China may have been the fact that Japan's iron and steel industrial circles view the China market as the second largest market after the United States, and have positively endeavored to open up sales outlets for their products there.

Since both Japanese and West European countries are planning to increase production of iron and steel, it is quite possible that there will be intense sales competition between them on the Chinese market.

4. Nonferrous Metals

As shown in Table IV-2, while the amount of other goods imported have either shown no fluctuations or have decreased, only nonferrous metals have rapidly increased, accounting for more than 50 percent of goods imported from Britain, and about 30 percent of those of West Germany, clearly showing that China has heavy demands for them. Metals that China has always desired are copper, aluminum, nickel, platinum and zinc. Recently, the amounts of copper imported from Britain, West Germany and Japan have rapidly increased. It is conceivable that the increase in imports of nonferrous metals was a result of an increase in demands for them in accordance with an improvement in the technological level of Chinese industry; however, as can be seen in Table IV-3, the exports of tungsten and antimony have decreased.

5. Grain

The imports of grains show a slight decrease, with wheat accounting for more than 80 percent of all grain imported. And, in spite of annually reported rich crops of wheat in China, no trend toward a decline in the imports of grain has been observed. During 1966–1969, the amounts of wheat imported by China totaled an average of 4.65 million tons annually, occupying a 13–16 percent share in the total amount of goods imported. The reason there has been no decrease in the amount of wheat imported is attributed to the following: a) its use as food reserves, b) the acquisition of foreign exchange by exporting comparatively cheap wheat, c) reduction of expenditures for procurement and transportation (domestic products are consumed inland and imported products are supplied to big cities on the northeastern coast) and d) an insufficient increase in food production. Judging from these factors it is safe to say that the amount of wheat to be imported will not decrease for some years to come.

C. GROWTH POTENTIAL OF THE CHINESE MARKET

The scope of China trade is decided by the tempo of the nation's domestic economic development; consequently, its size as an export market, or the volume of demands for imports on the part of China will be determined by the level of that nation's internal economic activities. China decides within the scope of its economic program how much raw material and machinery must be imported in order to maintain a desirable rate of growth for its domestic investments as well as industrial and agricultural production.

Although the imports of raw materials for iron and steel as well as machinery are fundamentally decided by the volume of domestic demands, they are also dependent on the development of demands for foodstuffs in China (the necessity to import grains and chemical fertilizers). As mentioned before, since the imports of wheat and chemical fertilizers are not expected to abruptly decline, the ratio of iron and steel and machinery imports to total imports is expected to maintain a trend similar to that observed during the third five-year program. However, aside from transportation equipment and those requiring highly advanced technology, the imports of machinery are not expected to increase in the immediate future due to the rise in China's augmented self-sufficiency, the necessity to import grains and chemical fertilizers as well as to increase the imports of nonferrous metals.

As has already been mentioned, since competition from western nations poses a problem for Japan, in order for her to make a forecast on the growth potential of the China market, it will be necessary for Japan to know and understand the development of the Chinese economy and changes in the composition of goods to be imported and, at the same time, study the methods utilized by western nations in their approaches to the Chinese market.

Japanese competition with western countries is likely to intensify in like proportion with the increase in China's dependence for foreign trade on non-communist bloc countries (about 80 percent in 1969). However, since Japan-China trade which accounted for about 20 percent of all Chinese trade in 1970 is not expected to drastically increase unless there is a rapid expansion in China's foreign trade, it is of the utmost importance for Japan to gain an insight into China trade policy and the methods used by western nations, in order to expand Japanese trade with China in the future.

The following are two examples of a number of long-range forecasts which have been made on Chinese economy and trade:

1. Dernberger's Projection

Robert F. Dernberger, a professor at Michigan University submitted a report on "China Trade Prospects and United Policy" to the National Committee of the United States on Sino-American relations, which was a long-range forecast (1965/67–1980) on the Chinese economy as shown in Table IV-5, based on the most optimistic hypothesis possible. According to his projection, China's economic growth rate (net national product) by 1980 will be 7.7 percent annually.

2. Professor Ishikawa's Projection

A long-range projection for the Chinese economy made by Professor Shigeru Ishikawa of Hitotsubashi University, Tokyo, appeared in a Japanese economic monthly "The Study of Economy," Vol. 21, No. 3, in July, 1970. He contends that as a most optimistic hypothesis, the economic growth rate can be increased if the planning authorities enforce a rigid economic system, and that it is possible for China to attain a 6.2 percent annual increase in her economic growth rate by 1981 without necessitating

Table IV-5 — Economic Standard and Structure of China in 1980

	Absolute Value		Growth Rate (%)	
	Renminbi Term (Billion Yuan)	US Dollar Terms (Billion Dollar)	1965/67 = 100	Annual Rate
Gross Investments	622	253	379	9.3
Net Output	2,580	1,049	302	7.7
(Breakdown) Agriculture	1,201	488	242	6.1
Industries	1,378	560	386	9.4
Military	294	120	330	8.3
Heavy Industry	495	201	372	9.2
Light Industry	589	239	440	10.2

SOURCE: *"China Trade Prospects and United Policy"* by the National Committee of the United States on United States-China Relations.

Table IV-6 — China's Import Dependency (%)

Year / Import Dependency	Import Dependency	
	Eckstein's Estimates	Data from the Joint Economic Committee of the United States Congress
1952	3.1	3.9
53	3.7	4.5
54	4.0	4.3
55	3.9	5.2
56	3.9	4.0
57	3.5	3.6
58	4.1	3.3
59	4.2	3.1
1960		3.4
61		3.1
62		3.0
63		2.9
64		3.3
65		3.6

SOURCES: (1) A. Eckstein's *"Communist China's Economic Growth and Foreign Trade."* Import Dependency in relation to the Gross National Product.

(2) *"An Economic Profile of Mainland China"* by the Joint Economic Committee of the United States Congress.

an increase in the per capita income of the nation.

These two projections indicate that the maximum growth rate for the Chinese economy during the 1970's will be 6 to 8 percent from the most optimistic standpoint.

According to a projection made by Professor Alexander Eckstein of Michigan University, China's degree of dependency on imports in relation to her gross national product (GNP), has been fluctuating around 4 percent as shown in Table IV-6. This degree of dependency is on almost the same level as that of the Soviet Union, and is considerably lower than that of East European countries whose dependency is on a level of 10 percent.

However, it is a mistake to come to the hasty conclusion that import trade does not exert a significant influence on the Chinese economy based on the observation that China apparently depends little upon imports. Capital goods compose an overwhelming share in the composition of goods imported, and China has been importing machinery, equipment and industrial raw materials which are very important for the growth of the national economy.

Robert Dernberger, anticipating a decrease in China's dependence upon trade, calculated the level of imports in 1980 on the assumption that the degree of dependency upon imports in relation to the GNP will be 4 percent (degree of dependency on import is actually lower than 4 percent), and predicts that imports in 1980 will amount to $4,900 million, showing a 164 percent (annual rate: 9.2 percent) increase over the 1969 level. It is also further assumed that the rivalry between China and the Soviet Union for import partners will continue, and that the present level of 8 percent in trade between East and West will be maintained without any fluctuation.

Table IV-7 — Economic Standard and Structure of China in 1980

	Absolute Rate	Commodity Composition	Gross Rate (%)	
	Billion Dollars	(%)	1965/67 = 100	Annual Rate
Total Imports	49	100	272	6.9
Foodstuffs and Beverages	2.5	5	100	—
Crude Materials, Animals and Vegetables	5	10	500	11.1
Textiles	2.5	5	150	2.7
Minerals and Metals	15	30	375	9.2
Chemicals	7	15	250	6.3
Machinery and Equipment	12	25	350	8.7
Other Industrial Products	2.5	5	250	6.3
Others	2.5	5	250	6.3

SOURCES: *"China Trade Prospects and United Policy"* by the National Committee of the United States on United States-China Relations.

V. REOPENING OF JAPAN-CHINA TRADE

A. OPENING OF FRIENDLY TRADE

For about two years after the discontinuance of Japan-China trade relations in May 1958, trade between the two countries was at a total standstill. During that period China, burdened with food and economic problems resulting from the conversion of Cooperatives into Peoples Communes on the domestic front and from an intensified confrontation with the Soviet Union on the external scene, was secretly working on a switchover in its policy toward Japan.

Resumption of trade relations between Japan and China was achieved in the form of "consideration" trade agreed upon in 1959 between the Japan Socialist Party and the General Council of Trade Unions (Sohyo) of Japan and the All-China Federation of Trade Unions. This particular formula of trade between the two countries was worked out in such a manner that China has taken into consideration the desire of Japan's minor enterprises, which greatly depend upon the supply of Chinese products including straw plait, lacquer, talc, sweet chestnuts, herb medicine and various Chinese food products. Those companies which needed these Chinese products were made direct partners of this particular formula of trade, which authorized no profit-making activities of trading firms and other export and import-related organizations. In return, Japan exported agricultural machines, transportation equipment, agricultural chemicals and others.

Consequently, although the amount of "consideration" trade doubled in the next year, it was only $200.000 to $300.000 in value at the most. In the latter half of 1960 the movement for the resumption of overall trade between Japan and China finally started gaining momentum. On August 27, 1960, Chinese Premier Chou En-lai presented Kazuo Suzuki, managing director of the Japan-China Trade Promotion Association, with the "three-point trade principle" for trade with Japan.

In accordance with the principle, China employed a trade formula wherein China designated a Japanese trading firm considered to be friendly toward China as a "friendly trading firm," and carried out private business individually with so-designated trading firms.

This particular formula of Japan-China trade is called a private individual trade, or more commonly the "friendly trading formula." It became a basic pattern which controlled trade between the two countries until the LT trade, which will be touched upon later, was initiated in 1962.

The reason China began private trade with Japan in 1960 in the form of friendly trade, which represented a step forward from the so-called consideration trade, could certainly be attributed to China's domestic economic situation at the time.

In fact, China's "great step forward" movement, which was adopted as one of China's economic policies, bogged down somewhat and on the other hand, the country was dealt a serious blow by poor agricultural production due to a series of natural calamities which began around 1959. Furthermore, relations with the Soviet Union had been declining since the summer of 1960, with Russian technical experts returning home from China. In order to promote the development of the domestic economy under such circumstances, China was forced to import materials and technology from abroad to some extent. It was necessary to reopen trade with Japan to satisfy these requirements.

In line with the activation of friendly trade between Japan and China in accordance with Chou En-lai's "three-point trade principle," the Japanese Government also worked out measures to cooperate in trade with China. It removed sweet chestnuts, lacquer and bristles from the list of compulsory barter trade items, while maintaining the principle of a compulsory barter trade system. On December 16, 1960, the Japanese Government approved a one-way cash settlement system for imports from China as a provisional and trial step. In addition, Japanese ships started serving China in December.

In response to the resumption of Japan-China trade through the friendly trading formula, China also approved an increase in the number of Japanese friendly trading houses. Japanese trading firms also participated in the Canton Trade Fair held in the spring of 1961. As if to respond to these initiatives on the part of China, the Japanese Government repealed the principle of maintaining a compulsory barter trade system on April 15,

1961, and formally approved the one-way cash settlement formula for imports from China.

Thanks to the Japanese Government's easing of restrictive measures in trade with China, Japanese exports of all but a few products listed on the Coordinating Committee for Export Control (COCOM) list were decontrolled, while imports from China were only subject to prior approval of the Minister of International Trade and Industry. The Japanese Government's intention was to approve, in principle, imports of Chinese products, except for iron ore, coking coal, soybeans, salt and other critical items based on the terms of the government's trade policy.

As a result, friendly trade between Japan and China got off to a favorable start in 1961; however, Japan-China trade based on this particular formula failed to 'achieve the expected results in the first half of 1961 due to a lack of mutual understanding of economic conditions as well as changes which had taken place in the business transaction systems of the two countries as a result of a more than two year interruption in trade relations; the excessive competition among Japanese firms at the Canton Trade Fair; and due to subsequent troubles over imports of coking coal and salt. In the latter half of the same year however, China's increased understanding of the so-called Japanese friendly trading firms helped put Japan-China trade, beginning with the 1961 autumn Canton Trade Fair, onto the right track registering a two-way trade of $47.56 million.

Compared with 1961, the initial year of friendly trade between Japan and China, 1962 witnessed further growth in trade between the two countries, with annual trade figures totaling $84.84 million. Japanese exports to China, in particular, doubled over the preceding year thanks to a sharp growth in shipments of steel materials to that country.

Japanese authorization of deferred payments for exports of steel materials and fertilizers in May 1962, also substantially contributed to the expansion of trade between the two countries. Japanese participation in the Canton Trade Fair was as active as in the previous year, with trade contracts concluded during the fair amounting to $8.75 million. When follow-up contracts signed in Peking after the fair were added, total trade involving the Canton Trade Fair reached approximately $20 million. More than 80 Japanese friendly trading firms took part in the autumn Canton Trade Fair and the amount of import and export contracts concluded surpassed that of the spring fair.

B.   AN OUTLINE OF LT TRADE

Under the friendly trade formula, China unilaterally designated some Japanese trading firms as friendly trading firms and only those so-designated by China were authorized to take part in trade with China.

China, which initially looked upon friendly trade between Japan and China as being beneficial, gradually came to believe in due course that this particular trading practice held a variety of inconveniences as well as shortcomings. Those firms designated by China as friendly trading firms were mostly financially-weak small and medium-scale enterprises. Quite a few major trading firms in Japan formed "dummy" companies to engage in trade with China. Consequently, most of the friendly trading turned out to be nothing other than a temporary transaction involving only a small amount of business. It was found to be of little use for continuous operation of programmed transactions. As demands for Japanese industrial plants, heavy machinery, fertilizers, and the like increased, such small-scale trade through the friendly trading firms made it impossible for China to carry out the planned transactions that she desired. Under such circumstances, China actively approached influential figures of the ruling Liberal Democratic Party (LDP) of Japan in 1962, resulting in visits to Peking of Kenzo Matsumura, Tatsunosuke Takasaki and others of the ruling party.

In September 1962, a party led by Liberal Democratic Dietman Kenzo Matsumura visited China at the invitation of Chinese Premier Chou En-lai. Admitting that it would be difficult to conclude a Japan-China governmental trade agreement although hoping for an early signing of such an agreement, China made a realistic proposal that both countries proceed for the time being with private trade with a view to expanding it progressively in the years to come.

Key points of the Chinese suggestion presented at that time were as follows:

Firstly, that both Japan and China carry out an overall trade with respect to key trade items including barter as well as deferred payment transactions. The key trade items China desired included Japanese exports of chemical fertilizers, agricultural chemicals, steel materials, alloy steel materials, chemical fiber plants and connected know-how in addition to patents and agricultural machinery. Chinese exports were to include coal, salt, iron ore, soybeans, corn and herb medicine.

Secondly, that both countries be required to set up a unified liaison organization to carry out specific negotiations for enforcement of such transactions. Since Japan had few objections to these points, a mission headed by Tatsunosuke Takasaki, also a Liberal Democratic Dietman, visited Peking for negotiations to work out specific points of the Chinese suggestion. As a result, a memorandum was exchanged on November 9, 1962, between Takasaki and Liao Cheng-chih, the Peking representative, for the development of the aforementioned long-term overall trade between Japan and China. The trade formula based on the memorandum is generally called LT trade. The letters L and T stand for the initials of Liao and Takasaki.

In the annals of postwar Japan-China trade relations, the opening of LT trade was really an epoch-making event. It rapidly expanded in size and in parallel with friendly trade conducted by the two countries.

Immediately after the signing of the memorandum initiating LT trade, representatives of the so-called Japan-China friendly organizations of Japan visited Peking and concluded on December 27, 1962, with representatives of the China Committee for the Promotion of International Trade, an agreement relating to friendly trading between Japan and China.

Thanks to this agreement, continued operation of the friendly trade agreement previously concluded between the two countries was confirmed, despite the inauguration of LT trade. The agreement also called for the holding of a Japanese Merchandise Fair in Peking and Shanghai during 1963 and a Chinese Merchandise Fair in Tokyo and Osaka in the following year.

The outline of LT trade called for Japan-China trade amounting to £36 million (about $100 million) of imports and exports annually, in order to develop long-term overall trade for a period of five years, from 1963 to 1967. Major Japanese exports included steel materials (special steel materials included), chemical fertilizers, agricultural machinery and industrial plants. Included in the Chinese exports were coal, iron ore, soybeans, corn, miscellaneous beans, salt and tin. Specific trade conditions based on the contents of an annual program were to be worked out by the two countries at annual negotiations between the Japanese and Chinese parties concerned.

Special arrangements for the initial year of LT trade were decided during a series of visits to Peking of representatives from Japanese industries involved in trade with China from late 1962 to early 1963.

As for Japanese exports, a Chinese request for a deferred payment system was authorized by the Japanese Government for the first time. A one and one half-year down payment-free deferred payment term was authorized for exports of ammonium chloride and farm equipment, while payment for steel material exports were based on a term of two-year deferred payments without a down payment.

Although the Japanese Government was originally reluctant to authorize deferred payments for exports to China on the grounds that there was no precedent, it approved the plan on condition that this particular payment arrangement would be effective only for the initial year of LT trade and that it would not be considered a precedent. As for plant exports to that country, there was the projected export of Kurashiki Rayon Company's vinylon manufacturing plant. After detailed studies on the matter, which was the first case of Japanese plant exports to China, the Japanese Government authorized deferred payments with a 2.5 percent down payment, plus a grace period of five years following the actual shipment for this particular plant export.

During the initial year of LT trade, two-way trade between Japan and China failed to reach the $100 million mark; however, it got off to a fine start with successful trade contacts accounting for 88.8 percent of the targeted figures for exports and 10.3 percent for imports, resulting in total trade of 92.8 percent of the projected figures.

Trade negotiations for the second year of LT trade were held in Peking in September 1963. At the negotiations Japan set an export goal of $74 million, excluding plant exports, as compared with $65 million for the initial year and an import target of $40 million, a sharp increase compared with the $25 million for the first year of LT trade.

Newly included in Japanese imports for the second year of LT trade were pig iron and buckwheat. With regard to payments for Japanese exports of the so-called medium-term deferred payment items such as ammonium chloride, agricultural machinery and steel materials, payments for ammonium chloride were to be made within one year of the shipment, while those for agricultural machinery and steel materials were given terms calling for a 20 percent down payment with the balance being paid in four installments over a period of two years. As for industrial plant exports, the shipment of another vinylon manufacturing plant was projected.

Trade negotiations for the second year of LT trade made favorable progress. In particular, on a contract basis Japanese exports attained 100 percent of the targeted figure, with total import and export contracts concluded surpassing the initial year to reach 93.1 percent of the targeted goal. The total amount of the contracts was to surpass $100 million in value only two years after the initiation of LT trade.

In response to a final decision on the second year program of LT trade and the favorable proceedings for implementation of the program, a

Japanese mission including Liberal Democratic Dietman Kenzo Matsumura and Kaheita Okazaki, of the Japan-China Overall Trade Liaison Association, visited Peking in April 1964, when the Chinese Economic and Trade Fair was being held in Tokyo, and exchanged with Liao Cheng-chih a memorandum for mutual establishment of the Takasaki and Liao Liaison Offices in Tokyo and Peking respectively and mutual dispatch of their respective representatives. Based on this memorandum, the liaison offices of Japanese and Chinese representatives were established in February 1965, ushering Japan-China trade into the second phase of its development.

Thus, the addition of LT trade to favorable development of the so-called friendly trade between the two countries contributed to a substantial growth in Japan-China trade in 1963, with the total amount of trade for the year registering $137 million on the customs clearance basis. The figure was close to the all-time postwar high in Japan-China trade which was established in 1956. In 1964, Japanese exports and imports registered $152.61 million and $157.75 million, respectively, resulting in total trade of $310.36 million between the two countries, a two-fold increase over the preceding year. As a result, the trade balance between the two countries which had been heavily in favor of Japan was greatly improved for the first time in six years following 1958.

Thanks to the continued favorable development of friendly trade and LT trade, which form the "two wheels of a cart," Japan-China trade was expected to make further development; however, a new obstacle to the expansion of trade between the two countries came into the picture in 1965 in the form of the Japanese Government's measure to discontinue the extension of the Export-Import Bank of Japan loans to help finance deferred payments for exports of industrial plants to China.

As for deferred payment exports of industrial plants to China, there was the case in which the extension of the Export-Import Bank of Japan loans was authorized under the administration of the Ikeda* Cabinet in 1963. It involved the export of Kurashiki Rayon Company's vinylon manufacturing plant. However, with the inauguration of the Cabinet headed by Prime Minister Eisaku Sato in 1965, the Japanese Government refused to authorize the extension of Export-Import Bank of Japan loans to finance Hitachi Shipbuilding & Engineering Company's projected export of a freighter to China on the grounds that it would violate the contents of the so-called "Yoshida Letter." Instead, the Japanese Government approved export of the freighter to China with the condition that it

*Japanese Prime Minister from 1960 to 1964.

be financed by private loans.

The Japanese Government's action angered Chinese officials who claimed that Japan accepted the interference of Taiwan into Japan-China trade. It subsequently cancelled the previously concluded plant export contracts, casting dark clouds over the subsequent development of Japan-China trade.

The issue involving the Export-Import Bank of Japan loans has remained unsettled to this date. As a result, Japan-China negotiations for the fourth year of LT trade held later in 1965 failed to achieve the expectations of the Japanese.

VI. RECENT JAPAN-CHINA TRADE

A. RECENT TRADE DEVELOPMENT

Recent trade between Japan and China has witnessed extremely favorable growth since 1964, as shown by Table VI-1.

Table VI-1 — Developments in Recent Japan-China Trade

(Unit: $1,000)

Year	Japan's Exports	Japan's Imports	Total	Percentage with the Previous Year	
1964	152,739	157,750	310,489	(+)	119.3
1965	245,036	224,705	469,741	(+)	51.3
1966	315,150	306,237	621,387	(+)	32.3
1967	288,274	269,439	557,733	(−)	10.2
1968	325,438	224,185	549,623	(−)	1.5
1969	390,803	234,540	625,343	(+)	13.7
1970	568,878	253,818	822,696	(+)	31.6
*1971	578,000	322,000	900,000	(+)	8.2

*Figures for 1971 are estimated.

The actual performance of Japan-China trade for fiscal year 1970 chalked up $822.69 million in total trade volume, up 32 percent over the preceding year. Japanese exports amounted to $568.87 million, which represented an increase of 45.6 percent over the previous year, hitting a record high surpassing that of 1968. On the other hand, Japanese imports totaled $253.81 million, up 8.2 percent in comparison with the preceding year, far below the $362.37 million and $269.74 million registered in 1966 and 1967, respectively (including $51.36 million in payment for imports of rice in 1966 and $33.98 million for the same in 1967). Even if the imports of rice are not included, the figures for Japan's imports from China still stand at a high level.

In terms of trade balances, Japan had a marked excess of exports in trade with China following fiscal year 1965, with a sharp export surplus in fiscal 1970 amounting to $315.06 million, a $159.34 million increase over the surplus of the previous year. As a result, Japan realized an aggregated $620.67 million in export surpluses during the years that followed fiscal 1964.

It may safely be said that Japan's successive export surpluses over the past six years in trade with China shows that, similar to West German trade with that country, Japan is on the way to increasing exports rather than imports in trade with China. However, one of the reasons given for this imbalance is the fact that China's enhanced capacity for export to Japan has not kept pace with her massive demands for Japanese goods.

As for the principal commodities traded between the two nations in 1970, metals and metal products (mainly steel), chemical products including chemical fertilizers, a variety of machines, textile fibers and products were exported to China by Japan. These four principal export items accounted for 98.5 percent of Japan's exports to China during 1969, and 97.4 percent in 1970. Conceivably, this tendency will remain unchanged for the time being; however, of these four principal items, metals dropped 1.6 percent, textile fibers and products went down 0.8 percent, and chemical products dipped 7 percent in comparison with the previous year, while the exports of machinery climbed upward by 8.5 percent over 1969.

Foodstuffs, textile fibers and products accounted for 81.4 percent of China's overall import volume. Unlike exports, the import volume of key commodities varies with developments in the Chinese economy. The following, which show the shares these various items held in relation to the entire import volume of Chinese trade for 1966 and 1970, is provided for reference:

| | Percent of Chinese Imports in: | |
	1966	1970
Foodstuffs	40.8%	26.4%
Textiles	8.7	24.1
Raw Materials	28.6	30.9
Iron and Steel	7.0	0.1
Mineral Fuels	4.9	2.5
Pine Resin	1.4	5.3

Table VI-2 — Change in the Composition of Japanese Goods Exported (1965 to 1970) to China   (Unit: $1,000)

Year / Item-wise	1965 Amount	1965 %	1966 Amount	1966 %	1967 Amount	1967 %	1968 Amount	1968 %	1969 Amount	1969 %	1970 Amount	1970 %
Textile and Textile Products	27,667	11.3	25,300	8.0	24,989	8.7	18,165	5.6	17,693	4.5	21,232	3.7
Chemical Products	92,589	37.8	115,652	36.7	98,650	34.2	111,707	34.3	122,394	31.3	138,280	24.3
Metal and Metal Products	48,880	20.0	113,306	35.9	113,892	39.5	154,219	47.4	195,944	50.1	276,076	48.5
Machinery Equipment and Appliances	61,814	25.2	53,657	17.0	44,009	15.3	32,917	10.1	48,301	12.4	119,164	20.9
Others	14,086	5.7	7,185	2.3	6,754	2.3	8,430	2.6	6,472	1.7	14,126	2.6
Total	245,036	100.0	315,150	100.0	288,294	100.0	325,438	100.0	390,804	100.0	568,878	100.0

Table VI-3 — Change in the Composition of Goods Imported (1965 to 1970) from China (Unit: $1,000)

Year / Item-wise	1965 Amount	1965 %	1966 Amount	1966 %	1967 Amount	1967 %	1968 Amount	1968 %	1969 Amount	1969 %	1970 Amount	1970 %
Foodstuffs	81,241	36.2	124,945	40.8	90,577	33.6	72,589	32.4	53,805	22.9	66,975	26.4
Textile and Textile Products	11,592	5.2	26,636	8.7	39,051	14.6	41,063	18.3	59,889	25.5	61,297	24.1
Raw Materials for Metal	3,733	1.7	6,859	2.2	5,485	2.0	1,947	0.9	2,511	1.1	2,629	1.0
Raw Materials and Others	73,988	32.9	87,570	28.6	84,909	31.5	79,198	35.3	82,181	35.0	78,320	30.9
Mineral Fuels	9,309	4.1	15,021	4.9	17,140	6.4	5,403	2.4	4,947	2.1	6,422	2.5
Chemical Products	5,952	2.7	7,793	2.5	8,693	3.2	9,942	4.4	16,115	6.9	23,181	9.1
Iron and Steel	24,209	10.8	21,556	7.0	9,608	3.6	1,454	0.6	208	0.1	90	0.1
Nonferrous Metals	6,958	3.1	3,810	1.2	2,540	0.9	1,559	0.7	873	0.4	795	0.3
Others	7,713	3.4	12,047	3.9	11,436	4.2	11,030	4.9	14,011	6.0	14,109	5.6
Total	224,705	100.0	306,237	100.0	269,439	100.0	224,185	100.0	234,540	100.0	253,818	100.0

Table VI-4 — Japan's Foreign Trade and Japan-China Trade

(Unit: $1,000)

Year	Japan's Exports to China (A')	Japan's Exports to the Rest of the World (B')	A'/B' (%)	Japan's Imports from China (A'')	Japan's Total Imports (B'')	A''/B'' (%)	Japan's Imports from China (A)	Japan's Total Exports and Imports (B)	A/B (%)
1960	2,726	4,054,537	0.1	20,729	4,471,132	0.5	23,455	8,545,669	0.3
61	16,639	4,235,596	0.4	30,895	5,810,432	0.5	47,534	10,046,028	0.5
62	38,460	4,916,159	0.8	46,020	5,636,524	0.8	84,480	10,552,683	0.8
63	62,417	5,452,116	1.1	74,599	6,736,337	1.1	137,016	12,188,453	1.1
64	152,739	8,673,191	2.3	157,750	7,937,543	2.0	310,489	14,610,734	2.1
65	245,036	8,451,742	2.9	224,705	8,169,019	2.8	469,741	16,620,761	2.8
66	315,150	9,776,391	3.2	306,237	9,522,702	3.2	621,387	19,299,093	3.2
67	288,294	10,441,572	2.8	269,439	11,663,087	2.3	557,733	22,104,659	2.5
68	325,438	12,971,662	2.5	224,185	12,987,243	1.7	549,623	25,958,905	2.1
69	390,803	15,990,014	2.4	234,540	15,023,536	1.6	625,343	31,013,550	2.0
70	571,708	19,363,347	3.0	253,769	18,873,543	1.3	825,477	38,236,890	2.2

Of Japan's total foreign trade, trade with China has risen to a level exceeding two percent since 1964. It is a well known fact that Japan's trade with other nations has recently grown to such proportions that it has become one of the wonders of the world. Above all, the fact that Japan-China trade is gradually coming to influence the expansion of Japanese trade with the rest of the world, bears eloquent witness to the remarkable growth rate of Japan-China trade.

The ratio of Japan's export and import volume in trade with China, to Japan's entire foreign trade volume from 1960 to 1970 is shown in Tables VI-2, 3, and 4.

B.   NEGOTIATIONS OVER JAPAN-CHINA TRADE

Friendly trade relations between Japan and China were reopened with the so-called "friendly trade" between the two countries agreed upon in 1961 and LT (Liao-Takasaki) memorandum trade initiated in 1963, and have since been conducted under these two formulas. The former was carried out in accordance with the "Agreement on Friendly Trade," with the parties being named the China Committee for the Promotion of International Trade, and the Japan Association for the Promotion of International Trade respectively. This agreement aimed at the expansion of friendly trade between Japan and China and provided for the conduct of friendly trade through economic and trade exhibitions in both countries and also personnel exchanges between the two nations.

On the other hand, the objective of the LT Memorandum Trade Agreement was to carry out overall trade between both nations, dealing with principal commodities based on long-term projects which Japan and China were to decide annually. In addition to the establishment of a unified Liaison Agency designed to assist trade between Japan and China, there are also provisions for the granting of benefits such as medium or long-term deferred payments for the trade of producers' goods as the occasion may demand. Under the first 5-year program, both Japan and China intended to conduct two-way trade transactions amounting to US $500 million.

The Liao-Takasaki Memorandum Trade Agreement was signed on November 9, 1962. Based on actual trade performances, LT trade totaled approximately US $730 million by the end of the first five-year period. However, it is regrettable that Japan-China trade did not continue to register as sharp a growth rate as was originally expected due to the outbreak of the issue involving the so-called "Yoshida Letter" centering around the financing of Japanese industrial plant exports with the aid of the Import-Export Bank of Japan's 5-year loan on a deferred payment basis. However, as far as the so-called friendly trade between China and Japan is concerned, Japanese merchandisers received much advertising at Japan Industrial Fairs held in Peking and Shanghai in 1963, 1965 and 1968, respectively. For the Chinese side, economic and trade fairs were held in Tokyo and Osaka in 1964, and in Northern Kyushu as well as Nagoya in 1966, thus aiding the promotion of mutual trade between Japan and China. As a result, friendly trade between Japan and China progressed smoothly along with LT trade.

However, LT trade was renamed "Japan-China Memorandum Trade" in 1968 due in part to the Great Cultural Revolution and to problems the Japanese side had with LT trade. The new agreement concluded between the Japan-China Memorandum Trade Office of Japan, represented by Kaheita Okazaki and its Chinese counterpart, represented by Liu Hsi-wen, was based on the same provisions as that of LT trade, but was different in that the former stipulated a year-by-year revision of Japan-China trade agreements. However, another noticeable difference from the days of LT trade was the inclusion of a statement in a joint communique by both nations which took on some political overtones due to Chinese dissatisfaction with Japan's attitude in her trade with China.

The trade agreement revised in 1971 calls for the following:

Total: Approximately $70 million in both exports and imports.

Exports: Chemical fertilizers, special steel, ordinary steel, raw materials for the chemical industry and a variety of machines including agricultural equipment and the like.

Imports: Soybeans, salt, eggs, mixed beans, buckwheat, corn, etc.

Note: In the past, coal, iron ore, scrap iron, rice, tin, tobacco leaves and meat were listed as import items.

Lastly, under the Japan-China Memorandum Trade Agreement, provisions were made for the establishment of Japan-China Memorandum Trade Offices having the characteristics of private trade representative offices in Tokyo and Peking for the purpose of serving as liaison agencies, in addition to an exchange of newsmen between the two countries.

C.   JAPAN-CHINA TRADE PROBLEMS

1.   Political Influence

The greatest problem facing current Japan-China trade is the lack of diplomatic relations between the two nations, a factor which is liable to produce conflicts over their respective diplomatic policies.

The following are the items upon which China has insisted in concluding the agreements on private trade, the LT and Friendly Trade Agreements, between the two countries in the past:

a. The Three-Point Political Principles with Regard to Japan

Japan shall not block the normalization of political relations between the two countries, take a hostile attitude toward China or engage in behind the scenes maneuvering to set up "two Chinas."

b. Strict Adherence to the Three-Point Guidelines for Trade with China

Trade with China should be conducted based on a government-level agreement; however, if both nations come to show a friendly attitude toward each other prior to the conclusion of a governmental agreement, private trade agreements may be concluded on an individual basis, with the exception of those trade commodities which are given special consideration in view of the needs of small and medium-sized enterprises.

c. Chou En-lai's Four Conditions for Trade with China

The Chinese side declared that as of April 1970, it would suspend all trade with Japanese enterprises including pro-China Japanese enterprises, unless they agreed to abide by Chou En-lai's "Four-Point Conditions for Japan-China Trade." The Japanese enterprises to which these apply are as follows:

(1) Japanese manufacturers or trading firms which, while engaged in trade with the People's Republic of China, make bids to invade North Korea by giving assistance to South Korea, or those that aid Taiwan in launching counteroffensives against mainland China.

(2) Japanese enterprises having massive investments in South Korea or Taiwan.

(3) Japanese enterprises that assist the United States in making air raids on Vietnam, Laos and Cambodia by manufacturing bombs for the United States.

(4) US-Japan joint venture enterprises and their subsidiaries.

d. Oppose the Japan-US Security Treaty and Joint Japan-US Communiques

e.   The Five-Point Principles of Peace

(1) Mutual respect for the sovereignty and the territories of the other nation.

(2) Mutual non-aggression.

(3) Non-interference in the internal affairs of the other nation.

(4) Peaceful coexistence.

(5) Inseparability of politics and economics.

Over the past ten years or more, these political assertions of China, whether concerning friendly trade or memorandum trade, have exerted far-reaching influence over Japan-China trade. In connection with this, Japan, parallel with West European nations, has been pursuing trade policies aimed at solving discrepancies in trade with China on a case-by-case basis. In other words, Japan, as a member of the free world nations, adopted the principles of the United Nations, and in terms of politics as well as economics, has subscribed to the formula of gradually improving her relations with China.

In more concrete terms, Japan endeavored to actively improve her political relations with China through the establishment of the Dietmen's League for the Promotion of Japan-China Trade and the Japan Association for the Promotion of International Trade, with the accent on improving them through the offices of memorandum trade following the resumption of trade between the two nations.

Up to the present, the Great Cultural Revolution in China has exerted no perceptible influence on the enactment of Japan-China trade, and even after LT trade was renamed the "Japan-China Memorandum Trade," massive efforts were made to maintain friendly trade relations between Japan and China.

Later, the Dietmen's League for Normalization of Japan-China Relations, with Dietman Aiichiro Fujiyama of the ruling Liberal Democratic Party as chairman, was established in December 1970, by a suprapartisan group comprised of the members of the Lower and Upper Houses of the Japanese Diet. Thus, both nations faced a turning point in their political relations in February 1971, when Fujiyama and other Japanese representatives as well as Kaheita Okazaki, representative of the Japan-China Memorandum Trade Office, conferred with Chinese leaders. As a result, both sides reached the conclusion that the time had come to consider a date for breaking the stalemate in Japan-China relations as well as concrete methods for carrying out such a policy.

Conceivably, Japan-China trade will gradually take a more clearly defined course since the world political scene is taking a more favorable turn as witnessed by the easing of strained United States-China relations and China's entry into the United Nations.

2. Issue Involving Japan Export-Import Bank Loans

Following the Japanese Government's approval of Kurashiki Rayon Company's export to China of a complete rayon-vinylon plant and the decision to finance the export with the aid of Export-Import Bank of Japan loans in 1963, Taiwan embarked on a campaign protesting these measures, which in turn developed into a diplomatic issue involving both Japan and Taiwan in 1964, and the latter took a series of diplomatic steps aimed at partially suspending her trade with Japan.

Former Japanese Prime Minister Shigeru Yoshida, in talks with Chang Chun, Secretary of the Presidential Agency of the Taiwanese Government, during his visit to Taiwan in March of 1964, reportedly stated that Japan did not intend to extend the benefits of deferred payments for exports destined for China through the Import-Export Bank of Japan. This is what has been termed the "Yoshida Letter."

Late in March 1965, China informed Japan that she intended to cancel already signed contracts for the export of Nichibo Company's vinylon plants, freighters from Hitachi Shipbuilding & Engineering Company and fertilizer plants of Toyo Engineering Company, giving the "Yoshida Letter" as the reason for the cancellations.

These factors once again led to trouble between the two countries. The Chinese side did not agree with Takeo Miki, then Japanese Foreign Minister, who stated that the "Yoshida Letter" was Yoshida's private letter and such an individual opinion could not be binding on the Japanese Government. This dispute, however, seriously affected both LT and MT trade, and following this, the rate of MT trade to total Japanese imports from China gradually decreased by the year, to fall below 10 percent in 1970.

At the time of the dispute, China placed orders for a total of 33 large-scale industrial plants with West European countries, but because of the discord, Japan lost a favorable opportunity to export such plants to China.

With regard to the extension of long-term loans to other nations, it is a practice in West European countries for city banks or syndicated banks to provide financing with their own capital under the stipulation that some type of security be provided by an export insurance agency. On the contrary, Japanese banks, with the exception of the Export-Import

Bank of Japan, are characterized by the fact that they do not finance any long-term deferred payments; therefore, it is necessary to have a clear understanding that in actuality, the Export-Import Bank of Japan for the most part assumes the characteristics of a commercial bank.

3. Export-Import Imbalance

Trade between Japan and China which began in 1950 was characterized by a chronic excess of Japanese imports from China until 1964; however, beginning in 1965, Japanese exports to China began to exceed her imports, and the margin of Japan's excess exports to China was the greatest ever in 1970, representing an increase of slightly less than $160 million over the preceding year. This could be attributed to two main economic factors, namely — a massive demand on the part of China for Japanese goods, and the fact that freight rates on the Japan — China route are one fourth those on the West Europe — China route.

However, Japan itself retains control of various factors which have resulted in a stagnant development of Japanese imports from China; that is, problems involving the protection of domestic agriculture. Included in such difficulties are a surplus production of rice, an increased fruit output, the protection of coastal fishermen, the maintenance of fair prices, and the prevention of damage caused by blight and insects. In addition, Japanese domestic price fluctuations make it difficult for Japan to purchase Chinese goods.

In order to correct this imbalance, it is necessary for Japan to strive to import as many goods as possible from China and, by blazing a new trail, call for China's cooperation in increasing her exports to Japan. In particular, it is highly probable that additional Chinese exports to Japan will center around foodstuffs, textile fibers and raw textile materials and products. In like manner, there is the possibility of Japan purchasing meat, eggs, foodstuffs — sweet chestnuts, nuts, dried persimmon, raisins, jam, canned foods, vegetables — frozen and dried; marine products — frozen lobster, hair-tail, sea eels, sea bream, mackerel, sardines, salmon, jellyfish; miscellaneous beans — red beans, french beans, peas and broad beans, grain and feeds — beet pulp, soybeans, and peanut lees.

As for textiles, raw silk is most likely to top the import list followed by silk-related raw materials such as silk spinning yarn, floss-silk and acetic acid yarn, secondary textile products such as jackets, blouses, sweaters, women and children's clothing and raw materials for textiles such as flax and angora rabbit and goat furs.

In addition to the aforementioned goods, there is the possibility that there will be a phenomenal increase in the exports of the items listed below, depending upon the efforts made by both nations.

Raw materials used in making steel — coking coal, fluorspar and tin metals; raw materials for industrial purposes — anthracite coal, soybeans, skin and feathers, salt, bristles and inorganic chemical medicines; miscellaneous goods — barley straw, basketwork, furniture, personal ornaments and stationary. Thus, there is the likelihood that the problems concerning the imbalanced Japan-China trade volume will be on their way to being solved.

4. Account Settlement Formulas

Account settlements in trade between Japan and China were conducted under the barter formula based on the British pound sterling until 1958. However, after the resumption of trade between the two countries, this formula was changed to one demanding cash payment based on the pound. French franc-based account settlements have been extremely rare. Therefore, both Japan and China become justifiably uneasy whenever uncertainty arises over the value of the pound. It is true that there were some cases in which yen clauses were incorporated into deferred payment agreements. Nevertheless, it is usually necessary to contract future bookings on the basis of the pound. Accordingly, the situation is such that deferred payments and usuance bills inevitably become more expensive since they depend upon the future parity of the pound.

Although West European nations are usually able to effect settlements through their own currencies, Britain, France, Switzerland and West Germany, in addition to their own currencies, began using the Chinese yuan for the mutual settlement of accounts in April 1970. Under this system, currency quotations are decided on the basis of fixed rates for the Swiss franc and the Chinese yuan, with account settlements being conducted at the branch office of the Bank of China in London. Apparently the balance of yuan holdings can be exchanged into the currencies of the respective countries in London at the end of each month.

The Montreal Bank of Canada, in October 1970, following in the footsteps of the four West European nations, also decided to introduce this formula for the settlement of accounts based on the Chinese yuan.

Meanwhile, in mid-1969, both Japan and China began conducting negotiations for the settlement of yen or yuan accounts based on the pound for LT as well as Memorandum Trade, but this proposal was rejected by the Chinese side in March 1970, presumably due in part to the prevailing opinion in various fields that the value of the yen was the equivalent of the United States dollar. However, trade settlement formulas between the two countries became multi-faceted with President Nixon's statement in April of 1971 to the effect that use of the dollar would be permitted in trade settlements with China. Therefore, there is the possibility of the United States dollar appearing in trade settlements between Japan and China, as opposed to the settlement of accounts based on the yen or yuan.

On the other hand, the Japanese side is showing signs of liberalizing the settlement of accounts through a revision of the regulations concerning account settlement standards and a lifting of restrictions on 14 foreign currencies. Therefore, it appears that the adoption of a formula for the settlement of accounts based either on the yen or the yuan, is gradually becoming more feasible.

5. Japan's Export Competition with West European Nations

Japan's advantage over West European nations lies in her exports to China of deadweight and bulky cargos as well as perishable goods, but she faces intensified competition with European countries in connection with the exports of high-priced goods, lightweight commodities, small-sized and technology-intensive products. Furthermore, Japan has experienced extreme difficulty in the exports of commodities whose brand names are not well known in China due chiefly to the lack of diplomatic relations between the two countries. Consequently, it will not be an easy matter for Japan to overcome these difficulties in order to cope with the competition from West European countries, since it will be necessary for Japan to further refine her technology, speed up delivery dates, intensify after-sales services and ease conditions for account settlements if she is to increase her exports to China.

Furthermore, it will require a great deal of effort on the part of Japan to bring this about since China places profound trust in a variety of the well known machines and chemical products of West European nations.

6. The Outlook for Japan-China Trade

The three factors of politics, economics, and trade must be taken into consideration in order to make a long-range forecast for Japan-China trade.

Like West Germany, Japan has yet to resume diplomatic relations with China, although relations between the two countries have been maintained on a private basis through two Japanese organizations, the Association for Memorandum Trade and the Association for the Promotion of International Trade. Nevertheless, it is difficult for Japan to stabilize trade with China since it naturally follows that Japanese trade with China will differ from that of other countries with which China has diplomatic relations. Furthermore, it is also quite natural that China should give preferential treatment to the countries with which she has formal relations such as those of Western Europe and Canada. However, with the United States-China rapprochement and the efforts being made by the League of Dietmen for the Normalization of Japan-China Diplomatic Relations, the gap between the two nations will presumably be narrowed, leading to a further lifting of trade restrictions.

In view of the fact that the Chinese economy has achieved its growth with the main stress on an increase in the production of foodstuffs and its GNP stands at more than US$130 billion, presumably the Chinese economy will widely diffuse into other areas and witness accelerated growth. China's economic development will probably be closely related with the Japanese economy in the form of trade, marine transportation and personnel and technical exchanges.

China's trade policy places stress on the protection of its domestic industry through state controls and protectionist customs duties. However, in the future it is anticipated that China will bring its conditions for trade with other countries more in line with those of West European nations.

Japan-China trade will most probably be conducted on the basis of the hitherto mentioned vague but inseparable conditions set by China for her foreign trade. Japan's exports to China will be roughly classified into the following items: iron and steel, chemical products including chemical fertilizers, machinery and raw materials for textiles. Characteristic of Japanese exports to China is the fact that these items alone accounted for 98.5 percent of the entire volume of Japan's exports to China in 1970. In connection with this, an estimate has been made of possible Japanese exports of these items to China over the next five years.

a. Iron and Steel

Japanese exports of this item to China in 1970 amounted to 157 million tons, or some $273 million in value. At the present time, since the value of Chinese imports of iron and steel is considered to be at a level of $280 million, this is the highest amount Japan can expect to export. However, it is anticipated that Japan will be able to increase her iron and steel exports to China at a growth rate of five percent yearly to reach $300 million, in view of the fact that it is presumed the Chinese side will increase its lump sum purchases of items from overseas countries during her fourth 5-year program.

b. Chemical Products

The exports of chemical products stood at $138.20 million in 1970, but chemical fertilizers have reached their saturation point and in the future the exports of chemical products will center around organic and synthetic chemical products. The exports of other chemical products including chemical fertilizers are projected to slightly exceed the present export volume during the next five years.

c. Machinery

The exports of machinery totaled $102 million in 1970 with the main items being machines for industrial and transportation purposes with vehicles as the core, and at present the export of these items is expected to increase. However, the exports of optical machines and electrical machinery are leveling off, partly because Japan is competing with West European nations in her exports of these items to China, and partly due to these items being subject to the restrictions of the Coordination Committee for Export Control (COCOM). Consequently, future growth in Japanese machine exports to China will depend greatly on the success of plant exports of synthetic textile manufacturing machines, chemical fertilizers, ships and the like, as well as whether deferred payments will be permitted. If deferred payments are permitted, Japan will be able to boost her export volume of these items to $200 million; however, United States entry into the China market may somewhat affect Japan's exports of these goods.

d. Textile and Textile Products

Japan has encountered difficulties in increasing her export volume to China for these items for the past several years, and total export amounts have leveled off at around $20 million, reflecting a gradual build-up of China's synthetic fiber and textile industry. Conceivably, Japan's exports of this item will only slightly rise and remain at a level hovering slightly over the present one during the next five years because China is more enthusiastic about purchasing raw materials for chemical fibers and intermediate textile products rather than synthetic textile products.

e. Japan's Imports from China

With respect to the prospects for Japan's imports from China over the next five years, the principle items breakdown into foodstuffs, raw materials, textile fibers and products as well as chemical products, which accounted for 90.5 percent of Japan's total imports from China during 1970. Foodstuffs imported in 1970 stood at $6.7 million, which is not considered bad since neither rice nor corn was imported. Furthermore, Japan is expected to need some 1.5 million tons of feed by 1972. In addition, the imports of various beans, fish and vegetables is expected to increase, boosting the import volume to a level of $100 million.

The imports of textiles and textile products stood at only $61 million in 1970. Japan's demands for the following goods are on the increase and at the same time Japan faces competition from West European nations who want to import raw materials such as raw silk, silk spinning yarn, acetic acid yarn, floss-silk and angora rabbit and goat furs. Presumably, the import of these goods will not register a sharp increase in the immediate future. However, it is anticipated that the imports of textiles and textile products will rise to $100 million within the next five years.

The imports of raw materials chalked up $78 million for 1970, with the main items being soybeans and salt. Japan encountered difficulty in increasing her soybean imports due to the fact that the price was set according to international price levels, and rising soybean prices in China giving further impetus to a rise in the cost of importing them. Nevertheless, Japan will have no difficulty increasing soybean imports to around 500,000 tons over the next five years if the price should become as ideal as those of the United States. However, in order for China to do this, it will be necessary for her to increase the area allocated for growing soybeans.

As far as chemical products are concerned, Japan's imports of rosin have hit an all-time high of $13.4 million. In the future, Japan will be faced with the necessity of purchasing massive amounts of inorganic medicines, mainly acids and sodas, in order to balance Chinese imports of Japan's organic synthetic chemical products, since China has almost reached self-sufficiency in the inorganic pharmaceutical industry. Further, it will be necessary for Japan to make spot purchases of these items for at least the time being. It is assumed that Japan will be able to import around $30 million worth of these items.

Due to China's lack of surplus raw materials for making steel such as pig iron, coking coals and tin metals, it is expected that Japan will only make sample purchases of these items for the present; however, it is doubtful that much can be expected for the imports of these items even after the next five years.

In addition to the items above, prospective purchases of flourspar and anthracite coal which are among the main goods imported from China, are both expected to grow $7 million during the next five years.

7. Circumstances Leading to Japan-China Memorandum Trade

It is necessary to take a backward glance at the procedures by which Japan-China trade has been conducted in the past with special emphasis directed toward developments in LT trade, prior to setting out on an explanation of current Japan-China Memorandum Trade (MT Trade).

In June 1952, following the Korean War, the first Japan-China trade agreement was concluded by Kei Hoashi and other Japanese representatives with Peking officials. With the conclusion of the second agreement in October 1953, between a suprapartisan League of Dietmen headed by Masanosuke Ikeda and the Chinese Government, and the third concluded between Tien Jen-min, Ikeda and Shozo Murata (then Chairman of the Association for the Promotion of International Trade) during the Chinese official's visit to Japan during May of 1955, Japan-China trade was well on its way toward expansion. Afterwards, namely since the latter half of 1957, agreements for specific items were concluded in rapid succession, including those covering salt, chemical fertilizers and iron and steel. There was remarkable enthusiasm on the part of Japanese industries for the export of iron and steel, and, under the 5-year long-term barter trade agreement, Japan was to import 2.1 million tons of coking coal and 2.3 million tons of iron ore worth £200 million in 1962, the last year of the agreement, in return for Japanese exports of steel materials corresponding to the total volume of the items imported. This agreement, the fourth Japan-China Trade Agreement, was signed on March 5, 1957, as a result of two trips to China made by M. Ikeda for negotiations. Total trade volume increased from $16 million in 1952 to around $150 million by 1957; however, in April of 1957, in the midst of confirming and implementing the fourth trade agreement, the Chinese expressed dissatisfaction with a reply from the Japanese Government and refused to implement the program. Then, with the outbreak of the "Chinese National Flag Incident" at Nagasaki, Japan, Japan-China trade was completely suspended as of May 10, 1957.

In 1959, the Japan Socialist Party (JSP) and the General Council of Japanese Trade Unions (Sohyo), made arrangements for trade with the

All-China Federation of Trade Unions, and both sides agreed to conduct trade geared to the needs of Japan's small and medium-sized enterprises centering around commodities such as raw lacquers, sweet chestnuts ard Chinese herb medicines.

After this, Chinese Premier Chou En-lai conferred with Kazuo Suzuki, then managing director of the Association for the Promotion of Japan-China Trade and announced China's "three-point guidelines for trade with Japan," based on China's three political principles with regard to Japan (see Attachment 2).

The Chinese side, in accordance with these principles, designated certain Japanese trading firms and enterprises it deemed friendly to Peking as trade partners and followed a formula under which pro-Peking Japanese companies would proceed with their trade transactions on an individual basis with the Chinese side. This eventually took the form of the current friendly trade.

Although the trade volume fell sharply to $23 million in 1960, it rose to register some $84 million in 1962; however, Japanese companies designated as being friendly to Peking in the initial stages of friendly trade were mostly small and medium-sized enterprises. Consequently, friendly trade was limited to temporary transactions on a case-by-case basis and trade volume was comparatively small. As a result, it was not possible for either side to make sufficiently planned transactions.

In September 1962, senior politicians of the Liberal Democratic Party represented by Kenzo Matsumura, Yoshimi Furui and Seiichi Tagawa, conferred with Premier Chou En-lai during their visits to China (see Attachment 3).

The Chinese side, although intent on concluding a government-level trade agreement, came through with a realistic proposal for the adoption of a gradual and cumulative formula designed to gradually expand Japan-China trade on a private basis since they deemed it difficult to immediately realize a government-level agreement.

Based on this new proposal, a Japanese mission led by Tatsunosuke Takasaki, senior politician of the Liberal Democratic Party, and Kaheita Okazaki, visited Peking in October 1962. This resulted in the initialing of a memorandum regarding long-term overall Japan-China trade and matters agreed upon on November 9 in Peking between Takasaki and Liao Cheng-chih, the Chinese representative (see Attachment 4).

a. The Significance of the Trade Agreement

The Chinese side regards both memorandum and friendly trade as having equally great importance, and, as a matter of course, does not consider one without the other. First of all, as can be seen in the three-point guidelines for trade with Japan and the LT agreement signed by Takasaki and Liao Cheng-chih, the principles of the Chinese side were based on a realistic way of thinking as seen by the fact that China adopted a cumulative trade formula during the first stages of her trade with Japan, realizing that a government agreement was not possible from the very outset. The conclusion of this agreement favorably affected LT trade as well as Japan trade as a whole, and led to a rapid expansion of Japan-China trade. Furthermore, the fact that a senioɪ politician of the LDP concluded the long-term agreement, which was tantamount to a semi-governmental agreement with the Peking regime, gave Japanese industrialists a sense of security, enabling them to tackle the problems of Japan-China trade in earnest.

Secondly, LT trade was designed to ensure long-range transactions of key commodities.

Thirdly, China's state-run trade has enabled Chinese corporations to conduct trade with Japan on a completely coordinated basis through one unified channel; on the other hand, Japan has been placed in a far weaker position in her trade with China since her trading firms are not united and make contacts with the Chinese side individually.

In addition, the exchange of newsmen has helped promote mutual contact and understanding in other aspects of Japan-China relations.

However, most important of all is the fact that both sides have been attempting to make political approaches to the other through trade.

The famous English historian Arnold Toynbee is reported as having said, "I highly evaluate the leaders of Japan's ruling party who have a channel in the form of LT trade which has enabled them to make contact with their Chinese counterparts, despite the lack of formal diplomatic relations between the two nations."

b. LT Trade

Kenzo Matsumura conferred with Liao Cheng-chih during his visit to China in May 1966, to discuss the future course of action after termination of the first LT Trade Agreement on December 31, 1967. On that occasion, the two politicians agreed in principle to continue memorandum trade. On his visit to Peking in 1967, Kaheita Okazaki and Chinese representatives decided to concretely carry out the matters agreed upon between both sides regarding arrangements for continuing memorandum trade (see Attachment 5).

However, at the time, China was in the midst of the Great Cultural Revolution and the activities of the leaders of Chinese Government offices were up for review by the Chinese general public; thus, judging from the state of affairs, it was not considered feasible to complete a long-term trade agreement at that time. In addition, Liao Cheng-chih, representative of the Liao Trade Office was suffering from poor health, and a succession of other incidents following the summer of 1968 led to strained relations between Japan and China.

In consideration of the fact that contrary to expectations the LT trade, which was based on the gradual and cumulative formula, produced no noticeable effects on Japan-China trade due to China's hardline policy towards foreign countries during the Great Cultural Revolution, as well as Japan's passive attitude toward Japan-China trade shown by the "Yoshida Letter," it was only natural for the Chinese side to have had doubts about and take a cautious attitude toward LT trade.

On November 7, 1967, the Chinese Government suddenly sent a telegram to Kenzo Matsumura requesting him to visit Peking by November 10. However, Matsumura was unable to meet the deadline due to a delay in settling the procedures for his trip to Peking. Consequently, he did not visit China, but a Japanese LT trade delegation went in his behalf in February, 1968.

c. MT Trade in 1968 (First Year)

Politicial talks were held between the Japanese and Chinese delegations in connection with memorandum (MT) trade for 1968, on February 8, 1968. The members of the Japanese delegation were Yoshimi Furui, Kaheita Okazaki and Seiichi Tagawa and others; the members of the Chinese delegation were Liu Hsi-wen, Wan Hsiao-yun and Sun Ping-hua.

The Japanese side briefed the Chinese delegation on their basic thinking with regard to Japan-China trade. They conveyed the expectations on the part of the Japanese people for increased Japan-China trade and stressed the necessity of continuing LT trade. The Chinese delegates strongly insisted on the three-point political principles and the inseparability of politics from economics, and contended that the Sato Cabinet's policy of separating politics from economics was proof of its policy of viewing China as an enemy. In addition to upholding the contentions of the Chinese side, the Japanese delegation expressed the desire to extend the term of the agreement to five years as opposed to the one-year proposal of the Chinese side. The Japanese delegation also demanded that both sides hold consultations to arrive at counter-measures to cope with the problem of account settlements in connection with the uncertainty over the pound sterling.

After these conferences, the MT Trade Agreement signed in 1968 differed from the LT Trade Agreement in the following respects:

(1) The period of the agreement was temporarily reduced from the previous five years to one year.

(2) The Japanese side agreed to abide by the "three-point political principles" and the inseparability of politics and economics, upon which the Chinese side insisted, and to regard them as principles to be observed in the conduct of relations between Japan and China.

(3) The "Takasaki Office" was renamed the "Japan-China Memorandum Trade Office" and the "Liao Office" became the "China-Japan Memorandum Trade Office."

Many improvements had to be made in negotiating the second LT trade agreement, including the problem of settling accounts. Japan had trouble breaking even in her trade with China due to the uncertainty over the stability of the pound, which placed her at a disadvantage in international competition with West European countries which were allowed to use their own currencies in trade with China. Accordingly, the Japanese side considered writing into the agreement a provision for the settlement of accounts by means of the currency of a third country not utilizing the pound, or on the basis of yen, equivalent in value to the pound. Technically speaking, although they knew there would be a lot of difficulties involved in bringing this about, at the least the Japanese side desired to sound out the Chinese side on this matter.

Furthermore, there were inequalities disadvantageous to Japan such as defective provisions written into the contracts concerning the methods of making remittances for account settlements and the parties responsible for paying indemnities for damages. In addition to these there were many other problems which had to be settled by Japan such as problems relating to exports of industrial plants and the "Yoshida Letter."

The "Yoshida Letter" was sent by former Japanese Prime Minister Yoshida to Chang Chun, Chief Presidential Secretary of the Taiwan Government in May 1964, allegedly stating that funding for plant exports to China would not be provided by the Export-Import Bank of Japan "during 1964." As a result, although it was possible to export Kurashiki Company's vinylon plants, which had already been approved by the Chinese Government, it was impossible to export some items tentatively contracted for such as Nichibo Company's vinylon plants, freighters of the Hitachi Shipbuilding & Engineering Company and urea (fertilizer) plants manufactured by Toyo Engineering, since funding could not be procured through the Export-Import Bank of Japan. Furthermore, following this, other trade talks on plant exports did not bear fruit, and Japan had no other alternative than to look enviously on trade talks for plant exports between West European nations and China.

In terms of Japanese imports, items mentioned in the LT Memorandum Trade Agreement but not imported included meat and leaf tobacco.

As for meat, prior to the suspension of Japan-China trade in 1958, Japan sent several survey missions to China to inspect the condition of Chinese livestock in order to prevent epidemics from occurring in China. As a result, the mission reported that hygienic conditions for domestic animals had improved much more than had been expected. The Chinese authorities concerned have also provided Japan with monthly reports on the hygienic conditions of domestic animals for the past several years, and Japanese firms are now trying to obtain permission from the government to import domestic animals from China.

d. MT Trade in 1969

Since MT Trade which went into effect in 1968 was based on a one year agreement, it was necessary to establish regulations concerning settlements for the following year in order to maintain stability in transactions and the continuance of trade. For this purpose, Seiichi Tagawa and Mimaharu Okubo visited China in October of 1968 for unofficial negotiations with Chinese officials. In February 1969, a Japanese mission composed of Yoshimi Furui, Kaheita Okazaki, and Seiichi Tagawa, was dispatched to China and conducted negotiations which lasted 50 days concerning the MT Trade Agreement for the coming year. However, these negotiations encountered extremely rough-going and unofficial as well as official talks and meetings of lesser officials were also held more than twenty times during this period.

On April 4, 1969, both sides signed a joint communique and trade agreement. However, both had to reduce this trade considerably; Japan had to suspend rice imports due to surplus domestic production while China had to drastically reduce the export of corn, coal, iron ores and the like to Japan.

Additionally, the problem of settling accounts on the basis of the yen or yuan came up for discussion between Japanese and Chinese representatives (Chen, vice-president of the Bank of China, represented the China side) amidst an air of uncertainty over the pound and the French franc. It was decided during the discussions that both sides would continue negotiations on this subject through the respective MT trade offices after the conclusion of the talks.

e. MT Trade in 1970

In March 1969, several confrontations between China and the Soviet Union occurred; however, with the death of North Vietnamese President Ho Chi Minh in September, a China-Soviet summit conference was held, and subsequently talks on the border issue were held in October, temporarily averting a crisis.

On the other hand, China criticized the joint Japan-US communique issued after talks between Prime Minister Eisaku Sato and United States President Richard Nixon in November 1969, referring to it as a "revival of Japanese militarism." Under such adverse conditions which had existed from quite some time before, an advance party composed of Yoshimi Furui, Shunichi Matsumoto and others had visited China early in March 1969 for negotiations on MT trade for fiscal year 1970, and conferred with Chinese delegates such as Liu Hsi-wen, Hsu Ming, Yen-Fu, Wu Shu-tun and others. The main body of the Japanese delegation which included Kenzo Matsumura, Kaheita Okazaki, Aiichiro Fujiyama, Hideji Kawasaki, Seiichi Tagawa, Yosaburo Naito and Yasumi Kurogane, also joined in the talks at the half-way point. As in previous talks, the discussions began and ended with political overtones. During these particular talks, the Chinese side showed a tough attitude toward the reversion of Okinawa to Japanese rule, which was disclosed in the aforementioned Japan-US joint communique issued in November, 1969.

f. MT Trade in 1971 (The 4th Year)

In the middle of February 1970, a Japanese delegation headed by Kaheita Okazaki which included Yoshimi Furui and Seiichi Tagawa, conferred with Liu Hsi-wen, Hsu Ming, Wu Hsiao-tung, Lin Pah and Chong Ming of the China-Japan Memorandum Trade Office and came to an agreement after 20 days of negotiations. This is attributed to the fact that both sides were in agreement on many points in the initial stages of the talks during which time they expressed their opinions.

During the discussions of political problems during these talks, the following problems came up for debate: militarism movements in Japan, the Japan-Taiwan-South Korea Liaison Committee, the development of natural resources in the shallow water areas near the Chinese seashore and the normalization of Japan-China diplomatic relations.

In negotiating trade arrangements, it was decided that Japan-China trade would be on the same level as that of the previous year; however, at a later conference between Japan's MT trade delegation and Premier Chou En-lai, the Premier made a statement suggesting the expansion of MT trade, which resulted in both sides agreeing to raise the trade volume for fiscal year 1971 at the ensuing talks between delegate Okazaki and Liu Hsi-wen.

The Fujiyama Delegation (the Dietmen's League for Normalization of Japan-China Relations

This delegation headed by Aiichiro Fujiyama and including Seiichi Tagawa, Ryoichi Nagata and Yasumi Kurogane, visited China together with the MT trade delegation, and conferred with Wan Kuo-chuan, Wu Hsiao-ta and Wan Hsiao-yun of the People's Republic of China Association for the Promotion of Friendly Relations with foreign countries, in an effort to help assist the Japanese trade delegation in trade negotiations with China.

g. Negotiations Concerning Problems in Settling Accounts

Japan and China decided in April 1968, to add the French franc to the currencies used in account settlements in trade between the two countries in order to cope with the chronic instability of the pound. Immediately afterwards, however, the franc suddenly decreased in value, seriously affecting Japan-China trade. Since that time, the Japanese side has been searching for an account settlement formula which would not be affected by fluctuations in foreign currencies.

In negotiating MT trade for fiscal year 1969, the Chinese side countered with a proposal opposing Japan's proposed settlement of accounts in Japan-China trade; however, although the plans of both sides were in basically the same vein, that is, exports on the basis of their own currencies and account settlements based on the pound, no agreement was reached due to differences in formulas for converting the yen or the yuan into the pound. Nevertheless, negotiations were continued afterwards and were also held at the Canton Trade Fair in October 1969, but again no agreement was reached although many compromises were made on both sides.

In a bid to effect a compromise with the Chinese side, Japanese representatives proposed the adoption of a formula almost similar to the Chinese one during MT trade negotiations, but in the end, this was refused by the Chinese authorities who stated they had no intention of concluding an agreement for the settlement of accounts.

Thus, the one-year-old negotiations for the settlement of accounts ended in a stalemate.

Attachment 1

Premier Chou En-lai's Four Conditions for Japan-China Trade

After the signing of the MT Trade Agreement for fiscal year 1970 on April 19, 1970, a Japanese delegation led by Kenzo Matsumura conferred with Premier Chou En-lai, Li Hsien-nien and Kuo Mojo at the People's Convention Hall in Peking. At that time, Chou En-lai presented China's four guidelines for foreign trade during discussions on the international situation and Japan-China relations. It was stipulated that —

1) China will not conduct trade with those Japanese firms which, while engaged in trade with China, simultaneously assist the Republic of Korea or Taiwan.

2) China will not carry on trade with Japanese enterprises investing in the Republic of Korea or Taiwan.

3) China will not make transactions with any Japanese enterprise engaged in the supply of weapons and ammunition to assist the United States in its war of "aggression."

4) China will not engage in trade with US-affiliated joint ventures located in Japan.

The official statement by China read in part:

"The Taiwan problem is one of the fundamental problems facing both China and Japan. Short of solving this problem, there is no point in conducting Japan-China trade. China is ready to terminate any and all agreements in Japan trade should there be a violation of the aforementioned principles, in spite of whether they are of a friendly trade or a memorandum trade nature. As we have stated before, we cannot aid militarism in achieving its objectives."

Wu Hsiao-tung gave a detailed briefing on China's principles regarding Japan-China trade at the Canton Trade Fair on May 2, 1970, and stated that Premier Chou En-lai, in his talks with representatives of Japan's pro-China trade organizations and the delegation headed by Kenzo Matsumura, outlined the four-point conditions for Japan-China trade. He explained them in detail at that time.

1) China will discontinue trade with any Japanese firm engaging in trade with her if they should aid any Taiwanese faction of "bandits" led by Chiang Kai-shek in invading China or should help South Korea violate the sovereignty of North Korea.

2) China will have no economic relations with Japanese trading firms or manufacturers with capital investments in Taiwan or South Korea.

3) China will have absolutely nothing to do with Japanese enterprises providing ammunition for United States "aggression" in Vietnam, Laos or Cambodia.

4) China will not conduct trade with any US-Japan joint venture or any United States subsidiary based in Japan.

China's trade with Japanese companies, whether it be of the friendly or memorandum type, must come up for review to determine whether it meets the standards prescribed in the four-point conditions for Japan-China trade. The conditions stipulate that —

"If it should be discovered that any Japanese trading firm or manufacturer is in violation of even one of the clauses in the four-point conditions, China will not conclude any contracts with the offender. Furthermore, if any attempt should be made to deceive China, contracts already concluded will be immediately terminated upon discovery thereof."

Chou En-lai added that China insists on the promotion of two-way trade between the two countries based on the three-point political principles regulating Japan-China relations as well as the three guidelines for trade with Japan, and firmly adheres to a policy of politics being inseparable from economics. He further added that if Japanese trading houses and manufacturers show a willingness to faithfully abide by the four-point conditions, China will gladly conduct trade with them on the basis of the principles of equality and reciprocity. The Chinese Premier further hinted at the possibility of China opening trade with any Japanese trading firm participating in the "Japan-Taiwan Cooperation Committee," if they would withdraw from the committee, make statements acknowledging their "criminal acts" and promise not to violate the four-point conditions again in the future.

Thus, Chou En-lai's four-point guidelines for Japan-China trade gradually took form at the Canton Trade Fair in 1970, and various Japanese enterprises went on record as agreeing to conduct Memorandum Trade according to Chou's four conditions, and commitments to conduct Memorandum Trade according to Chou's four conditions, and commitments to that effect were provided through the Japan-China Memorandum Trade Office. With this development, Japan-China trade entered a new phase; however, the implementation of the MT Trade Agreement for fiscal year 1970 was delayed considerably in comparison with the previous year.

After the turn of 1970, China turned toward the direction of further progress and development as well as putting the finishing touches on the Great Cultural Revolution. During this time, reconstruction of the Chinese

Communist Party had been well under way; Communist Party locals of the various ministries were consolidated and party committees for the local administration of the various provinces were created. Thus, the executive structure of the central government gradually began to fulfil its functions, and China entered a period in which she had to prepare to add the last touches to the fourth five-year plan.

As for China's relations with foreign countries, most of the Chinese diplomats who had been temporarily repatriated during the Great Cultural Revolution, were reassigned to their overseas posts within the year. The Chinese Government, taking the initiative, expanded its foreign diplomacy and the number of foreign diplomats invited from abroad registered a sharp increase.

Attachment 2

Premier Chou En-lai's (3-Point Guidelines for Trade with Japan)

The remarks made by Premier Chou En-lai in his talks with Kazuo Suzuki, executive director of the Association for the Promotion of Japan-China Trade, on August 27, 1960, constitute China's basic political posture toward trade with Japan, and were as follows:

"You have talked a great deal about Japan-China trade; therefore, I too would like to refer to China's policy with regard to trade with Japan. I will talk about the 'three-point guidelines' for Japan-China trade, because the Japanese seem to like to use the phrase. These 'three-point principles' or 'guidelines' were born of the continued struggle against Nobusuke Kishi's* policy of hostility toward China. Until now, Japan and China have sought to develop mutual trade under agreements concluded by the private organizations of both nations. However, during his administration, Nobusuke Kishi contended that such a formula for China-Japan trade would not work. Furthermore, he would not recognize the implementation of any private agreement nor would he guarantee them, and went as far as to destroy them with his 'hostile policy' toward China. Therefore, we had no other choice than to suspend trade between our two countries for over two and a half years, since we could not condone Kishi's policies. It would be for the common good if we were able to gradually promote trade based on the aspirations of the peoples of both China and Japan. However, before this, we will have to observe the attitude the Ikeda cabinet takes toward trade between China and Japan. The gist of the three-point principles for trade with China are as follows:

1) Governmental agreements
2) Private contracts
3) Individual consideration

First of all, guarantees will not be provided for any agreement unless it is signed by both the Chinese and Japanese Governments. The reason for this is that in the past, the Japanese Government would not guarantee any agreement made on a private basis. Further, a government level agreement can only be signed when both governments have made moves toward establishing friendly and normal relations. Otherwise, it is impossible to conclude any agreement. With regard to relations between the two countries, as comrade Liu Ning-yi stated during his stay in Tokyo, we are

*Japanese Prime Minister from 1957 to 1960

determined to stand firmly beside China's three-point political principles. These principles, far from being excessive demands on the Japanese Government, are quite fair. The Japanese Government should not take a hostile attitude toward China since China recognizes the existence of Japan and rejoices in the progress made by the Japanese people. Furthermore, if there is to be negotiations between the two countries, China will naturally have to deal with the Japanese Government. However, the Japanese Government does not take a similar attitude toward its negotiations with China. Unwilling to recognize the 'new China' nation, the Japanese Government takes a hostile attitude toward our newly born country and recognizes Taiwan, and that Taiwan represents China. Furthermore, the Japanese Government is not willing to make the government of 'new China' the other party of her negotiations.

Secondly, the Japanese Government should refrain from behind the scenes maneuvering to create 'two Chinas' by riding on the 'coat-tails' of the United States. The President of the United States, whether he is elected from the Democratic or the Republican party will probably set out on the establishment of 'two Chinas.' According to a report from a Taiwanese Government-affiliated newspaper based in Hong Kong, the Republican party is taking a passive wait-and-see attitude on its contemplated creation of 'two Chinas,' while the Democratic party will take the initiative in doing this if it should come to power. I believe that this is only natural; however, we will of course oppose any such action on the part of the Democratic party or Japan's trying to cater to the favor of the Democratic party.

Thirdly, we request the Japanese Government not to prevent China-Japan relations from moving toward normalization. China's three-point political principles are extremely fair and we believe that the Japanese will be able to understand if they put themselves in our position.

1) The Chinese Government, far from being hostile toward Japan, hopes for friendly relations with her.

2) China recognizes 'one Japan' without seeking to create two; furthermore, the Chinese Government makes it a principle to negotiate with only the Japanese Government.

3) We have persistently given encouragement, support and aid to moves toward the normalization of relations between China and Japan.

Therefore, why does the Japanese Government follow a policy that is diametrically opposed to that of the Chinese Government? In regard to the new Japanese Government, we do not welcome the statements made by either Prime Minister Hayato Ikeda or Foreign Minister Zentaro Kosaka relating to China policies. We will observe the course the Japanese Government takes in the future.

The Japanese Government led by Nobusuke Kishi was criticized twice on our part for its policies toward China; once in 1957 during the period in which I served as director of the Diplomatic Ministry of the Chinese Government, and a second time in 1958, the year in which Vice Premier Chen Yi held the post. In the meantime, the Japanese Government based its policies toward China on a series of actions taken by Kishi, who regarded China as a country hostile toward Japan. Therefore, we will continue to observe whether Prime Minister Ikeda adopts the policies of the Kishi government.

Under these circumstances, we have come to the conclusion that any agreement between our two countries should be concluded by the respective governments, and that stable relations between both nations cannot be ensured through any agreements concluded on a private basis. Any such agreement must include provisions for trade, fishery, mail and transportation. Is it impossible for both nations to conduct trade without an agreement? The answer is no. If conditions are established, we will be able to open trade with Japan based on any contract signed on a private basis. For example, a Japanese enterprise and a Chinese corporation can take a friendly attitude toward each other, hold talks based on mutual needs, sign a contract and make arrangements for mutual trade within a given period. If the contract is discharged faithfully, smooth relations between the two countries will be maintained and Japan-China political relations will move in a favorable direction. If this should come about, any short-term contract may be converted into a long-term one. I am making reference to these matters with future developments in Japan-China relations in mind.

In addition, special consideration has been given to individual small and medium enterprises for the past two years. In any case where these enterprises face any specific difficulty, it is proper and fitting that the General Council of Trade Unions of Japan (Sohyo) and the All-China Federation of Trade Unions consider what is in the best interest of these enterprises and take measures to rescue them from their predicaments. Furthermore, if the need arises, these two organizations will be permitted to increase the trade volume of this 'consideration trade.' Concerning this point, comrade Liu Ning-yi provided a report to Japanese representatives during his stay in Tokyo. I would like you to inform us through the China Committee for the Promotion of International Trade, what you believe to be a feasible 'friendly trade' profitable to both sides in terms of the three-point guidelines for trade with Japan. The members of this committee have a clear understanding of these principles. Mr. Suzuki, after returning home and discussing this with your friends and Japanese companies having connections with this committee, you will find this to be true.

We would like to add that we will continue to maintain our stand against the new Japan-US Security Treaty, which is directed against China and the Soviet Union as potential enemies of the United States and Japan, threatening the security of Southeast Asia as well as the peace of the Far East and Asia. We also support the struggles of the Japanese people now being staged in order to establish a democratic and neutral Japan — independent and peaceful — in opposition to the Japan-US Security Treaty. It is desired that Mr. Suzuki convey the Chinese people's feeling of respect and support to the Japanese people."

Attachment 3

Joint Communique After Talks Between Kenzo Matsumura and Premier Chou En-lai (September 19, 1962)

Premier Chou En-lai and Vice Premier Chen Yi held friendly and frank talks with Kenzo Matsumura, counsellor to the ruling Liberal Democratic Party, for three consecutive days, beginning September 16, 1962. The Chinese side, in addition to affirming that China rigidly adheres to its three-point political principles, the three-point guidelines for trade and the principle of the inseparability of politics and economics, insisted that all of these principles continue to remain valid. Both sides also came to the agreement that Japan as well as China should strive to bring about normal political and economic relations between the two nations through a gradual and cumulative formula.

Attachment 4

Concerning the Memorandum Issued by Tatsunosuke Takasaki and Liao Cheng-chih on November 9, 1962

"In order to bring to fulfillment the objectives of expanding and promoting trade between China and Japan as discussed by Kenzo Matsumura and Premier Chou En-lai in September 1962, and to enable both nations to promote mutual private trade on the basis of the principles of equality and reciprocity under a gradual and cumulative formula, Tatsunosuke Takasaki and Liao Cheng-chih do hereby exchange the following memorandum."

1) Both sides agree to strive for the promotion of long-term as well as all-around mutual trade and shall designate the period from 1963 to 1967 for the implementation of the first five-year program, during which an annual trade volume averaging £36 million in value will be conducted.

2) The principal commodities which each side will export have been decided as follows:

Japan — steel products including special steel products, chemical fertilizers, agricultural insecticides and herbicides, agricultural machines, plants and others.

China — coal, iron ore, soybeans, corn, miscellaneous beans, salt, tin, and others.

3) Individual transactions citing this memorandum will be in the form of separately signed contracts between the Japanese firm/organization concerned and the Chinese Corporation for the Promotion of Foreign Trade.

4) Account settlements for transactions based on this memorandum will be in either the pound sterling or a L/C (Letter of Credit) based on other foreign currencies or guarantees on the basis of an L/C, whichever is agreed upon by the two countries.

5) Both parties, after due consultation, will decide upon a method of effecting deferred payments on certain commodities which Japan exports to China as well as installment payments on industrial plants.

6) Both sides will endeavor to promote the technical exchanges and tie-ups necessary for the execution of this memorandum.

7) Both sides will, after due consultation, decide upon inspection procedures for commodities, arbitration and other matters necessary for the implementation of this memorandum.

8) This memorandum, or any agreement or contracts based on it, are

not to be cancelled without the consent of both parties concerned.

9) This memorandum, or any agreement or contracts based on it, may be amended or adjusted after consultations on both sides.

10) This memorandum is effective from the date of signature to December 31, 1967, with extension of the period optional and upon the mutual consent of the parties concerned.

11) Two copies of this memorandum shall be prepared, one in Japanese, and the other in Chinese, both of which are equally valid.

November 9, 1962
Peking

Tatsunosuke Takasaki   Liao Cheng-chih

Attachment 5

Agreement Reached Between Kenzo Matsumura
and Liao Cheng-chih (May 19, 1966)

1. Both parties agree in principle to continue LT Memorandum Trade in accordance with the agreements concluded between Liao Cheng-chih and Tatsunosuke Takasaki, during the period from 1963 to 1967.

2. Both parties agree to make concrete arrangements for Memorandum Trade when Kaheita Okazaki, representative of the Takasaki Memorandum Trade Office meets with Chinese Government representatives during his visit to China next year.

3. Both parties agree to contact each other at any time should any unforeseen incidents occur.

VII. JAPAN-CHINA TRADE ORGANIZATIONS

A. THE DEVELOPMENT OF PRIVATE TRADE AGREEMENTS

Trade between Japan and China is not based on governmental agreements, but entirely on private business arrangements such as the following:

The first Japan-China Trade Agreement concluded between the Japanese representatives to an International Economic Conference and the China Committee for the Promotion of International Trade; the second agreement concluded between the representatives of the Dietmen's League for the Promotion of Trade between China and Japan; the third agreement between the Japan Association for the Promotion of International Trade, a delegation of the Japan-China Export-Importer's Association, the Dietmen's League for the Promotion of Trade between China and Japan and the China Committee for the Promotion of International Trade; the "friendly trade formula," a result of the "Friendly Trade Agreement" signed in 1962 between the Japan Association for the Promotion of International Trade, the Western Headquarters of the Japan Association for the Promotion of International Trade, the Japan-China Association for the Promotion of International Trade and Friendship and the China Committee for the Promotion of International Trade; the LT Trade Agreement (LT Trade) between Tatsunosuke Takasaki's office and Liao Cheng-chih's office; and the Memorandum Trade Agreement (MT Trade) beginning in 1968 between the representatives of the Japan-China Memorandum Trade Office and its Chinese counterpart.

Consequently, during transactions with China, there are various conditions applicable since trade is conducted on the basis of memorandum trade agreements which have been concluded by private groups; namely, participation in one of these groups is the first stipulation and trade must be conducted according to the agreements worked out by the respective private group.

The first to the fourth trade agreements were on a barter trade basis, and stipulated that a balance would be maintained with respect to the total volume of imports and exports, and that merchandise would be classified according to importance based on the principle of a product for product exchange of items of equal value. It was further stipulated in this transaction formula that Japanese businessmen were to deal directly with Chinese foreign trade corporations within the framework of this agreement.

The "Friendly Trade Agreement," the first official agreement concluded in 1962, after a period of interrupted trade between the two nations, merely pointed out that China would trade on an individual basis with those firms it considered to be friendly to China, and was not an agreement for the transaction of trade of a barter nature, but one which allowed China to arbitrarily choose her trading partners.

LT trade which originated during one of Kenzo Matsumura's visits to China, was agreed upon by Tatsunosuke Takasaki and Liao Cheng-chih in 1962, and called for barter trade in general to be the mainstay of long-term deals in addition to other kinds of transactions including those on a deferred payment basis, with the two sides establishing centralized organizations for the uniform supervision of business, namely, trade based on the principle of reciprocity.

In such fashion, the trade between China and her respective partners has been worked out according to the discretion of the parties concerned on a private business basis.

Therefore, it is essential to take full note of the fact that if a Japanese company hopes to participate in trade with China, it is necessary to do so under one of these trade formulas. A brief outline of three Japanese organizations now playing a major role in Japan-China trade follows along with their system of conducting that business.

B. ACTIVITIES OF JAPAN-CHINA RELATED ORGANIZATIONS

1. The Japan-China Memorandum Trade Office, Incorporated

Address : Kotohira Kaikan Bldg.
1, Shiba, Kotohira, Minato-ku, Tokyo
Tel: (503) 4681

Representative: Kaheita Okazaki

This office replaced the old Takasaki office that was set up for LT trade. It was incorporated after the creation of MT trade.

The Japan-China Memorandum Trade Office has its liaison office in Peking. It is the successor of the Takasaki Peking Liaison Office and was born out of the "memorandum" concluded by K. Okazaki, representing the Takasaki office and Liao Cheng-chih of the Chinese in April 1964. Its Chinese counterpart is in Kioi-cho, Chiyoda-ku, Tokyo, which also underwent a name change from the Liao Cheng-chih Tokyo Liaison Office to the China-Japan Memorandum Trade Tokyo Liaison Office.

The Japan-China Memorandum Trade Office is the Japanese organization responsble for the negotiation of annual trade agreements with China within the context of the Memorandum Trade Agreement, but the conditions of concrete transactions based on the plans as well as final contents of annual programs concerning the export and import of major products within memorandum trade are settled after negotiations between Japanese traders, representing their related industries, and their Chinese counterparts. The members of the delegation representing Japanese firms are a part of the China-Japan General Trade Liaison Association which includes:

The Japan Ammonium Chloride Fertilizer Association

The Japan Urea and Ammonium Sulphate Industry Association

The Japan-China Machinery Exporters' Associations

The Japan Soda Industry Association

The Japan-China Association of Agricultural Chemical Exporters

The Japan-China Iron and Steel Trade Liaison Association

The Foreign Steel-Making Raw Materials Committee

Special Steel Exporter Council

The All Japan Miso Cooperative Industrial Associations

The Japan-China Feed and Miscellaneous Beans Importers' Association

The Japan Noodle Industry Cooperative Association

The Japan-China Processed Products Traders' Association

The Chinese Egg Importers' Association

2. Japan Association for the Promotion of International Trade (KOKUBOSOKU)

Address: : Shin Nippon Building
2-6 Otemachi, Chiyoda-ku, Tokyo
Tel: (270) 3631

President: : Tanzan Ishibashi

Executive Director: Sadaji Hagiwara

The Association for the Promotion of Japan-China Trade was established in 1952 in an effort to clear away all political or diplomatic obstacles to the promotion of trade between China and Japan. In September 1954, the Japan Association for the Promotion of International Trade was established by unifying the functions of private organizations aiming at the formation of a movement to promote trade with socialist countries. However, not limiting itself to trade with China, the association also promotes trade with the Soviet Union and other socialist nations. Regarded as a friendly organization by the Chinese side, the Japan Association for the Promotion of International Trade signed a friendly trade agreement with the China Committee for the Promotion of International Trade, after a period of interrupted trade between the two countries. Since becoming one of the friendly trade organizations, the association, in addition to promoting friendly trade, has also cooperated in holding exhibitions and fairs for Chinese goods in Japan. Its main functions are concluding trade agreements, promoting personnel and technological exchanges, sponsoring sample exhibitions and acting as an intermediary in the conduct of transactions.

The Western Headquarters of the Japan Association for the Promotion of International Trade

Address: : Yasuda Trust & Banking Building
4-38 Kitahama, Higashi-ku, Osaka
Tel: (202) 0641

The association also has branch offices in Kobe, Nagoya, Kyoto, Kanazawa, Niigata, and other large Japanese cities.

C. FORMULAS FOR TRADE BETWEEN JAPAN AND CHINA AND THEIR DEVELOPMENT

1. Friendly Trade Formulas

In 1959, Japanese businessmen dealing in sweet chestnuts, lacquer, Chinese medicinal herbs, talc, straw plait and materials for Chinese cooking, strongly requested the Chinese authorities through the Japan Socialist Party (JSP) and the General Council of Japanese Trade Unions (Sohyo) to supply them with these necessary materials, indispensable for the operation of their businesses. As a result, the Chinese side permitted "consideration" trade for Japanese small and medium enterprises in need, and transactions began with a $300,000 volume of lacquer and chestnuts to be imported by Japan in 1959, which was further expanded to around $800,000 by 1960. Japan, in return, exported agricultural machinery, agricultural chemicals, rubber belts, and the like to China. The Chinese side only permitted transactions with those manufacturers in need of goods and did not allow trading firms to play an active role. This trade became the forerunner of the "friendly firms trade formula" which was developed in the following year. Thus, in the strictest sense of the word, trade between Japan and China was never actually halted, since there was always trade via Hong Kong as well as this "consideration" trade.

At the conference between Premier Chou En-lai and Kazuo Suzuki, who was then managing director for the Association for the Promotion of Japan-China Trade, in Peking on August 27, 1960, there was an offer on the part of the Chinese Premier to the effect that, in addition to the "consideration dealings" in Japan-China trade, the two sides could conclude trade contracts based on the mutual friendship of the parties concerned; however, it was also noted that in actuality, trade between the two countries should be based in principle on a government agreement. Thus, friendly trade was born out of Premier Chou En-lai's offer, and made possible the individual negotiation of trade contracts on a private basis as well as continuous transactions if both parties agreed. The "Friendly Trade Agreement" was officially signed in 1962 by the China Committee for the Promotion of International Trade and three Japanese organizations designated as "friendly" toward China (Japan-China Trade Promotion Association, the Japan Association for the Promotion of International Trade and the Western Headquarters of the Japan Association for the Promotion of International Trade).

The Friendly Trade Agreement specified that the Chinese side would selectively enter into business with any firm it designated as a "friendly trading firm" from an officially promulgated list of Japanese trading firms or manufacturers desiring to engage in trade with China, and recommended by the Japanese organizations or individuals considered to be friendly to China related to the Japan General Council of Trade Unions (Sohyo), the Japanese Socialist Party (JSP) or the Liberal Democratic Party.

Transaction methods on an individual basis included invitations to attend the Canton Trade Fair to negotiate trade contracts as well as visits to Peking to negotiate business contracts with various corporations handling the commodities being traded. Trade transactions are in principle based on free competition, but in practice, some priority is given to negotiations for particular items.

a. Trade Formulas Relating to Friendly Trade

Friendly trade was based on the so-called "three political principles and the three principles for trade" and any firm hoping to enter into business with China had to have the recommendation of the three Japanese organizations mentioned previously (Japan-China Trade Promotion Association, the Japan Association for the Promotion of International Trade and the Western Headquarters of the Japan Association for the Promotion of International Trade), who had signed agreements with their Chinese partners, and then be designated as a friendly firm by the Chinese authorities. Once the status of a friendly firm is acquired, that company is invited to participate in the Canton Trade Fair or other commercial exhibitions, providing an effective way to do business with China. (1962 was the first year in which actual business talks were held at the fair.)

Originally, the friendly firms were composed mostly of friendly Japanese firms and organizations, the "dummy" companies of large organizations or trading firms, but gradually banks, shipping companies and others also participated, followed by large trading companies themselves, and a sector of the manufacturers as well. Subsequently, friendly trade rapidly became more complete than at first both in quantity as well as quality of the firms participating.

As of March 1971, approximately 335 firms had been designated as friendly firms engaged in trade with China; among them, 300 were trading houses and 35 included banks, insurance houses, inspection offices, shippers or shipping agents, warehouse representatives and their advertising agents and others.

The friendly trade agreement simply allows trading houses and organizations to engage in trade with Chinese corporations but does not specify the commodities to be handled or the manner in which trade transactions are to be conducted. Consequently, all types of commodities can be considered open to trade with the exception of one group which was specified under the LT Trade Agreement but not opened for transactions under current MT trade.

Most trade negotiations are held in Canton during the Export Commodities Fair, but in the event talks are stalemated, arrangements may be made to continue them in Peking.

Although it may be said that all types of goods are freely transacted, in reality, rather than ordinary trade, barter type transactions seem to be more desirable and Chinese corporations display particular preferences to certain trading firms. Due to this tendency, there are some prefectures in Japan where the local administrations assemble friendly trading firms into one organization, thereby facilitating the negotiation of trade contracts in large volume as well as ensuring a balance between imports and exports.

In the beginning, the friendly trading firms faced many hardships since most were hastily established financially weak enterprises for trade with China; many suffered huge losses in exports when contracts were broken, and as a consequence, were completely restructured in the process.

Recently, however, many major trading firms and manufacturers have embarked on China trade. The trade contract volume has also increased considerably, and commodities traded as well have changed to include everything from light industrial farm and marine products and heavy machinery to soybeans. In the past, LT (MT) trade and friendly firm trade had been operated in parallel, but recently, stress has been put on the latter and transactions under this formula have been increasing remarkably.

b. Export-Import Contracts

Once trade negotiations and contracts have been concluded with the Import-Export Corporation of China, both parties concerned are required to exchange contracts along the following lines:

First of all, trade contracts must begin with the sentence:

"In order to promote friendship and economic exchanges between the peoples of China and Japan based on the three principles set down by Premier Chou En-lai, we hereby conclude

the following contract for the enactment of friendly trade between our two countries ..... ."

The remainder of the contract is exactly like other conventional
ones and lists details concerning specifications and descriptions of
goods, quantity, price per unit, total value, insurance, packaging,
shipping port and arrival ports, etc.

Terms of payment for the Japanese side as a rule stipulate that
letters of credit (L/C) will be forwarded 25 days prior to the shipping
date for imports, and 10 days for Chinese imports from Japan.

Although L/C conditions stipulate cable transfer of funds at sight for
Japanese imports from China, the same does not apply in reverse.

There are two types of letters of credit, those that are irrevocable
and those that are transferrable, with the expiration date for either
being 15 days after the date of the bill of lading. The shipping
documents are nearly the same as those for a third country; ships are
prohibited to enter American or Taiwan ports, and the ships booked by
the sellers must be approved by the buyer beforehand. Japanese ships
are directed to strictly observe Chinese navigational laws.

Shipping notices are to be forwarded to the buyer immediately by
the Japanese and within 48 hours by the Chinese side; the seller is held
responsible and forced to make compensation for all damages incurred
in case the buyer was unable to obtain an insurance policy due to the
seller's failure to cable a shipping notice in advance.

The seller is responsible for any delays in shipment except when a
letter of credit has not been received or there has been an accident
beyond human control.

Inspections of goods at loading ports conducted by the Chinese
Merchandise, Survey and Inspection Bureau as well as those conducted
by the same agency at ports of discharge are final. And, in the case of
exports, the Japanese side can submit claims against any inspection
results conflicting with the terms of contracts concluded with the ports
of discharge. However, any such claims must be made within 90 days;
60–90 days for textiles, and 30 days for machinery, agricultural,
marine and mining products.

Allowances for variations in value for shipping are around five
percent of the total value for China; however, there are no such
allowances provided for Japan.

Accident clauses exclude penalties for non-delivery in the event of
wars and natural disasters such as floods, fire and the like, provided
official certificates verifying the accident are sent by airmail after

prompt notification by cable. Events beyond human control also include strikes. Furthermore, penalties for delays in delivery are applicable only to Japanese exports.

Any discrepancies or conflicts in this regard are to be worked out in negotiations between the parties concerned. Arbitration is conducted based on the "defendant country principle," by the Arbitration Commission of the Chinese Committee for the Promotion of International Trade and the Japanese International Trade Arbitration Association.

2. LT Trade Formulas

As mentioned previously, friendly trade contains many flaws ranging over methods of inspection, arbitration, disasters beyond human control, as well as settlement conditions overly advantageous to the Chinese. Furthermore, most friendly trading firms were newly established small and medium sized companies which often had no influential connections within the Japanese domestic market, subsequently limiting the expansion of trade for a time.

In an effort to solve these problems, after due consultation with the Japanese Government, Diet members Tatsunosuke Takasaki and Kenzo Matsumura and others visited China in 1962 and reached an agreement with Liao Cheng-chih, the Chinese representative, for the step by step expansion of trade through private efforts with the mutual understanding that a governmental agreement would be difficult at that stage.

This agreement called for the long-term barter trade of major items with provisions for deferred payments as well as the establishment of a centralized institution for the coordination of overall trade.

This memorandum (LT Memorandum Trade Agreement) was signed on November 9, 1962 after further discussions concerning the details for long-term transactions between Takasaki and Liao Chen-chih. The important point of this agreement is that although the Chinese Government maintained that all private trade contracts were left up to the China Committee for the Promotion of International Trade and declined to overtly involve itself in the negotiations, the Chinese Foreign Trade Ministry assumed a dominant role during all stages of negotiation.

In addition, the agreement also once again stressed fundamental Chinese trade policy; that is, maintaining a balance between exports and imports while expanding trade between the two nations.

With the conclusion of this agreement, Japan-China trade rapidly expanded; the insecurity and mistrust which had surrounded it to that date was eliminated. The Japanese Government as well as the governing party called the move a positive step and promised cooperation. In addition, the export of a vinylon plant to China on a 5-year deferred payment basis was permitted.

Thus, trade between the two countries developed to a scale equal to trade with any other third country; manufacturers and trading companies adopted a positive attitude and changed the old "dummy" company transaction formula into one in which genuine efforts were made toward making direct transactions with China.

This agreement, however, irritated the US and the Nationalist Chinese Government in Taiwan, especially deteriorating the trade relations between Japan and Taiwan, and eventually prompted the late Prime Minister Shigeru Yoshida into delivering the so-called "Yoshida Letter" to Taiwan's President Chiang Kai-shek, which developed into a problem that has lingered until the present day.

a. Outline of the Memorandum and Trade Formulas

The LT trade system, based on the memorandum signed between Tatsunosuke Takasaki and Liao Cheng-chih, mapped out a plan for the exchange of staple commodities and permitted Japanese exports of chemical fertilizers, urea, ammonium sulphate, ammonium chloride, agricultural insecticides and herbicides, processing materials, ordinary steel, special steel, plants and know-how as well as patents, and Japanese imports of soybeans, corn, coking coal, iron ore, pig iron, salt and tin ingots.

LT trade in reality was a long-term contract which covered the five years from 1963 to 1967; however, before the start of each fiscal year during that period, the representatives of the two respective offices met to formulate tentative trade plans for the following year. These served as estimates for the other organizations affiliated with the Japan-China General Trade Liaison Office, such as the commodity councils, which then concluded contracts on an item-by-item basis with Chinese officials.

Based on the commodities conference agreement, Japanese manufacturers and consumers, which have been designated as friendly trading firms, make detailed trade contracts with Chinese corporations and actual trade activities begin.

b. Contracts and Transactions

LT trade contracts were more favorable in content toward the Japanese than those contracted under the terms of friendly trade. Furthermore, in contrast with friendly firm trade which obliged the other party to recognize China's three trade principles, LT trade merely required the traders to abide by the principle of mutual benefit and reciprocity and did not entail political principles. In addition, the disadvantages to the Japanese side in the way of methods of inspection and arbitration procedures were for the most part corrected. For instance, concerning arbitration, the principle of holding arbitration meetings in the country of the defendant was adopted. Settlement methods were based on the correspondent agreements concluded between Japanese banks and the Bank of China and the dispatch of shipping documents could be handled directly by the banks of both countries after establishing letters of credit rather than sending them via London as before. Furthermore, the Japanese side no longer needed the approval of the Chinese side prior to chartering ships to carry its exports to China.

Regarding terms of payment, friendly trade required the establishment of letters of credit 20 days prior to shipment, while LT trade shortened this period to 15 days.

Basic decisions on LT transactions are made by a council of manufacturers who also set down the framework within which export is to be conducted; the member makers then entrust the job of fulfilling their export quotas to affiliated trading firms, leaving little room for the activities of general trading houses. This point is the notable difference between friendly trade and ordinary trade through a trading house; that is, any firm desiring to trade with China must be a member of a friendly trade organization.

c. Deferred Payment Exports

LT trade also made provisions for deferred payments for industrial plants, machinery and equipment, steel and the like at the request of the Chinese; the Japanese Government, as well, apparently desired to permit deferred payments within the framework of LT trade. Nevertheless, deferred payments created all sorts of complicated political problems. For example, the Japanese Government gave the Kurashiki Rayon Company permission to export a vinylon plant valued at $20 million to China at 25 percent down and the remainder payable over a period of five years with financing provided by the Export-Import Bank of Japan. However, the Nationalist Government in Taiwan strongly protested this transaction insisting that it was economic assistance, and opposed the export of a Nichibo textile plant in the following year as well as negotiations for a Toyo Engineering urea plant and negotiations then going on for the export of a freighter with Hitachi Shipbuilding & Engineering Company, using the "Yoshida Letter" to support their objections. The Japanese Government, at a loss over how to deal with the Taiwan Government, was finally forced to shelve the problem after a period of fruitless searching, leaving it unsolved.

Except for industrial plants, deferred payments are permitted for the exports of steel, machinery and fertilizers; steel and machinery are transacted on the basis of payment terms requiring a 20 percent down payment, with the balance payable over a period of two years.

It was agreed that payment for ammonium chloride would be effected within one year.

As insurance for deferred payments, the Bank of China issues letters of credit or letters of guarantee, with the bills payable at its head office in Peking.

The interest rates on deferred payments are 5 percent annually, with the exception of those financed by the Export-Import Bank of Japan and other commercial banks which range between 7 and 8 percent.

3. The Development of Friendly and MT Trade

Friendly trade and MT trade developed hand in hand during the period from 1963 to 1970. The ratio between the two with respect to total trade volume over this period are expressed in Table VII-1.

The so-called two wheels of friendly firm's trade and LT trade (renamed MT trade in 1968) contributed to the rapid development of Japan-China trade with the trade volume steadily increasing from $84.48 million in 1962 to $137 million in 1963 and $310 million in 1964. Trade declined somewhat during 1967 and 1968, but resumed an upward trend to reach $625 million in 1969 and $822.69 million in 1970. It is estimated that total trade for 1971 will total $900 million.

As shown in Table VII-1, friendly firm's trade witnessed remarkable growth in the years following 1964, and both exports and imports registered a high increase rate with a large variety of goods, more so than MT trade which was confined to a listing of traditional major commodities. The items which MT trade concentrated upon included ammonium chloride, ammonium sulfate and urea for export, noodles, corn,

Table VII-1 — Total Japan-China Trade and LT (MT) and Friendly Trade

(Unit: $1,000)

Year	Total Volume of Foreign Trade (1)	LT (MT) Trade (2)	Friendly Trade (3)
1963	137,016	64,115 (46.7%)	72,901 (53.3%)
1964	310,489	128,427 (41.1%)	182,026 (58.6%)
1965	469,741	179,186 (38.1%)	290,555 (61.9%)
1966	621,387	205,228 (33.0%)	416,159 (67.0%)
1967	557,733	153,483 (27.5%)	404,250 (72.5%)
1968	549,623	115,920 (21.1%)	433,703 (78.9%)
1969	625,343	69,600 (11.7%)	555,743 (88.9%)
1970	822,696	70,000 (8.5%)	752,696 (91.5%)
1971	900,000	84,220 (9.1%)	815,780 (90.9%)

NOTE: (1)   The total volume of foreign trade is based on the customs clearance basis.

(2)   LT (1963—1967) and MT (1968—1970) trade are estimates based on the contract basis.

(3)   Friendly trade: (1)—(2)

salt, iron ore, and coking coal for import on the part of Japan. The main items commonly shared by both friendly and memorandum trade were ordinary steel, special steel, agricultural chemicals, processed materials and machinery for export, and broad beans, miscellaneous beans, pig iron, tin and the like for import.

D. CHINESE TRADE CORPORATIONS

Trade corporations in China are government owned with the exception of a few which are privately owned. However, whether government or private, Chinese trade corporations adopt a reciprocal settlement system under the guidance of the Chinese Foreign Trade Ministry and faithfully follow the plans of the State Economic Commission in their business activities.

The major Chinese trade corporations are as follows:

1. China National Cereals, Oils and Foodstuffs Import and Export Corporation

Major items handled include the following:

Cereals, vegetable oils for food or industrial use, oil seeds, oil cake and animal feeds, salt, grain, livestock, meat and meat products, animal fats, egg and egg products, fresh fruit and fruit products, marine products, canned foods, sugar and sugar products, liquors, dairy products, vegetables, seasonings and the like.

Head Office: 82 Tung An Men Street, Peking, China,
with branches in major Chinese cities
and Hong Kong.

2. China National Native Produce and Animal By-Products Import and Export Corporation

Major export items:

Tobacco leaves, tobacco products, medicinal herbs, all types of tea, coffee, cocoa, dried fruit, logs and lumber, perfumes, oil, spices, ceramics, handicrafts, and the like, pig hair, horse hair, fur, fur carpets, untanned leather, feathers, wool, cashmere wool, carpets, leather products, livestock and the like.

Head Office: 82 Tung An Men Street, Peking

3. China National Light Industrial Products Import and Export Corporation

The products handled include assorted items for daily use including paper, office and school items, toys, musical instruments, sporting goods, sanitary ware, construction materials and electrical appliances.

Head Office: 82 Tung An Men Street, Peking

4.   China National Textiles Import and Export Corporation

Major items handled include the following:

Cotton, raw silk, artificial fibers, synthetic fibers, cotton cloth, silk fabric, wool fabric, bast fiber fabric, other textile items, cotton and woolen products.

5.   China National Chemicals Import and Export Corporation

Major items handled include the following:

Rubber, tire and rubber products, petroleum and its products, chemical fertilizer, agricultural chemicals, medical and pharmaceutical products, surgical instruments, chemical medicines, dyestuff, pigments, and other products.

6.   China National Machinery Import and Export Corporation

Major items handled include the following:

Lathes, presses, drills, planing machines, molding machines, heavy oil engines, gasoline engines, turbines, boilers, mining machinery, metallurgical machinery, presses and pumps, cranes, transportation equipment (engine driven vehicles, ships, etc.) agricultural machinery as well as agricultural tools, printing machines, knitting machines, construction machinery and other light industrial machinery, electric machinery as well as heavy industrial equipment (generators, motors, transformers, rectifiers, etc.) electronic communication equipment, scientific instruments (optical, physical, electronic, navigational, meterorological, etc.), various heavy industrial meters, laboratory equipment, precision measuring instruments, metal cutting tools, handicrafts, ball and roller bearings, hard alloys, cinematographic equipment and materials, photographic equipment and materials.

Head Office: Erh Li Kou, Hsi Chiao, Peking

7.   China National Metals and Minerals Import and Export Corporation

Items handled include steel plates, steel pipes, high quality steel, rails, metal products, iron alloys, pig iron, iron ore, nonferrous metals, precious metals, rare metals, nonferrous metal ores, etc.

Head Office: Erh Li Kou, Hsi Chiao, Peking

VIII. BUSINESS PRACTICES OF JAPAN-CHINA TRADE

Since Japan has no government-level agreement with the government of China, as has been mentioned frequently in the previous chapters, she must resort to different procedures than in her trade with countries of the free world, and must obtain certain qualifications in order to trade with China. At present there are only two ways of entering into trade with China; one is to become a friendly firm, and the other is to conduct transactions through the memorandum trade formula. Furthermore, special attention should be paid to the fact that Japan, in addition to being a member of COCOM (Coordinating Committe for Export Controls), has special export restrictions placed on her trade with China as a result of her relations with the United States, thus creating complicated procedures which include prohibiting clauses not to be found in transactions with any other country.

Promoting exports to China is also quite difficult and different from methods of dealing with the countries of the free world in that not only is it extremely difficult to go to China, but at the present stage, individual trading firms or manufacturers will find it close to impossible to hold individual exhibitions in China or to advertise in Chinese newspapers or other media in an effort to promote their goods in that country. This is significant in that it means they must participate in co-sponsored exhibitions of commodities such as the Canton Trade Fair.

Once again, special problems arise in the enactment of contracts or in trade negotiations held at the Canton Trade Fair since trade is state-operated in China. Therefore, it is necessary to give an explanation regarding qualifications which must be obtained in order to engage in trade with China, procedures for obtaining entry visas, export-import restrictions, the circumstances surrounding the sponsoring of exhibitions as well as export and import contracts and methods of participating in the Canton Trade Fair.

A. QUALIFICATIONS FOR JAPAN-CHINA TRADE AND TRAVEL PROCEDURES

1. Qualifications for Traders

Japan-China trade is conducted through two different channels, friendly trade and memorandum (MT) trade. In order to participate in friendly firms trade, a firm is requested to abide by the three political principles and obtain the recommendation of, as well as become a member of one of the friendly firms (e.g., the Japan-China Friendship Association or the Japan Association for the Promotion of International Trade) in order to obtain the designation of a friendly firm. In addition, the Memorandum Trade Agreement specifies that transactions with China are to be carried out through one of the business organizations forming the Japan-China General Trade Liaison Council. Consequently, a firm must either become a member of this council or arrange for a member firm or consumer organization to conduct trade transactions on its behalf. Although the MT trade formula differs from friendly trade in that it allows Japan to choose the enterprises which will handle its trade with China, the Chinese side still reserves the right to accept or reject the Japanese choice. In reality, the majority of leading firms as well as those engaged in MT trade with China are designated as friendly firms with only a few exceptions.

If any Japanese manufacturer, for example a machinery manufacturer, desires to take part in trade with China. he must first join an industrial association related to that firm's line of business (e.g., the Machine Tool Industry Association, the Textile Machinery Industry Association, etc.), which is a substructural organization of the Japan-China Machinery Trade Association, one of the organizations forming the mainstay of the MT trade system, and then as a member of that particular industrial association, enter trade negotiations with the Chinese side. Furthermore, there have been recent moves within Japanese industrial circles to invite Chinese corporations or their technicians to visit Japan to promote technological exchange as well as business negotiations. It therefore naturally follows that any firm desiring to participate in trade with China must become a member of one of the aforementioned organizations.

As of March 1971, there were 301 trading firms, 14 banks, six insurance companies, 20 shipping warehouses and inspection agents, and four travel companies, making a total of 345 business firms engaged in friendly firms trade with China.

The present status of Japan-China trade demands that a firm first be designated as a friendly trading firm before it can enter into trade with China, and after being qualified as a friendly firm, the respective company must send one of its representatives to China to negotiate trade transactions; however, since the Chinese Government is not yet recognized by Japan, special procedures are required.

2. Travel Procedures

Unlike other countries, special procedures are required in making applications to visit China, mainly due to the fact that there are no formal diplomatic relations between China and Japan, in addition to the fact that trade is state-managed. Owing to the fact that it is virtually impossible to conduct actual transactions through correspondence, cable or telephone, the most effective means of concluding trade agreements with China is by participating in the Canton Trade Fair. The most commonly employed method of transaction is to have the people in charge of China trade at the respective company visit the country and directly negotiate with Chinese officials for the ultimate conclusion of trade agreements.

One of the prime requirements necessary for making a trip to China is an invitation from the Chinese national trade corporation concerned or the China Committee for the Promotion of International Trade. Generally speaking, those making their first business trip to China usually apply for this invitation through a Japanese organization considered friendly toward China. Upon receipt of the invitation, the firm or the individual concerned must submit an application form to the Foreign Ministry in order to obtain permission to visit a communist country. At present, this application stating the purpose of the visit must be channelled through the Foreign Ministry, the Immigration Bureau of the Justice Ministry and other related ministries including the Ministry of International Trade and Industry (MITI), for consideration before a passport is issued. The application must include destination, the purpose of the visit as well as a brief record of the applicant indicating whether he has received an invitation.

It usually takes two to three weeks to complete all the necessary procedures since passport applications must be submitted to the offices of the government agencies in the local areas for screening. However, since there are no representatives of the Chinese Ministry of Foreign Affairs in Japan, entry visas for China must be obtained in Hong Kong.

Following completion of the necessary entry procedures with the aid of the China Travel Service in Hong Kong which usually takes two or three days, the visitor then travels by train from Kowloon, and crosses the border at Lowu to enter China.

The Chinese travel office in Hong Kong provides the passenger with declaration forms for his personal effects and the amounts of foreign currency he has with him. It is imperative that these two forms be accurately filled out since Chinese customs officials check all visitors on the basis of these documents. In addition, the "declaration of foreign currencies" form is taken into custody at customs but returned after verification; this document is absolutely necessary whenever one desires to exchange traveller's cheques or cash for Chinese currency.

After the necessary declarations and inspections are completed at customs, one can change his foreign currency into Chinese yuan at the People's Bank of China conveniently located within the customs building. Upon return, the traveller should pay special attention to the following items:

a. Take the procedures necessary for the exchange of Chinese yuan back into foreign currencies if necessary.

b. Ensure that you have obtained permission to take souvenir items out of China beforehand.

c. Make arrangements for any luggage to be shipped separately.

One is inspected at the border when he enters and once again upon his departure, based on the declaration of personal belongings. Any items which are forbidden to be taken out of the country will be confiscated. Chinese money may not be taken out of the country, and all yuan must be converted into Hong Kong dollars prior to crossing the border. After completing exit procedures, the traveller must walk from the Chinese side of the border back to Lowu.

Visits to China for the purpose of sightseeing are being permitted and there are Japanese travel agents which have been set up for the purpose of handling these affairs with their Chinese counterparts. The following are Japanese travel agencies, affiliated with the China International Travel Service, which handle the processing of papers necessary to make the China trip, as well as hotel reservations and other services.

      a. China-Japan Heiwakanko Company

          Head Office: Tokyo, Japan   Tel: 833-4651

                       Osaka   Tel: 251-9779

      b. China-Japan Travel Company

                   Tokyo   Tel: 503-4641

      c. New Japan International, Ltd.   Tel: 561-9861

    d. Western Japan Travel Agency
                Osaka   Tel: 364-0912

Personal Items That Require Special Attention:

1) **Short Term Travelers** (6 months or less)

a) Declaration forms stating the items in one's possession must be completed at the Customshouse prior to going through customs inspection.

b) Personal items essential to the visitor during his trip and in a reasonable quantity do not have to be declared and are exempt from customs duties and standard trade taxes; a limited amount of clothing, foodstuffs, toys and local products as well as items for daily use and bona fide gifts not to exceed 50 yuan in total value is permissable after applicable standard trade taxes have been paid. Any items exceeding the limits mentioned above are not permitted to be brought in or out of the country as personal effects.

c) Valuable items such as watches, cameras, pens and radios, registered at the customshouse at entry must be brought out again on the visitors return trip.

2) The following items demand extra special attention:

a) **Chinese money:**

The People's Republic of China forbids any of its currency being brought in or taken out of the country; illegal possession of China's national currency discovered during entry or exit will be confiscated.

b) **Foreign currencies and traveller's cheques:**

Foreign currencies and travellers cheques in one's possession must be explained by the declaration of foreign currencies form verified at the port of entry and a certificate issued by the Bank of China granting permission to carry them.

c) **Gold, platinum, silver and other precious metals such as personal ornaments:**

Only those items which have been brought in and declared at entry may be carried out at exit.

d) **Lottery or raffle tickets:**

Forbidden.

e) **Exposed and undeveloped photo-films, cinema-film:**

May not be taken out of China.

f) All materials such as books, newspapers, publications, maps, magazines, notes, drafts, negative films or photos, records, tapes, etc., detrimental to Chinese politics, culture and morals are not to be brought into the country.

g) Scientific books, publications, drafts, notes, exposed and undeveloped films, photos, records, tapes and the like touching upon Chinese national secrets, may not be taken out of the country.

h) No items of artistic value pertaining to the Chinese Revolution, history or culture, may be taken out of the country. Furthermore, to take any ancient artistic items or books out of the country one must have the permission of the Chinese Cultural Agency.

B. TRADE FAIRS

The third Japan-China Trade Agreement concluded in May 1955, provided for the holding of sample exhibitions in both countries.
Exhibitions for Chinese products were held in Tokyo and Osaka late in the same year, and exhibitions displaying samples of Japanese products were held in Peking and Shanghai during the fall of 1956, contributing greatly to the promotion of transactions between the two countries, especially in the area of machinery.

Exhibitions of Japanese products were held in Wuhan and Canton in 1958 in accordance with the Fourth Japan-China Trade Agreement, but at that time, trade between the two countries was suspended, and all items on exhibition had to be brought back to Japan forcing Japanese enterprises to suffer huge losses.

After friendly trade was resumed in 1962, exhibitions were sponsored first for the exhibition of Japanese goods in Peking and Shanghai in 1963, and Tokyo and Osaka for Chinese commodities in 1964. Exhibitions have been held alternately in Japan and China since that time.

These exhibitions offer the most ideal places for advertising, negotiations and the exchange of technical know-how, since there are few other means of doing this within the framework of Japan-China trade.

The Japanese Government also cooperated by co-sponsoring an exhibition of Japanese industrial products in China at a cost of ¥100 million.

1. 1965 Japanese Industrial Fair in Peking and Shanghai

The agreement signed in December 1962 by three Japanese organizations, the Japanese Association for the Promotion of International Trade, the Association for the Promotion of Japan-China Trade, the Western Headquarters of the Japan Association for the Promotion of International Trade, and the China Committee for the Promotion of International Trade, provided for the sponsoring of trade exhibitions in both countries. As a result, trade exhibitions of Japanese products were held in Peking and Shanghai in 1963, and in Tokyo and Osaka in 1964 for Chinese commodities. In August 1964, the two countries exchanged an agreement concerning future exhibitions, which paved the way for the Japanese Industrial Trade Fair held in Peking and Shanghai in 1965, and the Chinese exhibition in Tokyo and Osaka in 1966.

The exhibition of Japanese industrial products in China in 1965 was co-sponsored by the three Japanese organizations mentioned above, in conjunction with the Japan-China Export-Importers' Cooperative, and held from October 4 through 20 in Peking, and from December 1 through 21 in Shanghai. These Japanese industrial exhibitions are extremely helpful to those who desire to enter into trade with China because there are few other similar opportunities.

Manufacturers, traders, wholesalers, business organizations and local self-governing bodies were allowed to participate freely in the 1965 Japanese Industrial Fair in China. Among the products displayed were the best Japanese industries had to offer, in the hopes of filling varied and diverse Chinese demands for the third 5-year economic program. This exhibition cost a total of ¥500 million, with the Japanese Government contributing ¥110 million and prefectural as well as municipal government organizations providing one-third to one-half of the cost including contributions toward the costs of maintaining booths.

This exhibition witnessed an increased participation of leading businesses and the number of important commodities also notably increased in comparison with the previous exhibition. The success of this exhibition owed a great deal to the unreserved cooperation on the Chinese side which contributed to making this Japanese sample exhibition the largest ever held by Japan overseas.

One of the outstanding aspects of Japanese industrial exhibitions is the efficient way in which Chinese spectators and industrialists, those who have demands for products, utilize the occasion for technical exchanges as well as the viewing of products on display. The exhibitions also offer the opportunity for frequent discussions and the exchange of technical ideas between Japanese specialists dispatched to China with their companies products, and their Chinese counterparts.

Following the 1965 exhibition, mission after mission of technical experts and specialists were sent from China to Japan in order to view Japanese factories, contributing much to the expansion of trade between the two nations.

2. 1969 Japanese Industrial Fair in Peking and Shanghai

In accordance with an agreement signed by the Japanese Association for the Promotion of International Trade and the China Committee for the Promotion of International trade for the Japanese Industrial Fair in Peking and Shanghai in 1969, and based on the agreement concerning the promotion of friendly trade between the peoples of China and Japan, and the "Conference Summary Record" signed in March 1968, the 1969 Japanese Industrial Fair was held in Peking (the Shanghai Fair was later called off) from March 22 to April 11 under the auspices of the Japan Association for the Promotion of International Trade and the China-Japan Import-Exporters' Cooperative.

The fair was held in accordance with the three Chinese political and trade principles as well as the inseparability of political and economic affairs. It aimed at providing an opportunity for friendly transactions and economic exchanges and a rapid expansion of trade between the two countries by presenting to China the most up-to-date products and technology Japanese industry had to offer to aid in the development of the Chinese economy.

The following are Japanese products which were displayed at the fair:

a. Metal Machine Tools and Manufacturing Equipment

(1) Machine tools, metal processing machinery and related tools and parts.

(2) Furnaces for industrial use, casting and forging equipment, metallurgical equipment and the like.

b. Industrial Machinery for the Following Industries

Chemical, mining, textile, wood processing, food processing, printing, plastic processing and others.

c. Automation and Control Equipment

d. Electronic Industrial Equipment

e. **Scientific Apparatus**
   (1) Analysis
   (2) Measuring
   (3) Electronic application

f. **High Voltage Electrical Equipment Including Generators**

g. **Transport, Road Building and Agricultural Machinery**
   (1) Transport
   (2) Road building
   (3) Cargo handling
   (4) Agricultural machinery

h. **Metals and Metal Products**

i. **Chemical Products**

j. **Textile Products**

k. **Others**

Needless to say, an extensive exchange of technical information between the specialists dispatched by the Japanese manufacturers and the Chinese technicians was conducted during the period of the exhibition.

"Commemorative spot sales," registered a sale of Japanese products valued at £250,000 during the exhibition."

The rapid expansion of Japanese exports to China from $390,803,000 in 1969 to $568,878,000 in 1970 can only be attributed to the success of the 1969 exhibition which provided impetus to an increase in China's demands.

3. Chinese Economic and Trade Fair

According to the provisions of the agreement exchanged between China and Japan in December 1962, the Japan Association for the Promotion of Japan-China Trade, the Japan Association for the Promotion of International Trade and the Japan-China Import-Exporters' Association and the Western Headquarters of Japan Association for the Promotion of International Trade cooperated in and sponsored the 1964 "Chinese Economic and Trade Exhibition" at Harumi International Sample Exhibition Grounds in Tokyo and the International Sample Exhibition Grounds in Osaka. These exhibitions brought to Japan a delegation of Chinese officials led by the chairman of the China Committee for the Promotion of International Trade, together with machine tools, weaving machines, native produce, mining products, agricultural, forestry and marine goods, textiles, traditional handicrafts and the like. Souvenirs, handicrafts and other assorted items were sold on the spot.

Although the number of trade contracts concluded during the exhibition is unknown, it provided an opportunity for Japanese businessmen to learn about the actual state of the Chinese economy as well as to discuss trade dealings other than at the Canton Trade Fair.

4. 1966 Chinese Economic and Trade Fair

The 1966 Chinese Economic and Trade Fair was held for three weeks from October 1–21, in Kita-Kyushu and from November 19 to December 11, in Nagoya, attended by a delegation of 66 Chinese, mostly technicians. The list of Chinese items exhibited at these fairs is as follows:

Field	Items Displayed	Number
1. Geology	Various minerals and geological research devices	54
2. Metallurgy	Wheels, tires, various metallurgic and nonferrous metal products	288
3. Petroleum	Various oil and oil by-products	149
4. Coal	Coal and coal mining exhibits	118
5. Chemicals	Chemical fertilizers, agricultural chemicals, plastic raw materials, synthetic fibers, medical and pharmaceutical products, rubber products, cinema film, dye materials, etc.	276
6. Chemical Industrial Products	Chemical dyes and medicines	47
7. Construction	Architectural relief exhibits	3
8. Construction Materials	Marble, glass, transparent quarts products, cement, tile, etc.	75
9. Models of Irrigation and Water Power Stations		5
10. Railroad Models	Combustion engines and railroad cars	2
11. Machine Tools	Machine tools, electric machinery, meters, etc.	715
12. Therapeutic Machinery, etc.	X-ray machines, articial heart devices	6
13. Ship Models	Freighters, tankers and others	5

Field	Items Displayed	Number
14. Electronic Communications Equipment	Communications equipment, radio, television, computers, etc.	4
15. Power Engines	Diesel engines, tractors, large-size passenger vehicles	4
16. Precision Instruments	Electronic instruments, analytical instruments, measuring instruments	2
17. Light Industry	Vases, materials of an educational or cultural nature, toys	392
18. Woven Goods	Various types of cotton cloth, wool, silk and silk by-products	1,000
19. Carpets, Furs, Leather Goods and Wool Blankets, etc.		425
20. Tea and Local Products	Black tea, green tea, jasmin tea, etc.	535
21. Handicrafts	Ivory works, gems, bamboo, grass and wisteria braidings, mahogany made items, tablecloths, furniture, etc.	664
22. Other Light Industrial Products	Ceramics, glassware, salt, tobacco, paper, watches, etc.	352
23. Peking Handicrafts	Ivory, gems, pottery, paintings, etc.	171
24. Necklaces		
25. Household Tools		
26. Handicrafts	Ivory works, gems, musical instruments, etc.	844
27. Foodstuffs	Foodstuffs and food oils, canned foods, liquors, sugar, cakes, biscuits, etc.	349
28. Agriculture-Related Exhibits		59
29. Marine Products	Fishing boat models, fish specimens	42
30. Books	Books, paintings, records, etc.	3,148
31. Postage Stamps		83

Total Items Exhibited: 10,019

This exhibition made a great contribution to the deepening of mutual understanding between the two countries as well as familiarizing the Japanese people with Chinese-made commodities.

5. Canton Trade Fair

The Canton Trade Fair has been held twice yearly, during the spring and autumn since 1957; Japan began participating in the fair in 1961. Together with the expansion of trade, the number of participants from Japan as well as the volume of transactions has been steadily increasing. This trade fair has become an indispensable bargaining place for Japanese and European traders, and to participate in Japan-China trade has become synonymous with participating in the Canton Trade Fair.

Originally, the Canton Trade Fair was designed for the purpose of inviting overseas merchants in such places as Hong Kong and Southeast Asian countries, in an effort to promote Chinese exports, chiefly agricultural, local commodities, mineral ores and textile raw materials. As the Chinese economy developed, these products became more diversified to include cotton cloth and other textile products as well as machinery, which have been on the increase. Furthermore, recent visitors to the fair have not been limited to Chinese merchants from overseas, but also include thousands of Japanese traders and an increasing number of West Europeans.

Participants from Japan totaling 1,000 attended the spring 1971 fair in which the achievements of Chinese economic development were displayed, along with people from over 100 different countries, and competed against high pressure sales campaigns on the part of West European traders.

In the future, together with the strengthening presence of Western Europe, the possible participation of the United States will increase the importance of the fair and further sharpen competition.

C. PRIOR APPROVAL SYSTEM FOR EXPORTS AND IMPORTS

Japanese imports from China differ from those of other regions in that prior approval is required. Previously, China, North Korea, East Germany, Hungary and Albania were designated as compulsory barter areas requiring reciprocal trade contracts. However, in December 1960, it was decided that one-sided contracts could be concluded with these countries if authorized by the Japanese Ministry of International Trade and Industry, and the compulsory barter trade system was abolished in April 1961 with the exception of North Korea, which remained restricted until November 1962. At the same time, the Japanese Government applied Article 10 of the Import Trade Control Law (Bulletin No. 175 issued on April 10, 1961) requiring prior approval for the import of goods from these regions. Bulletin No. 522 issued on October 8, 1962, stipulated that the prior approval requirement would be applicable not only to imports from these regions but to shipments to them as well. Therefore, at present, special regulations applicable to trade with communist bloc countries having no diplomatic relations with Japan are the regulations on the export of strategic materials, and the prior approval requirement for imports.

In reality, however, in keeping with the progress of trade liberalization and requests for the simplification of approval application procedures, the Japanese Government has adopted a policy of automatically approving all of these applications, provided that they pose no problems of competition with other Japanese industries or overcompetition among the trading companies themselves. Nevertheless, eggs, walnuts and straw plaiting are not unconditionally approved at present due to the Japanese Government's policy of protecting domestic enterprises. Any application for import approval of commodities valued over £100,000 as well as those included in the following list must be submitted directly to the Import Section, International Trade Bureau of the Ministry of International Trade and Industry. (Note: Applications for import approval of other items must be forwarded through regional bureaus or offices of the Ministry of International Trade and Industry.)

- eggs and egg yolks (excluding those used for hatching purposes)
- human hair
- red beans
- broad beans and green peas
- other beans
- bananas
- walnuts
- corn
- soybeans
- matting and other carpetmaking or carpeting materials
- soybean oil cakes
- salt
- graphite (natural only)
- dolomite, including tar dolomite
- magnesite (excluding refind oxide magnesium)
- unburnt gypsum

- steel
- tungsten ore
- antimony ore
- coal (excluding anthracite coal from North Vietnam) as well as briquettes and the like
- mercury
- antimony trioxide
- albumen
- straw plait
- cotton
- iron ore
- antimony ingots, power and flakes, as well as scrap

D. CONTENTS OF EXPORT/IMPORT TRADE CONTRACTS

Two standard forms are employed in Japan-China trade; one for friendly trade and the other for memorandum trade. These two forms however have posed quite a few problems in the past when commodities requiring both contracts were involved.

Overcompetition is inevitable since a large number of Japanese businessmen must thread themselves through the sole business channel offered by China, the Canton Trade Fair. This leads to the concluding of disadvantageous contracts for both imports and exports especially since there are two different approaches depending on the type of trade concerned, friendly or memorandum. The former allows the Japanese enterprises to deal directly with individual Chinese corporations while the latter allows Japan's traders to form one united body for the negotiation of prices with China. There are some differences in price between the two trade methods, but they are negligible.

Since there are differences in the positions of the two participants in Japan-China trade, the Japanese position is relatively weak and Japanese traders are often forced to accept demands spelled out by the Chinese officials. For example, within a period of one year, Japan had to pay a price which nearly doubled for her imports of shrimp and lobster from China. It cannot be safely said that transactions with China are stable on a long-term basis when factors such as this are taken into consideration.

In addition to the troubles arising from disadvantageous competition conditions, other fundamental problems exist in Japan-China trade. For instance, the problem of what is termed "final" as far as ports of loading and unloading, and especially with regard to determining the quality of goods. Furthermore, another problem worth attention is the differences between the two countries' methods of weighing and inspection.

The fact that there are two standard forms for trade contracts in itself reflects the importance the two sides place on the wording of the contracts.

Arbitration for friendly firm trade is to be held in Peking and presided over by the Arbitration Commission of the China Committee for the Promotion of International Trade while that for MT trade is to be conducted in Peking by the same body, as well as Tokyo through the auspices of the Japan International Trade Arbitration Association.

In conclusion, it may be said that MT trade has lived up to the principle of reciprocity, allowing Japan to make inspections and file claims against breeches of contract, as well as the freedom to charter the ships she chooses.

Ⅸ. REFERENCE MATERIALS

Contract Form

Contract Number :   MT (70)
Contract Date   :
Place of Contract :   Peking
Buyers   :   China National Machinery Import & Export
                      Corporation
                      Erh Li Kou, Hsichiao, Peking
                      Cable Address: MACHIMPEX PEKING

Sellers:

In realization of the agreement for Fiscal   Memorandum
Trade, following negotiations conducted in a friendly atmosphere in
accordance with three political principles and the principle of the inseparability of political and economic affairs acknowledged in the communique
published   ,19   by the representatives of China and Japan's
Memorandum Trade Offices as well as the four China-Japan trade conditions set down by the Chinese Government, the two parties hereby agree
to conclude this Contract in accordance with the following articles.

(I)

Description of Goods		Unit	Quantity	Unit Price	Total
Total:					

(II)   Origin of Goods   :   Japan

(III)   Manufacturers   :

(IV)   Loading Port   :

(V)   Port of Destination:

(VI)   Shipping Date   :

(VII) Marking   :

All shipments shall be clearly marked with gross weight, net weight, cargo number, content and other markings as herein stipulated.

(VIII) Insurance:

Insurance shall be purchased by Buyers.

(IX)   Documents:

All documents as herein required shall be sent by Sellers to Buyers within   days prior to shipment.

(X)   Guarantee of Quality:

The Sellers shall guarantee all shipments to conform to articles 1 and 2 of this contract with regard to quality and condition. The guarantee shall be valid for a period of   months after arrival of goods at port of destination, and this period shall not be extended   months after the shipping date. Sellers shall be fully responsible for damage or defects occurring within the guarantee period as the result of defective design or workmanship on the part of the manufacturers when goods are subjected to normal use by the Buyers under conditions consistent with handling stipulated by the instruction manuals. Sellers shall be responsible for repair, replacement of parts, or substitution of goods without charge, upon demand of the Buyers substantiated by certificates issued by the Chinese surveyors. Consequent transportation expenses for replacement of the defective goods from the place of use, inspection costs as well as profit loss to Buyers, shall be remitted in full without delay by Sellers to Buyers.

Disputes against Buyers' claims shall be submitted within two weeks of receipt of Buyer's claims. Otherwise, claims by Buyers shall be considered valid.

(XI)   Inspection and Indemnity:

i) Inspection certificates issued by Japanese commodity inspection organs selected in advance with the mutual consent of Sellers and Buyers, after minute inspection of quality and quantity of goods with distinct explanation of standards used in inspection and results obtained thereof, shall be applied for by Sellers in advance of shipment effected.

ii) Inspection of quality and quantity of goods upon arrival at destination shall be entrusted to the Chinese Merchandise, Survey and Inspection Bureau by Buyers. Buyers reserve the right to lodge claims against damage or quality and quantity at variance with this contract within   days after arrival of goods at port of destination substantiated by certificates issued by Chinese inspection organs. Sellers shall be responsible for replacement free of charge, of all parts inconsistent with this contract, supplementing insufficient quantities, or lowering the market value of the goods on Buyers' demand, and shall remit to Buyers without delay all subsequent transportation costs for replacement goods to the port of destination, inspection costs and profit losses incurred thereby. Disputes against Buyers' claims shall be submitted by Sellers within two weeks upon receipt. Otherwise, claims by Buyers shall be considered valid.

iii) Reinspection shall be executed in accordance with the stipulations in Article X of this Contract.

(XII) Terms of Payment:

Buyers shall, within twenty days after receipt of cable sent by Sellers confirming export license number and shipment (for each lot), open an Irrevocable Letter of Credit at the Bank of China, listing the Sellers as the Beneficiary drawn at sight, payable in British pound sterling. Sellers shall negotiate payment of the shipment value by forwarding to the opening banks, as required per this Letter of Credit, documents in accordance with the provisions of Article XVI of this Contract. Expiry date of the Letter of Credit shall be 15 days after shipment date.

(XIII) Terms of Shipment:

1) FOB shipment shall be consistent with the provisions hereunder:

i) 30 days prior cable notice shall be sent to Buyers by Sellers within the period stipulated by this Contract, confirming contract number, description of goods, quantity, gross weight including packing, and measurement (if any one of the crates should weigh over 5 tons, all crates must be individually listed, including weight with packing, and measurement), and Sellers shall facilitate Buyers' selection of carrying vessels.

ii) Buyers shall entrust the selection of carrying vessels to the Chinese Ocean Shipping Company.

iii) Buyers shall be responsible for notifying Sellers by cable of name of scheduled carrying vessel, name of loading port as well as cable address and address of agent of vessel, within 10 days prior to said vessel's call at loading port. Sellers shall contact therewith the shipping agent without delay in order to facilitate shipment of goods.

iv) In all cases of goods being unavailable for shipment due to the Sellers' failure to effect delivery on schedule when vessel chartered by Buyers arrives at loading port on schedule, Sellers shall be responsible for demurrage and deadfreight. In the event chartered vessel does not arrive at loading port within twenty days in compliance with notice forwarded by Buyers, all warehouse costs at loading port on and beyond 21st day shall be at Buyers' expense and warehouse costs thus arising shall be paid by Buyers to Sellers in accordance with warehouse receipt.

v) **FOB Terms of Delivery**: 50 percent of all risks and loading charges until goods are taken overside shall be at Sellers' responsibility. Loading charges shall be defined as all costs incurred during the period goods are alongside until goods reach vessel's cargohold (this means from the place possible for onboard cranework to the designated space within the vessel's cargohold) including heavy lift charges for heavy lifts on land or on sea needed for the loading of heavy cargos. The cost shall not in any way include onboard arrangement cost, fixing cost and packing cost, or hatch opening-closing costs.

2) C & F Terms are as specified hereunder:

i) Sellers shall be responsible for loading goods on vessels voyaging straight from the loading port to the Chinese port as stipulated in Article VI of this Contract. Transshipment is prohibited.

ii) Carrying vessels shall not call at ports in the United States and/or in the Taiwan area before its arrival at Chinese ports. It is further stipulated that American vessels will not be permitted for use in shipment of cargos.

iii) If Sellers' chartered vessel is of Japanese nationality, the said vessel shall abide by the navigation regulations for Japanese ships in Chinese waters enforced by the Government of the People's Republic of China.

(XIV) Shipping Notification:

i) Upon completion of shipment, Sellers will immediately notify Buyers and the China National Foreign Trade Transportation Corporation (cable address: ZHONGWAIYUN) of contract number, description of goods, quantity, gross weight (of which cargo exceeding either 9t in weight, 3,400mm in length or 3,250mm in two dimensions, package inclusive weight, and measurements shall also be forwarded) invoice amount, name of carrying vessel, and vessel's departure date.

ii) Sellers shall be responsible for all damage and losses arising from failure to notify Buyers by cable within the appropriate time for purchasing insurance prior to shipment of goods.

(XV) Packing:

Goods shall be packed in strong, seawaterproof, shockproof and rustproof wooden crates, capable of withstanding long sea voyages and rugged transportation. All damage and losses resulting from insufficiency of packing shall be at Sellers' responsibility.

Documents as herein required shall be forwarded to the negotiating bank in order to receive proceeds after completion of shipment.

i) Clean on board Bills of Lading negotiable for the value of the goods "Freight Payable at Destination" (Freight Prepaid for C&F terms) made out in triplicate to order of Shipper and blank endorsed, distinctly marked "Notify China National Foreign Trade Transportation Corporation at Port of Destination."

ii) Commercial invoices in quintuplicate distinctly marked with contract number, description of goods, quantity, unit price, and total invoice amount. In the event of partial shipment, lot numbers should also be marked.

iii) Packing list in duplicate.

iv) Certificate of Inspection and List of Measurement and Weight: One each, issued by the Japanese commodity inspection organ previously decided by the mutual consent of both parties, or by the manufacturers.

v) Detailed instruction manual explaining the handling of the goods together with technical documents as specified in Article XIV of this Contract, one each, or one certificate to the effect that the aforementioned documents have been duly enclosed with the goods.

Sellers shall send on board of carrying vessel one single copy each of the i), ii) and iii) documents beneficiary to the China National Foreign Trade Transportation Corporation Office at the port of destination, who shall act on behalf of the buyer in taking delivery of goods. Sellers are further held responsible for sending one copy each of the documents herein mentioned to Buyers, and the China National Foreign Trade Transportation Corporation within 3 days after the carrying vessel's departure.

(XVII) Force Majeure:

Sellers shall not be responsible for any delay or failure to delivery goods on schedule due to Force Majeure, including wars, major floods or storms, fire, snow or earthquakes, which arise within the shipment period stipulated by this Contract regardless of whether this occurs in the production, loading or transportation stages. In the event any of the aforementioned incidents occur, Sellers shall inform Buyers by cable without delay at first knowledge, and documents verifying the event issued by the Chamber of Commerce and Industry of the area in which the aforementioned incident occurred, and/or by registered notaries public, shall be sent to Buyers within fifteen days from the date the aforementioned cable is sent. Sellers shall take all necessary measure in order to make up losses incurred by Buyers arising from non-delivery and at the same time shall inform Buyers in detail of the nature of measures effected. It shall be at Buyers' option to cancel the contract based on actual circumstance or mutual agreement with Sellers. In case of prolonged Force Majeure extending beyond ten weeks, Buyers reserve the right to cancel the order for the respective goods.

(XVIII) Penalty for Delays in Shipment:

A penalty of 1 percent of the total value of goods shall be paid to Buyers in all cases of delay in delivery within two weeks resulting from Sellers' responsibility other than Force Majeure. All delays under a period of two weeks are computed as two weeks. It is stipulated that the penalty shall be gradually increased another 1 percent every two weeks the delay in delivery continues. However, the penalty shall be held under 5 percent of the value of the goods. The Sellers shall remit the amount of the penalty to Buyers together with documents testifying to manufacturer's production progress 14 days prior to the scheduled period of delivery as stipulated by the Contract, and set another delivery date. In the event delivery is delayed over ten weeks, Buyers reserve the right to cancel the Contract for the said goods without submission to arbitration and a penalty amounting to 5 percent of the total value of the said goods shall be paid without delay by the Sellers to the Buyers.

(XIX)   Arbitration:

All disputes arising during execution of this Contract or related to this Contract shall be settled through negotiations between Sellers and Buyers. All claims which cannot be settled through negotiations between Sellers and Buyers shall be submitted to arbitration. Arbitration shall be mediated in the defendant country, in China by the Arbitration Commission of the China Committee for the

Promotion of International Trade in compliance with the commission's arbitration regulations, in Japan by the Japan International Trade Arbitration Association in compliance with the association's arbitration regulations. The arbitration board shall consist of one People's Republic of China national, one Japanese national, and one national from a third country selected by the mutual consent of both parties, should they not belong to the Arbitrators List of the Japan International Trade Arbitration Association. All arbitration decisions shall be final, and the two signing parties of this Contract shall fully abide by the decisions. The two signing parties shall obtain approval from their respective Governments, expediting all accommodations for the execution of arbitration and the travel of officials concerned, as well as guaranteeing their safety. The losing party shall bear all expenses thereof unless otherwise specifically instructed.

(XX) This Contract, commencing upon being duly signed by the Sellers and the Buyers, shall be made out in two copies, one each in Japanese and Chinese, each with equal force, and shall be kept by the hereby signing parties.

(XXI) Collaterals:

i) All damage, cost, indemnity or penalties held against Sellers in compliance with Articles VIII, XI, XVII and XIX of this Contract shall be remitted by Sellers directly to Buyers, and subtractions from the value of the goods shall not be permitted.

ii) All other clauses shall be conducted consistent with the provisions of the 1970 Memorandum Trade, with the three political principles and the principle of the inseparability of political and economic affairs acknowledged in the joint communique published by the representatives of China and Japan's Memorandum Trade Offices, as well as the Four Conditions for China-Japan Trade set forth by the Chinese Government.

Buyers: China National Machinery Import and Export Corporation

Sellers:

MAJOR CHINESE IMPORTS FROM THE WEST

Iron/Steel

Machinery and Equipment

Chemical Products

(1967 -- 1969)

I. IMPORT OF IRON AND STEEL – 1 –

1967 (1)

SITC Nos.	Description	Belg/Lux	France	W.Germ
67	**Iron and Steel**	4,719 37,936	12,871 83,519	88,297 526,528
672	**Ingot and Other Primary Forms (Including Blanks for Tubes and Pipes) of Iron or Steel**	– –	– –	359 1,309
672.5	Blooms, billets, slabs, sheet bars and roughly forged pieces of iron or steel	– –	– –	359 1,309
673	**Iron and Steel Bars, Rods, Angles, Shapes and Sections (Including Sheet Piling)**	– –	3,028 20,383	20,664 124,517
673.1	Wire rod of iron or steel, in coil	– –	– –	1,155 13,610
673.2	Bars and rods (excluding wire rod) of iron or steel; hollow mining drill steel	– –	2,828 18,722	19,036 106,210
673.4	Angles, shapes and sections (excluding rails), 80mm. or more, and sheet piling of iron or steel	– –	179 1,628	445 4,491
673.5	Angles, shapes and sections, less than 80mm., of iron or steel	– –	– –	– –
674	**Universals, Plates and Sheets of Iron or Steel**	4,371 37,016	7,686 52,191	29,993 250,412
674.1	Universal and heavy plates and sheets, more than 4.75mm. in thickness, of iron or steel (other tinned plates and sheets)	2,106 20,197	737 7,380	16,406 151,614
674.2	Medium plates and sheets, 3mm. to 4.75mm. in thickness, of iron or steel (other than tinned plates and sheets)	443 4,420	537 3,941	4,665 44,493
674.3	Plates and sheets, less than 3mm. in thickness, of iron or steel, not coated or clad	1,613 10,298	2,655 20,460	4,933 27,375

Top line — value in thousand dollars
Bottom line — quantity in metric tons

Italy	Neth	Brit	Norw	Swed	Austr	Japan	Austral	Total
19,214	412	17,281	—	12,448	1,536	102,671	3,840	263,289
135,867	2,223	127,979	—	25,161	2,732	583,775	31,633	1,557,353
—	—	—	—	—	—	148	—	507
—	—	—	—	—	—	1,131	—	2,440
—	—	—	—	—	—	—	—	359
—	—	—	—	—	—	—	—	1,309
2,076	—	5,267	—	3,572	—	10,572	194	45,373
17,017	—	49,732	—	10,429	—	...	2,504	2,224,582
—	—	2,749	—	—	—	3,950	194	8,048
—	—	34,377	—	—	—	...	2,504	50,491
1,902	—	2,513	—	3,557	293	6,583	—	36,712
15,418	—	15,309	—	10,405	487	...	—	166,551
—	—	—	—	—	515	—	—	1,144
—	—	—	—	—	1,044	—	—	7,163
161	—	—	—	—	—	—	—	161
1,572	—	—	—	—	—	—	—	1,572
13,833	412	10,427	—	6,060	—	45,301	3,646	121,729
103,702	2,223	76,684	—	11,122	—	...	29,129	562,479
2,969	—	4,757	—	4,417	—	4,214	—	35,606
28,363	—	39,950	—	9,055	—	40,397	—	296,956
3,799	—	2,904	—	1,111	—	6,723	—	20,182
37,965	—	25,489	—	1,426	—	73,191	—	190,925
5,285	—	1,950	—	532	—	24,495	1,405	54,852
25,164	—	6,658	—	641	—	...	13,088	103,684

I. Import of Iron and Steel — 2 —

1967 (2)

SITC Nos.	Description	Belg/Lux	France	W.Germ
674.7	Tinned plates and sheets	210 2,100	3,515 18,643	1,012 4,832
674.8	Plates and sheets, less than 3mm. in thickness, of iron or steel, plated, coated or clad (excluding tinned plates and sheets)	— —	242 1,767	2,977 22,098
675	**Hoop and Strip of Iron or Steel**	— —	289 2,040	3,664 20,568
677	**Iron and Steel Wire (Excluding Wire Rod)**	118 166	— —	1,855 4,416
678	**Tubes, Pipes and Fittings of Iron or Steel**	194 754	1,734 8,897	31,466 124,327
678.1	Tubes and pipes of cast iron	— —	— —	— —
678.2	Tubes and pipes of iron (other than of cast iron) or steel, seamless (excluding clinched)	153 471	900 2,942	30,042 119,256
678.3	Tubes and pipes of iron (other than of cast iron), welded, clinched, etc.	— —	799 5,900	1,424 5,070
678.5	Tube and pipe fittings of iron or steel	— —	— —	— —
679	**Iron and Steel Castings and Forgings, Unworked, N.E.S.**	— —	— —	296 979
679.3	Iron and steel forgings (including drop forgings) in the rough state	— —	— —	296 979

1968 (1)

SITC Nos.	Description	Belg/Lux	France	W.Germ
671	**Pig Iron, Spiegeleisen, Sponge Iron, Iron and Steel Powders and Shot and Ferro-Alloys**	— —	101 391	1 2
673.1	Wire rod of iron or steel, in coil	— —	1,421 18,842	1,878 23,190

Top line — value in thousand dollars
Bottom line — quantity in metric tons

Italy	Neth	Brit	Norw	Swed	Austr	Japan	Austral	Total
—	412	285	—	—	—	6,760	—	12,194
—	2,223	1,479	—	—	—	30,272	—	59,549
1,779	—	531	—	—	—	3,108	2,147	10,784
12,210	—	3,108	—	—	—	21,530	15,283	75,996
—	—	517	—	—	14	575	—	5,059
—	—	2,452	—	—	19	..	—	25,079
257	—	1,046	—	1,907	243	2,693	—	8,119
214	—	2,695	—	2,568	1,061	...	—	11,120
2,951	—	—	—	856	—	43,383	—	80,564
14,934	—	—	—	...	—	194,268	—	343,180
1,123	—	—	—	—	—	—	—	1,123
4,910	—	—	—	—	—	—	—	4,910
1,662	—	—	—	790	39	40,607	—	74,193
9,365	—	—	—	1,042	88	178,935	—	312,099
—	—	—	—	—	40	1,980	—	4,243
—	—	—	—	—	66	14,441	—	25,477
—	—	—	—	—	69	796	—	865
—	—	—	—	—	22	892	—	914
—	—	—	—	—	58	—	—	354
—	—	—	—	—	33	—	—	1,012
—	—	—	—	—	—	—	—	296
—	—	—	—	—	—	—	—	979

Top line — value in thousand dollars
Bottom line — quantity in metric tons

Italy	Neth	Brit	Norw	Swed	Austr	Austral	Japan	Total
—	—	7	...	—	—	—	70	179
—	—	...	20	—	—	—	225	638
193	—	4,355	—	—	—	—	8,788	16,635
937	—	57,362	—	—	—	—	...	100,331

SITC Nos.	Description	Belg/Lux	France	W.Germ
673.11	Wire rod of iron or steel	— —	1,392 18,793	1,806 22,774
673.2	Bars and rods (excluding wire rod) of iron or steel; hollow mining drill steel.	311 3,600	943 7,189	10,999 82,769
673.21	Bars and rods (excluding wire rod) of iron or steel, clad, plated.	311 3,600	610 5,720	7,105 67,775
673.4	Angles, shapes and sections (excluding rails), 80mm. or more, and sheet piling of iron or steel	— —	— —	— —
673.41	Angles, shapes and sections of iron or steel	— —	— —	— —
674	**Universals, Plates and Sheets of Iron or Steel**	613 5,249	2,055 13,998	13,983 116,973
674.1	Heavy plates and sheets, more than 4.75mm. in thickness, of iron and steel	328 3,261	3 35	6,529 69,327
674.11	Heavy plates and sheets of iron and steel, clad	328 3,261	3 35	6,124 66,732
674.14	Heavy plates and sheets of high carbon steel	— —	— —	204 1,504
674.2	Medium plates and sheets, 3mm. to 4.75mm. in thickness, of iron or steel (other than tinned plates and sheets)	— —	44 63	1,550 15,023
674.21	Medium plates and sheets of iron or steel, clad	— —	— —	1,456 14,969
674.3	Plates and sheets, less than 3mm. in thickness, of iron and steel, not plated	285 1,988	1,821 12,420	2,780 12,416
674.31	Plates and sheets of iron or steel, clad	236 1,742	750 7,366	548 3,644
674.7	Tinned plates and sheets	— —	— —	407 2,011
674.8	Plates and sheets, less than 3mm. in thickness, of iron or steel, plated, coated or clad (excluding tinned plates and sheets)	— —	187 1,480	2,717 18,196

Top line — value in thousand dollars
Bottom line — quantity in metric tons

Italy	Neth	Brit	Norw	Swed	Austr	Austral	Japan	Total
—	—	4,355	—	—	—	—	8,371	15,924
—	—	57,362	—	—	—	—	101,725	200,654
3,609	—	1,284	—	749	287	—	17,709	35,891
31,970	—	8,888	—	4,577	668	—	...	139,581
1,781	—	690	—	—	—	—	10,056	20,553
18,116	—	6,850	—	—	—	—	...	102,061
18	—	—	—	—	1,125	—	770	1,913
203	—	—	—	—	1,093	—	6,994	8,290
...	—	—	—	—	—	—	770	770
203	—	—	—	—	—	—	6,994	7,197
3,382	—	2,501	—	3,970	280	—	56,579	83,363
26,112	—	11,678	—	9,777	2,281	—	...	186,068
3,339	—	826	—	3,112	20	—	5,691	16,848
3,653	—	8,258	—	7,918	16	—	68,010	160,478
339	—	644	—	506	—	—	5,615	13,559
3,653	—	7,922	—	4,368	—	—	67,727	153,698
—	—	8	—	—	—	—	—	212
—	—	83	—	—	—	—	—	1,587
1,101	—	43	—	187	2	—	2,288	5,215
6,955	—	76	—	238	2	—	23,643	46,000
1,101	—	2	—	—	—	—	1,968	4,527
6,955	—	20	—	—	—	—	23,165	45,109
1,319	—	1,397	—	671	258	—	30,406	38,937
10,816	—	2,144	—	1,621	2,263	—	...	43,668
1,129	—	17	—	153	258	—	19,435	22,536
9,916	—	148	—	999	2,263	—	187,185	213,263
—	—	22	—	—	—	—	14,306	14,735
—	—	121	—	—	—	—	7,620	9,752
623	—	213	—	—	—	—	3,888	7,628
4,688	—	1,079	—	—	—	—	28,148	53,591

I. Import of Iron and Steel   – 4 –

1968 (3)

SITC Nos.	Description	Belg/Lux	France	W. Germ
674.81	Plates and sheets of iron or steel	— —	187 1,480	2,667 18,181
675.01	Hoop and strip of iron or steel, clad	909 7,389	— —	1,988 13,936
677	**Iron and Steel Wire (Excluding Wire Rod)**	406 3,185	325 482	2,894 10,614
678	**Tubes, Pipes and Fittings of Iron or Steel**	14 94	121 397	16,138 73,325
678.2	Tubes and pipes of iron (other than of cast iron) or steel, seamless (excluding clinched)	— —	121 397	15,878 72,088
678.3	Tubes and pipes of iron (other than of cast iron), welded, clinched, etc.	14 94	— —	260 1,237
679	**Iron and Steel Castings and Forgings, Unworked, N.E.S.**	— —	— —	375 1,261

1969 (1)

SITC Nos.	Description	Belg/Lux	France	W. Germ
67	**Iron and Steel**	1,977 —	6,396 —	46,474 —
671	**Pig Iron, Spiegeleisen, Sponge Iron, Iron and Steel Powders and Shot and Ferro-Alloys**	— —	— —	142 3,500
671.2	Pig iron (including cast iron)	— —	— —	142 3,500
671.5	Other ferro-alloys	— —	— —	— —

Top line — value in thousand dollars
Bottom line — quantity in metric tons

Italy	Neth	Brit	Norw	Swed	Austr	Austral	Japan	Total
623	—	213	—	—	—	—	3,888	7,578
4,688	—	1,079	—	—	—	—	28,148	53,576
243	—	107	—	22	—	—	2,264	5,533
1,826	—	750	—	99	—	—	21,042	45,042
550	61	771	—	396	110	—	4,382	9,895
892	366	1,778	—	448	500	—	...	18,263
94	—	15	—	519	12	—	45,611	62,524
663	—	34	—	389	4	—	276,340	351,246
92	—	10	—	518	12	—	40,891	57,522
663	—	13	—	389	4	—	235,874	309,428
2	—	3	—	—	—	—	4,628	4,907
...	—	17	—	—	—	—	40,350	41,698
—	—	—	—	—	—	—	—	375
—	—	—	—	—	—	—	—	1,261

Top line — value in thousand dollars
Bottom line — quantity in metric tons

Italy	Neth	Brit	Norw	Swed	Austr	Austral	Japan	Total
6,972	—	5,241	—	2,607	3,131	191	163,413	236,402
—	—	—	—	—	—	—	—	...
—	—	185	—	—	—	—	1	327
—	—	42	—	—	—	—	...	3,542
—	—	—	—	—	—	—	—	142
—	—	—	—	—	—	—	—	3,500
—	—	185	—	—	—	—	—	185
—	—	42	—	—	—	—	—	42

I. Import of Iron and Steel – 5 –

1969 (2)

SITC Nos.	Description	Belg/Luxs	France	W.Germ
672	**Ingots and Other Primary Forms (Including Blanks for Tubes and Pipes) of Iron or Steel**	— —	486 4,001	377 1,444
672.5	Blooms, billets, slabs, sheet bars and roughly forged pieces of iron or steel	— —	486 4,001	377 1,444
673	**Iron and Steel Bars, Rods, Angles, Shapes and Sections (Including Sheet Piling)**	101 1,146	984 7,890	7,261 54,918
673.1	Wire rod of iron or steel, in coil	— —	110 1,495	899 10,029
673.2	Bars and rods (excluding wire rod) or iron or steel; hollow mining drill steel	— —	866 6,275	6,358 44,859
673.4	Angles, shapes and sections (excluding rails), 80mm. or more, and sheet piling of iron or steel	— —	— —	— —
674	**Universals, Plates and Sheets of Iron or Steel**	501 4,640	4,811 27,478	24,114 180,819
674.1	Universals and heavy plates and sheets, more than 4.75mm. in thickness, of iron or steel (other than tinned plates and sheets)	— —	— —	8,329 67,470
674.2	Medium plates and sheets, 3mm. to 4.75mm. in thickness, of iron or steel (other than tinned plates and sheets)	— —	143 271	657 6,365
674.3	Plates and sheets, less than 3mm. in thickness, of iron or steel, not plated, coated or clad	— —	759 5,353	7,201 53,403
674.7	Tinned Plates and sheets	427 4,268	3,909 21,341	503 2,515
674.8	Plates and sheets, less than 3mm. in thickness, of iron or steel, plated, coated or clad (excluding tinned plates and sheets)	— —	— —	7,424 51,066
675	**Hoop and Strip of Iron or Steel**	977 6,678	— —	2,032 13,104
677	**Iron and Steel Wire (Excluding Wire Rod)**	291 1,088	— —	1,571 5,384

Top line — value in thousand dollars
Bottom line — quantity in metric tons

Italy	Neth	Brit	Norw	Swed	Austr	Austral	Japan	Total
—	—	—	—	—	—	—	342	1,205
—	—	—	—	—	—	—	2,819	8,264
—	—	—	—	—	—	—	327	1,190
—	—	—	—	—	—	—	2,658	8,103
3,403	—	3,336	—	213	2,750	—	—	18,048
29,880	—	28,934	—	639	4,200	—	—	127,607
207	—	1,446	—	—	—	—	8,143	10,805
956	—	16,783	—	—	—	—	...	29,263
3,112	—	1,890	—	213	—	—	28,473	40,912
28,083	—	12,151	—	639	—	—	...	92,004
—	—	—	—	—	2,718	—	319	3,037
—	—	—	—	—	4,088	—	3,055	7,143
2,884	—	1,349	—	1,728	—	191	75,495	111,133
28,514	—	5,332	—	7,130	—	1,004	...	254,917
1,688	—	738	—	1,372	—	—	15,581	27,708
10,715	—	2,741	—	5,691	—	—	166,448	253,065
233	—	—	—	108	—	—	5,188	6,329
2,576	—	—	—	116	—	—	49,775	59,103
—	—	—	—	247	—	191	39,230	47,628
—	—	—	—	1,324	—	1,004	...	61,084
—	—	510	—	—	—	—	7,860	13,209
—	—	2,432	—	—	—	—	37,873	68,429
921	—	—	—	—	—	—	7,636	15,981
6,915	—	—	—	—	—	—	52,366	110,347
—	—	—	—	—	—	—	—	3,009
—	—	—	—	—	—	—	—	19,782
606	—	283	—	618	366	—	2,722	6,457
750	—	730 "	—	921	706	—	...	9,579

I. Import of Iron and Steel – 6 –

1969 (3)

SITC Nos.	Description	Belg/Lux	France	W.Germ
678	**Tubes, Pipes and Fittings of Iron or Steel**	— —	— —	10,762 47,440
678.2	Tubes and pipes of iron (other than of cast iron) or steel, seamless (excluding clinched)	— —	— —	9,396 40,398
678.3	Tubes and pipes of iron (other than of cast iron), welded, clinched, etc.	— —	— —	1,366 7,042
679	**Iron and Steel Castings and Forgings, Unworked, N.E.S.**	— —	— —	215 818
679.3	Iron and steel forgings (including drop forgings) in the rough state	— —	— —	215 818

NOTES: 1) — represents none or figures less than one thousand dollars.

2) — represents those not listed in original statistics.

3) — values in general are on F.O.B. basis for exports and C.I.F. basis for imports, with some exceptions.

SOURCE: Supplement to the World Trade and Annual

Top line — value in thousand dollars
Bottom line — quantity in metric tons

Italy	Neth	Brit	Norw	Swed	Austr	Austral	Japan	Total
—	—	—	—	—	—	—	45,304	56,066
—	—	—	—	—	—	—	291,004	338,444
—	—	—	—	—	—	—	38,887	48,283
—	—	—	—	—	—	—	237,975	278,373
—	—	—	—	—	—	—	6,360	7,726
—	—	—	—	—	—	—	52,964	60,006
—	—	—	—	—	—	—	—	215
—	—	—	—	—	—	—	—	818
—	—	—	—	—	—	—	—	215
—	—	—	—	—	—	—	—	818

II. IMPORT OF MACHINERY AND TRANSPORT EQUIPMENT

1967 (1)

SITC Nos.	Description	Belg/Lux	France	W.Germ	Italy	Neth
7	**Machinery and Transport Equipment**	217 ...	34,993 ...	44,769 ...	15,324 ...	753 ...
71	**Machinery, Other than Electric**	— —	7,987 ...	37,642 ...	8,652 ...	410 ...
72	**Electrical Machinery, Apparatus and Appliances**	123 ...	2,561 ...	5,707 ...	1,132 ...	343 ...
73	**Transport Equipment**	— —	24,444 ...	1,420 ...	5,541 ...	— —
711	**Power Generating Machinery, Other than Electric**	— —	— —	1,552 174	468 70	— —
711.1	Steam generating boilers	— —	— —	— —	— —	— —
711.3	Steam engines (including stationary steam engines with self-contained boilers (generally known as loco-mobiles) and steam turbines)	— —	— —	— —	138 23	— —
711.4	Aircraft engines	— —	— —	— —	— —	— —
711.5	Internal combustion piston engines	— —	404 65	1,508 151	321 46	— —
711.6	Gas turbines, other than for aircraft	— —	— —	— —	— —	— —
711.8	Engines, n.e.s. (wind engines, hot air engines, water wheels and water turbines)	— —	..	— —	— —	— —

— 1 —

Top line — value in thousand dollars
Bottom line — quantity in metric tons

Brit	Den	Norw	Swed	Austr	Switz	Japan	Fin	Total
27,240	3,535	1,826	14,251	6,477	10,893	38,789	1,795	200,862
...	...	...	...	...	...	...	...	...
16,370	2,935	—	12,347	5,790	9,919	25,834	1,708	129,594
...	...	—	...	...	...	...	...	...
3,272	600	—	1,494	569	973	11,358	—	28,132
...	...	—	...	...	...	...	—	...
7,598	—	1.799	410	118	—	1,597	—	42,927
...	—	...	...	...	—	...	—	...
218	2,335	—	2,558	797	—	878	—	8,806
...	1,369	—	486	516	—	...	—	...
—	—	—	—	797	—	—	—	797
—	—	—	—	516	—	—	—	...
—	—	—	—	—	—	—	—	138
—	—	—	—	—	—	—	—	...
—	—	—	—	—	—	—	—	0
—	—	—	—	—	—	—	—	...
125	2,335	—	—	—	—	358	—	5,051
...	1,369	—	—	—	—	...	—	...
—	—	—	2,525	—	—	—	—	2,525
—	—	—	470	—	—	—	—	...
—	—	—	—	—	—	520	—	520
—	—	—	—	—	—	...	—	...

II. Import of Machinery and Transport Equipment – 2 –

1967 (2)

SITC Nos.	Description	Belg/Lux	France	W.Germ	Italy	Neth
712	**Agricultural Machinery and Implements**	– –	– –	– –	– –	– –
712.1	Agricultural machinery and appliances for preparing and cultivating the soil	– –	– –	– –	– –	– –
712.3	Milking machines, and other daily-farm equipment	– –	– –	– –	– –	– –
712.5	Tractors	– –	– –	– –	– –	– –
712.9	Agricultural machinery and appliances, n.e.s.	– –	– –	– –	– –	– –
714	**Office Machines**	– –	106 1	– –	– –	– –
714.1	Typewriters and check writing machines	– –	– –	– –	– –	– –
714.2	Calculating machines, accounting machines and similar machines incorporating a calculating device (including electronic computers)	– –	– –	– –	– –	– –
714.3	Statistical machines, e.g., calculating from punched cards	– –	– –	– –	– –	– –
714.9	Office machines, n.e.s.	– –	– –	– –	– –	– –
715	**Metal Working Machinery**	– –	3,143 1,187	26,068 6,577	3,323 1,641	105 20
715.1	Machine-tools for working metals	– –	3,143 1,187	14,059 3,037	2,876 1,478	105 20
715.2	Metal working machinery, other than machine-tools	– –	– –	12,009 3,540	447 163	– –
717	**Textile and Leather Machinery**	– –	– –	766 124	567 299	– –

Top line — value in thousand dollars
Bottom line — quantity in metric tons

Brit	Den	Norw	Swed	Austr	Switz	Japan	Fin	Total
152	—	—	—	—	—	—	—	152
122	—	—	—	—	—	—	—	...
—	—	—	—	—	—	—	—	0
—	—	—	—	—	—	—	—	...
—	—	—	—	—	—	—	—	0
—	—	—	—	—	—	—	—	...
129	—	—	—	—	—	—	—	129
113	—	—	—	—	—	—	—	...
—	—	—	—	—	—	—	—	0
—	—	—	—	—	—	—	—	...
1,617	—	—	—	—	—	468	—	2,191
28	—	—	—	—	—	...	—	...
—	—	—	—	—	—	—	—	0
—	—	—	—	—	—	—	—	...
1,396	—	—	—	—	—	451	—	1,847
23	—	—	—	—	—	(N) 35	—	...
206	—	—	—	—	—	—	—	206
5	—	—	—	—	—	—	—	...
—	—	—	—	—	—	—	—	0
—	—	—	—	—	—	—	—	...
4,176	—	—	572	515	8,136	5,700	—	51,738
1,018	—	—	92	274	1,181	...	—	...
3,617	—	—	572	—	8,136	2,625	—	35,133
879	—	—	92	—	1,181	(N)291	—	...
559	—	—	—	505	—	3,076	—	16,596
138	—	—	—	272	—	...	—	...
2,242	—	—	—	—	188	928	—	4,691
354	—	—	—	—	...	...	—	...

II.   Import of Machinery and Transport Equipment   – 3 –

1967 (3)

SITC Nos.	Description	Belg/Lux	France	W.Germ	Italy	Neth
717.1	Textile machines	— —	— —	694 113	522 283	— —
717.3	Sewing machines	— —	— —	— —	— —	— —
718	**Machines for Special Industries**	— —	2,721 729	376 119	1,176 1,116	— —
718.1	Paper mill and pulp mill machinery, paper cutting machinery and other machinery for the manufacture of paper articles	— —	2,658 616	— —	— —	— —
718.2	Printing and bookbinding machinery	— —	— —	— —	— —	— —
718.3	Food-processing machines (excluding domestic)	— —	— —	— —	— —	— —
718.4	Construction and mining machinery, n.e.s.	— —	— —	218 49	1,061 1,075	— —
718.5	Mineral crushing, sorting and moulding machinery; glass working machinery	— —	— —	104 55	— —	— —
719	**Machinery and Appliances (Other than Electrical)**	— —	1,591 383	8,861 3,258	3,051 1,268	292 69
719.1	Heating and cooling equipment	— —	— —	529 299	403 100	136 39
719.2	Pumps and centrifuges	— —	566 92	575 60	459 92	— —
719.3	Mechanical handling equipment	— —	193 118	377 144	717 546	— —
719.32	Fork-lift, trucks, etc.	— —	190 118	— —	— —	— —
719.5	Power-tools, n.e.s.	— —	134 20	1,303 346	— —	— —

Top line — value in thousand dollars
Bottom line — quantity in metric tons

Brit	Den	Norw	Swed	Austr	Switz	Japan	Fin	Total
2,241	—	—	—	—	188	877	—	4,522
353	—	—	—	—	...	...	—	...
—	—	—	—	—	—	—	—	0
—	—	—	—	—	—	—	—	...
281	178	—	1,329	—	115	1,105	1,016	8,297
110	48	—	626	—	19	...	426	...
—	—	—	—	—	—	—	1,016	3,674
—	—	—	—	—	—	—	426	...
—	—	—	—	—	114	560	—	674
—	—	—	—	—	19	...	—	...
—	100	—	—	—	—	—	—	100
—	27	—	—	—	—	—	—	...
189	—	—	160	—	—	332	—	1,960
89	—	—	42	—	—	...	—	...
—	—	—	1,090	—	—	179	—	1,373
—	—	—	570	—	—	...	—	...
7,682	366	—	7,886	4,456	1,416	16,657	686	52,944
1,613	161	—	2,672	2,161	...	...	276	...
1,165	213	—	—	—	—	5,094	668	8,208
302	92	—	—	—	—	...	271	...
156	—	—	619	561	—	4,832	—	7,768
29	—	—	192	134	—	...	—	...
326	—	—	2,853	2,594	—	1,435	—	8,495
185	—	—	1,119	1,546	—	...	—	...
—	—	—	—	—	—	419	—	609
—	—	—	—	—	—	...	—	...
—	—	—	1,598	—	561	522	—	4,118
—	—	—	253	—	37	...	—	...

II. Import of Machinery and Transport Equipment – 4 –

1967 (4)

SITC Nos.	Description	Belg/Lux	France	W.Germ	Italy	Neth
719.6	Other non-electrical machines (e.g., calendering machines, packing or wrapping machinery, weighing machinery, etc.	— —	— —	855 347	— —	— —
719.7	Bearings	— —	186 49	2,666 1,128	211 78	— —
719.8	Machinery and mechanical appliances, n.e.s.	— —	184 27	2,192 798	764 269	— —
719.9	Parts and accessories of machinery, n.e.s.	— —	268 48	364 134	434 156	— —
722	**Electric Power Machinery and Switchgear**	— —	456 155	237 47	739 205	— —
722.1	Electric power machinery	— —	361 136	143 35	459 169	— —
722.2	Electric apparatus for making and breaking or for protecting electrical circuits (switchgear, etc.)	— —	— —	— —	280 35	— —
723	**Equipment for Distributing Electricity**	— —	— —	117 15	— —	— —
723.1	Insulated wire and cable	— —	— —	117 15	— —	— —
724	**Telecommunications Apparatus**	— —	1,067 72	1,345 36	— —	— —
724.2	Radio broadcast receiver	— —	— —	— —	— —	— —
724.9	Other telecommunications equipment	— —	1,066 72	1,345 36	— —	— —
725	**Domestic Electrical Equipment**	— —	— —	— —	— —	— —

Top line — value in thousand dollars
Bottom line — quantity in metric tons

Brit	Den	Norw	Swed	Austr	Switz	Japan	Fin	Total
—	—	—	—	287	—	179	—	1,321
—	—	—	—	44	—	...	—	...
144	—	—	2,120	503	306	2,222	—	8,358
51	—	—	770	263	123	1,520	—	...
5,255	—	—	493	—	400	1,682	—	10,970
916	—	—	249	—	32	...	—	...
535	123	—	—	452	—	692	—	2,868
122	63	—	—	161	—	...	—	...
258	—	—	589	186	109	3,912	—	6,486
17	—	—	146	43	26	...	—	...
—	—	—	—	105	—	2,648	—	3,716
—	—	—	—	26	—	...	—	...
216	—	—	524	—	—	1,264	—	2,284
10	—	—	93	—	—	...	—	...
—	—	—	—	156	—	392	—	665
—	—	—	—	87	—	290	—	...
—	—	—	—	141	—	392	—	650
—	—	—	—	81	—	289	—	...
802	—	—	—	—	131	—	—	3,345
...	—	—	—	—	2	—	—	...
—	—	—	—	—	—	—	—	0
—	—	—	—	—	—	—	—	...
800	—	—	—	—	131	—	—	3,342
...	—	—	—	—	2	—	—	...
—	—	—	—	—	—	—	—	0
—	—	—	—	—	—	—	—	...

II.   Import of Machinery and Transport Equipment   – 5 –
1967 (5)

SITC Nos.	Description	Belg/Lux	France	W.Germ	Italy	Neth
726	**Electric Apparatus for Medical Purposes and Radiological Apparatus**	— —	157 12	216 10	— —	— —
726.1	Electro-medical apparatus	— —	— —	— —	— —	— —
726.2	X-ray apparatus	— —	156 12	214 10	— —	— —
729	**Other Electrical Machinery and Apparatus**	— —	783 49	3,792 655	355 113	115 3
729.2	Electric lamps	— —	— —	— —	— —	— —
729.3	Thermionic, etc. valves and tubes, photocells, transistors, etc.	— —	172 3	— —	— —	— —
729.4	Automotive electrical equipment	— —	— —	— —	— —	— —
729.5	Electrical measuring and controlling instruments and apparatus	— —	544 27	2,306 123	275 104	— —
729.6	Hand tools	— —	— —	— —	— —	— —
729.7	Electron and proton accelerators	— —	— —	— —	— —	— —
729.9	Electrical machinery and apparatus, n.e.s.	— —	— —	1,450 531	— —	— —
731	**Railway Vehicles**	— —	— —	625 130	— —	— —
731.1	Railway locomotives, electric	— —	— —	— —	— —	— —
731.2	Railway locomotives, battery operated or powered from an external source of electricity	— —	— —	— —	— —	— —
731.3	Railway locomotives	— —	— —	568 123	— —	— —

Top line — value in thousand dollars
Bottom line — quantity in metric tons

Brit	Den	Norw	Swed	Austr	Switz	Japan	Fin	Total
175	—	—	—	—	—	345	—	893
...	—	—	—	—	—	...	—	...
—	—	—	—	—	—	—	—	0
—	—	—	—	—	—	—	—	...
136	—	—	—	—	—	295	—	801
...	—	—	—	—	—	...	—	...
2,004	452	—	849	226	652	6,615	—	15,843
...	10	—	...	13	16	...	—	...
—	—	—	—	—	—	—	—	0
—	—	—	—	—	—	—	—	...
169	—	—	—	—	—	—	—	341
...	—	—	—	—	—	—	—	...
—	—	—	—	—	—	—	—	0
—	—	—	—	—	—	—	—	...
1,363	446	—	—	219	512	3,177	—	8,842
...	10	—	—	10	10	(N)4,110	—	...
—	—	—	—	—	—	—	—	0
—	—	—	—	—	—	—	—	...
—	—	—	—	—	—	—	—	0
—	—	—	—	—	—	—	—	...
379	—	—	798	—	125	3,322	—	6,074
...	—	—	459	—	6	...	—	...
—	—	—	254	118	—	—	—	997
—	—	—	152	75	—	—	—	...
—	—	—	—	—	—	—	—	0
—	—	—	—	—	—	—	—	...
—	—	—	174	—	—	—	—	174
—	—	—	70	—	—	—	—	...
—	—	—	—	—	—	—	—	568
—	—	—	—	—	—	—	—	...

II. Import of Machinery and Transport Equipment – 6 –

1967 (6)

SITC Nos.	Description	Belg/Lux	France	W.Germ	Italy	Neth
731.6	Railway and tramway freight and maintenance cars, not mechanically propelled	— —	— —	— —	— —	— —
731.7	Parts of railway locomotives and rolling-stock, n.e.s.	— —	— —	— —	— —	— —
732	**Road Motor Vehicles**	— —	12,652 6,638	605 185	5,535 4,147	— —
732.1	Passenger motor cars	— —	— —	— —	— —	— —
732.2	Buses	— —	— —	— —	— —	— —
732.3	Trucks	— —	10,784 5,982	— —	4,968 4,011	— —
732.4	Special purpose motor vehicles	— —	710 318	— —	— —	— —
732.5	Road tractors for tractor-trailer combinations	— —	— —	389 142	— —	— —
732.8	Bodies, chassis, frames and other parts of motor vehicles	— —	1,063 294	196 34	518 116	— —
733	**Road Vehicles Other than Motor Vehicles**	— —	— —	190 179	— —	— —
733.3	Trailers	— —	— —	190 179	— —	— —
734	**Aircraft**	— —	2,043 13	— —	— —	— —
734.1	Airplane, gliders and kites; rotochutes	— —	1,587 8	— —	— —	— —
734.9	Airships, balloons and parts of aircraft, airships and balloons (not including rubber tire, engines or electrical parts)	— —	455 5	— —	— —	— —

Top line — value in thousand dollars
Bottom line — quantity in metric tons

Brit	Den	Norw	Swed	Austr	Switz	Japan	Fin	Total
—	—	—	—	118	—	—	—	118
—	—	—	—	75	—	—	—	...
—	—	—	—	—	—	—	—	0
—	—	—	—	—	—	—	—	...
833	—	—	—	—	—	744	—	20,369
...	—	—	—	—	—	...	—	...
391	—	—	—	—	—	—	—	391
(N)172	—	—	—	—	—	—	—	...
—	—	—	—	—	—	—	—	0
—	—	—	—	—	—	—	—	...
—	—	—	—	—	—	464	—	16,216
—	—	—	—	—	—	(N)223	—	...
108	—	—	—	—	—	202	—	1,020
35	—	—	—	—	—	(N) 14	—	...
—	—	—	—	—	—	—	—	389
—	—	—	—	—	—	—	—	...
302	—	—	—	—	—	—	—	2,079
95	—	—	—	—	—	—	—	...
—	—	—	—	—	—	—	—	190
—	—	—	—	—	—	—	—	...
—	—	—	—	—	—	—	—	190
—	—	—	—	—	—	—	—	...
377	—	—	—	—	—	—	—	2,420
...	—	—	—	—	—	—	—	...
—	—	—	—	—	—	—	—	1,587
—	—	—	—	—	—	—	—	...
—	—	—	—	—	—	—	—	455
—	—	—	—	—	—	—	—	...

II. Import of Machinery and Transport Equipment   – 7 –
1967 (7)

SITC Nos.	Description	Belg/Lux	France	W.Germ	Italy	Neth
735	**Ships and Boats**	— —	9,712 19,657	— —	— —	— —
735.3	Ships and boats	— —	9,712 19,657	— —	— —	— —
735.8	Ships, boats and other vessels for breaking up	— —	— —	— —	— —	— —
735.9	Ships, and boats, n.e.s.	— —	— —	— —	— —	— —
861	**Scientific, Medical, Optical, Measuring and Controlling Instruments and Apparatus**	— —	586 28	4,896 261	212 21	— —
861.1	Optical elements	— —	— —	— —	— —	— —
861.3	Spectacles, microscopes and other optical instruments	— —	109 7	1,531 59	— —	— —
861.4	Photographic cameras (other than cinematographic) and flash-light apparatus	— —	— —	— —	— —	— —
861.5	Cinematographic cameras, projectors, sound recorders and sound reproducers	— —	117 1	— —	— —	— —
861.6	Photographic and cinematographic apparatus and equipment, n.e.s.	— —	— —	— —	— —	— —
861.7	Medical instruments, n.e.s.	— —	— —	— —	— —	— —
861.9	Measuring, controlling and scientific instruments, n.e.s.	— —	261 11	3,056 197	176 19	— —
864	**Watches and Clocks**	— —	234 ...	— —	214 ...	— —
864.1	Watches, watch movements and cases	— —	162 ...	— —	— —	— —
864.11	Pocket watches	— —	162 ...	— —	— —	— —

Top line — value in thousand dollars
Bottom line — quantity in metric tons

Brit	Den	Norw	Swed	Austr	Switz	Japan	Fin	Total
6,388	—	1,799	—	—	—	796	—	18,695
...	—	...	—	—	—	...	—	...
6,388	—	1,799	—	—	—	635	—	18,534
...	—	...	—	—	—	...	—	...
—	—	—	—	—	—	—	—	0
—	—	—	—	—	—	—	—	...
—	—	—	—	—	—	162	—	162
—	—	—	—	—	—	(N) 16	—	...
6,289	—	—	418	—	2,717	5,089	—	20,207
...	—	—	...	—	122	...	—	...
—	—	—	—	—	—	263	—	263
—	—	—	—	—	—	...	—	...
423	—	—	—	—	144	911	—	3,118
...	—	—	—	—	2	...	—	...
—	—	—	—	—	—	169	—	169
—	—	—	—	—	—	...	—	...
—	—	—	—	—	—	—	—	117
—	—	—	—	—	—	—	—	...
—	—	—	—	—	—	219	—	219
—	—	—	—	—	—	...	—	...
189	—	—	—	—	—	—	—	189
...	—	—	—	—	—	—	—	...
5,568	—	—	290	—	2,512	3,458	—	15,321
...	—	—	5	—	116	...	—	...
—	—	—	—	—	4,905	—	—	5,353
—	—	—	—	—	...	—	—	...
—	—	—	—	—	4,349	—	—	4,511
—	—	—	—	—	...	—	—	...
—	—	—	—	—	4,328	—	—	4,490
—	—	—	—	—	...	—	—	...

II. Import of Machinery and Transport Equipment — 8 —

1968 (8)

SITC Nos.	Description	Belg/Lux	France	W.Germ	Italy	Neth
864.2	Clocks, clock movements and parts	— —	— —	— —	214 ...	— —
891.1	Phonographs (gramophones), tape recorders and other sound recorders and reproducers	— —	— —	— —	— —	— —

NOTES: 1) — represents none or figures less than the unit figure of $1,000.

2) — represents those not listed in the original statistics.

3) — values in general are on f.o.b. basis for exports and CIF basis for imports, with some exceptions.

SOURCE: UN; Commodity Trade Statistics

Top line — value in thousand dollars
Bottom line — quantity in metric tons

Brit	Den	Norw	Swed	Austr	Switz	Japan	Fin	Total
—	—	—	—	—	556	—	—	770
—	—	—	—	—	...	—	—	...
—	—	—	—	—	—	112	—	112
—	—	—	—	—	—	...	—	...

II. Import of Machinery and Transport Equipment – 9 –

1968 (1)

SITC Nos.	Description	Belg/Lux	France	W.Germ	Italy	Neth
7	**Machinery and Transport Equipment**	506 ...	15,711 ...	27,336 ...	7,214 ...	488 ...
71	**Machinery, Other than Electric**	110 ...	5,714 ...	21,335 ...	4,604 ...	156 ...
711	**Power Generating Machinery, Other than Electric**	— —	784 126	— —	130 22	— —
711.1	Steam generating boilers	— —	— —	— —	— —	— —
711.5	Internal combustion piston engines, other than for aircraft	— —	783 126	— —	125 19	— —
711.6	Gas turbines, other than for aircraft	— —	— —	— —	— —	— —
714	**Office Machines**	— —	464 5	430 15	167 4	— —
714.2	Calculating machines, accounting machines and similar machines incorporating a calculating device (including electronic computers)	— —	405 4	343 7	162 4	— —
714.3	Statistical machines, e.g., calculating from punched cards	— —	— —	— —	— —	— —
715	**Metal-Working Machinery**	— —	1,769 426	13,710 4,355	2,910 1,202	— —
715.1	Machine-tools for working metals	— —	1,769 426	12,520 3,865	2,711 1,164	— —
715.2	Metal-working machinery, other than machine-tools	— —	— —	1,190 490	199 38	— —
717	**Textile and Leather Machinery**	108 52	391 111	269 61	186 35	— —

Top line — value in thousand dollars
Bottom line — quantity in metric tons

Brit	Den	Norw	Swed	Austr	Switz	Japan	Fin	Total
6,911	745	—	5,772	2,530	7,800	29,278	499	104,790
...	...	—	...	...	...	...	...	...
3,230	208	—	5,350	2,306	7,095	19,112	170	69,390
...	...	—	...	...	...	...	...	...
189	—	—	480	—	—	911	—	2,494
...	—	—	56	—	—	...	—	...
—	—	—	—	—	—	246	—	246
—	—	—	—	—	—	...	—	...
101	—	—	128	—	—	741	—	1,878
...	—	—	23	—	—	...	—	...
—	—	—	352	—	—	—	—	352
—	—	—	33	—	—	—	—	...
337	—	—	—	801	—	—	—	2,199
3	—	—	—	14	—	—	—	...
—	—	—	—	—	—	—	—	910
—	—	—	—	—	—	—	—	...
295	—	—	—	801	—	—	—	1,096
2	—	—	—	14	—	—	—	...
556	—	—	—	1,129	5,818	4,232	—	30,124
169	—	—	—	304	875	...	—	...
555	—	—	—	1,105	5,818	3,613	—	28,091
169	—	—	—	300	875	308	—	...
—	—	—	—	—	—	619	—	2,008
—	—	—	—	—	—	...	—	...
778	—	—	172	—	—	134	—	2,038
208	—	—	82	—	—	...	—	...

II. Import of Machinery and Transport Equipment – 10 –

1968 (2)

SITC Nos.	Description	Belg/Lux	France	W.Germ	Italy	Neth
717.1	Textile machines	108 52	383 111	203 56	142 25	— —
718	**Machines for Special Industries**	— —	911 1,160	201 64	266 175	— —
718.1	Paper mill and pulp mill machinery, paper cutting machinery and other machinery for the manufacture of paper articles	— —	152 58	— —	— —	— —
718.2	Printing and book-binding machinery	— —	— —	— —	129 54	— —
718.4	Construction and mining machinery, n.e.s.	— —	545 1,086	— —	132 120	— —
718.5	Mineral crushing, sorting and moulding machinery; glass working machinery	— —	214 16	— —	— —	— —
719	**Machinery and Appliances (Other than Electrical) and Machine Parts, N.E.S.**	— —	1,396 312	6,682 2,287	944 432	— —
719.1	Heating and cooling equipments	— —	— —	2,645 1,879	— —	— —
719.2	Pumps and centrifuges	— —	155 17	1,284 166	— —	— —
719.3	Mechanical handling equipment	— —	— —	— —	— —	— —
719.32	Other mechanical handling equipment and trucks	— —	— —	— —	— —	— —
719.5	Power-tools, n.e.s.	— —	— —	555 94	210 120	— —
719.6	Other non-electrical machines (e.g., calendering machines, packing or wrapping machinery, weighing machinery, etc.)	— —	— —	— —	— —	— —

Top line — value in thousand dollars
Bottom line — quantity in metric tons

Brit	Den	Norw	Swed	Austr	Switz	Japan	Fin	Total
778	—	—	172	—	—	128	—	1,914
208	—	—	82	—	—	...	—	...
114	—	—	153	—	104	983	—	2,732
34	—	—	35	—	17	...	—	...
—	—	—	—	—	—	—	—	152
—	—	—	—	—	—	—	—	...
—	—	—	—	—	—	774	—	903
—	—	—	—	—	—	...	—	...
—	—	—	—	—	—	124	—	801
—	—	—	—	—	—	...	—	...
—	—	—	—	—	—	—	—	214
—	—	—	—	—	—	—	—	...
1,225	—	—	4,471	283	1,008	12,700	135	28,844
357	—	—	1,393	57	...	...	46	...
201	—	—	—	—	—	833	—	3,679
27	—	—	—	—	—	...	—	...
181	—	—	—	—	—	3,365	—	4,985
51	—	—	—	—	—	...	—	...
125	—	—	490	113	—	1,650	104	2,482
56	—	—	165	32	—	...	38	...
—	—	—	—	—	—	118	104	222
—	—	—	—	—	—	...	38	...
—	—	—	1,063	—	428	1,088	—	3,344
—	—	—	91	—	24	...	—	...
122	—	—	—	—	—	124	—	246
12	—	—	—	—	—	...	—	...

II. Import of Machinery and Transport Equipment – 11 –

1968 (3)

SITC Nos.	Description	Belg/Lux	France	W.Germ	Italy	Neth
719.7	Ball, roller or needle-roller bearings	— —	576 220	1,868 869	493 209	— —
719.8	Machinery and mechanical appliances, n.e.s.	— —	322 31	— —	— —	— —
719.9	Parts and accessories of machinery, n.e.s.	— —	224 28	169 53	— —	— —
72	**Electrical Machinery, Apparatus and Appliances**	354 ...	1,030 ...	2,773 ...	134 ...	326 ...
722	**Electric Power Machinery and Switchgear**	273 50	— —	— —	— —	— —
722.1	Electric power machinery	— —	— —	— —	— —	— —
722.2	Electrical apparatus for making and breaking or for protecting electrical circuits (switchgear, etc.)	205 27	— —	— —	— —	— —
723	**Equipment for Distributing Electricity**	— —	— —	135 15	— —	— —
723.1	Insulated wire and cable	— —	— —	135 15	— —	— —
724	**Telecommunications Apparatus**	— —	— —	277 7	— —	— —
724.9	Telecommunications equipment, n.e.s.	— —	— —	269 6	— —	— —
726	**Electric Apparatus for Medical Purposes and Radiological Apparatus**	— —	— —	222 13	— —	— —
726.2	X-ray apparatus and other radiological apparatus	— —	— —	211 12	— —	— —
729	**Other Electrical Machinery and Apparatus**	— —	911 65	2,093 561	— —	106 2

Top line — value in thousand dollars
Bottom line — quantity in metric tons

Brit	Den	Norw	Swed	Austr	Switz	Japan	Fin	Total
—	—	—	2,762	—	344	4,010	—	10,053
—	—	—	1,108	—	156	2,271	—	...
366	—	—	—	—	207	412	—	1,307
113	—	—	—	—	13	...	—	...
120	—	—	—	—	—	1,218	—	1,731
72	—	—	—	—	—	...	—	...
2,490	530	—	118	219	705	6,514	181	15,374
...	...	—	...	...	...	...	...	...
164	—	—	—	132	112	1,701	181	2,563
22	—	—	—	33	36	...	168	...
—	—	—	—	—	—	1,173	181	1,354
—	—	—	—	—	—	...	168	...
120	—	—	—	—	—	528	—	853
7	—	—	—	—	—	...	—	...
255	—	—	—	—	—	456	—	846
253	—	—	—	—	—	340	—	...
255	—	—	—	—	—	451	—	841
253	—	—	—	—	—	339	—	...
596	—	—	—	—	—	—	—	873
...	—	—	—	—	—	—	—	...
596	—	—	—	—	—	—	—	865
...	—	—	—	—	—	—	—	...
—	—	—	—	—	—	183	—	405
—	—	—	—	—	—	...	—	...
—	—	—	—	—	—	138	—	349
—	—	—	—	—	—	...	—	...
1,423	450	—	—	—	531	4,123	—	9,637
...	9	—	—	—	14	...	—	...

II. Import of Machinery and Transport Equipment – 12 –

1968 (4)

SITC Nos.	Description	Belg/Lux	France	W.Germ	Italy	Neth
729-1	Batteries and accumulators	— —	— —	— —	— —	— —
729.3	Thermionic, etc. valves and tubes, photocells, transistors, etc.	— —	324 11	— —	— —	— —
729.5	Electrical measuring and controlling instruments and apparatus	— —	343 11	1,013 47	— —	— —
729.9	Electrical machinery and apparatus, n.e.s.	— —	151 30	1,021 511	— —	— —
73	**Transport Equipment**	— —	8,967 ...	3,208 ...	2,476 ...	— —
731	**Railway Vehicles**	— —	— —	— —	— —	— —
731.7	Parts of railway locomotives and rolling-stock, n.e.s.	— —	— —	— —	— —	— —
732	**Road Motor Vehicles**	— —	6,149 2,735	373 92	2,476 1,783	— —
732.1	Passenger motor cars (other than buses or special vehicles), whether or not assembled	— —	— —	— —	— —	— —
732.3	Buses (including trolley-buses), whether or not assembled	— —	4,490 2,374	— —	2,258 1,722	— —
732.4	Special purpose lorries, trucks and vans, whether or not assembled	— —	— —	— —	— —	— —
732.8	Bodies, chassis, frames and other parts of motor vehicles other than motorcycles (not including rubber tires, engines, chassis with engines mounted, electrical parts)	— —	— —	199 29	205 55	— —
734	**Aircraft**	— —	2,816 18	— —	— —	— —

Top line — value in thousand dollars
Bottom line — quantity in metric tons

Brit	Den	Norw	Swed	Austr	Switz	Japan	Fin	Total
—	—	—	—	—	—	1,870	—	1,870
—	—	—	—	—	—	...	—	...
—	—	—	—	—	—	—	—	324
—	—	—	—	—	—	—	—	...
911	450	—	—	—	483	1,623	—	4,823
...	9	—	—	—	11	2,739	—	...
393	—	—	—	—	—	2,221	—	3,786
...	—	—	—	—	—	...	—	...
1,191	—	—	304	—	—	3,653	148	19,947
...	—	—	...	—	—	...	...	...
—	—	—	—	—	—	1,870	—	1,870
—	—	—	—	—	—	...	—	...
—	—	—	—	—	—	1,806	—	1,806
—	—	—	—	—	—	10,201	—	...
762	—	—	239	—	—	1,782	—	11,781
...	—	—	187	—	—	...	—	...
116	—	—	—	—	—	—	—	116
53	—	—	—	—	—	—	—	...
—	—	—	199	—	—	501	—	7,448
—	—	—	174	—	—	254	—	...
—	—	—	—	—	—	237	—	237
—	—	—	—	—	—	12	—	...
568	—	—	—	—	—	1,015	—	1,987
185	—	—	—	—	—	...	—	...
—	—	—	—	—	—	—	—	2,816
—	—	—	—	—	—	—	—	...

II. Import of Machinery and Transport Equipment – 13 –

1968 (5)

SITC Nos.	Description	Belg/Lux	France	W.Germ	Italy	Neth
734.1	Airplane, gliders and kites; rotoshutes	— —	1,811 10	— —	— —	— —
734.9	Airships, balloons and parts of aircraft, airships and balloons (not including rubber tires, engines or electrical parts)	— —	1,005 8	— —	— —	— —
735	**Ships and Boats**	— —	— —	2,775 ...	— —	— —
735.5	Ships and boats, other than warships, tugs, special ships and ships for breaking up	— —	— —	2,775 ...	— —	— —
86	**Professional, Scientific and Controlling Instruments; Photographic and Optical Goods, Watches and Clocks**	— —	920 ...	4,613 ...	169 ...	— —
861	**Scientific, Medical, Optical, Measuring and Controlling Instruments and Apparatus**	— —	656 32	4,511 306	— —	— —
861.1	Optical elements	— —	— —	— —	— —	— —
861.3	Binoculars, microscopes and other optical instruments	— —	183 11	1,401 60	— —	— —
861.4	Photographic cameras (other than cinematographic) and flash-light apparatus	— —	— —	— —	— —	— —
861.5	Cinematographic cameras, projectors, sound recorders and sound reproducers	— —	127 1	— —	— —	— —
861.6	Photographic and cinematographic apparatus and equipment, n.e.s.	— —	142 8	— —	— —	— —
861.7	Medical instruments, n.e.s.	— —	— —	109 2	— —	— —

Top line — value in thousand dollars
Bottom line — quantity in metric tons

Brit	Den	Norw	Swed	Austr	Switz	Japan	Fin	Total
–	–	–	–	–	–	–	–	1,811
–	–	–	–	–	–	–	–	...
–	–	–	–	–	–	–	–	1,005
–	–	–	–	–	–	–	–	...
–	–	–	–	–	–	–	148	2,923
–	–	–	–	–	–	–	...	...
–	–	–	–	–	–	–	148	2,923
–	–	–	–	–	–	–	1	...
2,707	–	–	263	–	7,994	3,580	–	20,246
...	–	–	...	–	...	...	–	...
2,646	–	–	263	–	3,439	3,466	–	14,981
...	–	–	...	–	154	...	–	...
–	–	–	–	–	–	203	–	203
–	–	–	–	–	–	...	–	...
158	–	–	–	–	–	626	–	2,368
...	–	–	–	–	–	...	–	...
–	–	–	–	–	–	173	–	173
–	–	–	–	–	–	...	–	...
–	–	–	–	–	–	–	–	127
–	–	–	–	–	–	–	–	...
–	–	–	–	–	–	–	–	142
–	–	–	–	–	–	–	–	...
108	–	–	–	–	–	100	–	317
...	–	–	–	–	–	...	–	...

II. Import of Machinery and Transport Equipment — 14 —

1968 (6)

SITC Nos.	Description	Belg/Lux	France	W.Germ	Italy	Neth
861.9	Measuring, controlling and scientific instruments, n.e.s.	— —	171 9	2,891 243	— —	— —
862	**Photographic and Cinemato-grahic Supplies**	— —	— —	— —	115 40	— —
862.4	Photographic film, plates and paper	— —	— —	— —	101 19	— —
864	**Watches and Clocks**	— —	262 ...	— —	— —	— —
864.1	Watches, watch movements and cases	— —	253 ...	— —	— —	— —
864.11	Wrist watches	— —	— —	— —	— —	— —
864.2	Clocks, clock movements and parts	— —	— —	— —	— —	— —

1969 (1)

SITC Nos.	Description	Belg/Lux	France	W.Germ	Italy	Neth
7	**Machinery and Transport Equipment**	232 ...	11,961 ...	12,547 ...	10,344 ...	272 ...
71	**Machinery, Other than Electric**	9 ...	4,963 ...	9,964 ...	9,372 ...	123 ...
711	**Power Generating Machinery, Other than Electric**	1 ...	629 218	504 258	253 47	45 13
711.3	Steam engines (including stationary steam engines with self-contained boilers (generally known as locomobiles) and steam turbines)	— —	— —	243 235	— —	— —

Top line — value in thousand dollars
Bottom line — quantity in metric tons

Brit	Den	Norw	Swed	Austr	Switz	Japan	Fin	Total
2,291	—	—	243	—	3,308	2,173	—	11,077
...	—	—	4	—	151	...	—	...
—	—	—	—	—	—	—	—	115
—	—	—	—	—	—	—	—	...
—	—	—	—	—	—	—	—	101
—	—	—	—	—	—	—	—	...
—	—	—	—	—	—	4,552	—	4,814
—	—	—	—	—	—	...	—	...
—	—	—	—	—	—	3,946	—	4,199
—	—	—	—	—	—	...	—	...
—	—	—	—	—	—	3,946	—	3,946
—	—	—	—	—	—	...	—	...
—	—	—	—	—	—	607	—	607
—	—	—	—	—	—	...	—	...

Top line — value in thousand dollars
Bottom line — quantity in metric tons

Brit	Den	Norw	Swed	Austr	Switz	Japan	Fin	Total
5,853	682	665	5,116	—	4,906	44,376	—	96,954
...	...	...	...	—	...	...	—	...
2,755	233	—	4,244	—	4,687	30,297	—	66,647
...	...	—	...	—	...	...	—	...
160	11	—	119	—	91	3,004	—	4,817
...	...	—	31	—	6	...	—	...
—	—	—	—	—	19	3	—	265
—	—	—	—	—	1	...	—	...

II. Import of Machinery and Transport Equipment — 15 —

1969 (2)

SITC Nos.	Description	Belg/Lus	France	W.Germ	Italy	Neth
711.5	Internal combustion piston engines, other than for aircraft	1 ...	412 113	224 20	253 47	44 9
712	**Agricultural Machinery and Implements**	— —	41 15	176 149	6 1	— —
712.2	Agricultural machinery and appliances for harvesting, threshing and sorting	— —	— —	176 149	— —	— —
712.5	Tractors, other than road tractors for tractor-trailer combinations	— —	41 15	— —	— —	— —
714	**Office Machines**	— —	37 1	18 1	1 ...	2 ...
715.1	Machine-tools for working metals	— —	697 158	4,305 1,326	7,017 3,215	— —
715.2	Metal-working machinery, other than machine-tools	— —	— —	25 11	— —	— —
715.22	Rolling mills	— —	— —	— —	— —	— —
717.1	Textile machines	— —	16 1	292 119	153 47	— —
718.1	Paper mill and pulp mill machinery, paper cutting machinery and other machinery for the manufacture of paper articles	— —	57 15	432 118	— —	— —
718.2	Printing and book-binding machinery	— —	— —	213 49	224 52	— —
718.4	Construction and mining machinery, n.e.s.	— —	1,467 1,264	13 3	223 452	— —
718.42	Coal cutter and the parts	— —	1,467 1,264	13 3	223 452	— —
719.1	Heating and cooling equipments	— —	7 4	752 551	254 72	45 2

Top line — value in thousand dollars
Bottom line — quantity in metric tons

Brit	Den	Norw	Swed	Austr	Switz	Japan	Fin	Total
134	11	—	75	—	72	2,996	—	4,222
...	...	—	29	—	5	...	—	...
11	—	—	—	—	—	1,220	—	1,454
7	—	—	—	—	—	...	—	...
—	—	—	—	—	—	—	—	176
—	—	—	—	—	—	—	—	...
10	—	—	—	—	—	1,220	—	1,271
7	—	—	—	—	—	(N) 93	—	...
125	—	—	—	—	7	76	—	266
3	—	—	—	—	...	...	—	...
1,009	189	—	836	—	4,251	4,579	—	22,883
302	99	—	81	—	494	(N) 490	—	...
20	—	—	—	—	—	592	—	637
7	—	—	—	—	—	...	—	...
—	—	—	—	—	—	455	—	455
—	—	—	—	—	—	...	—	...
513	—	—	359	—	29	302	—	1,664
233	—	—	187	—	4	...	—	...
3	—	—	31	—	—	15	—	538
...	—	—	7	—	—	...	—	...
35	—	—	—	—	79	494	—	1,042
4	—	—	—	—	15	...	—	...
42	—	—	—	—	—	823	—	2,568
37	—	—	—	—	—	...	—	...
42	—	—	—	—	—	815	—	2,560
37	—	—	—	—	—	...	—	...
11	7	—	15	—	2	501	—	1,594
2	1	—	3	—	...	...	—	...

II. Import of Machinery and Transport Equipment – 16 –

1969 (3)

SITC Nos.	Description	Belg/Lux	France	W.Germ	Italy	Neth
719.14	Industrial and laboratory furnaces and ovens, non electric	— —	7 4	— —	— —	— —
719.2	Pumps and centrifuges	— —	197 18	859 36	58 6	— —
719.21	Pumps for liquids	— —	150 9	721 30	22 1	— —
719.3	Mechanical handling equipment	— —	111 11	637 547	1 ...	4 2
719.5	Power-tools, n.e.s.	1 ...	8 1	382 74	16 5	5 ...
719.6	Other non-electrical machines (e.g., calendering machines, packing or wrapping machinery, weighing machinery, etc.	— —	4 ...	707 333	1 ...	— —
719.7	Ball, roller or needle-roller bearings	— —	1,575 755	271 78	1,038 414	21 9
719.8	Machinery and mechanical appliance, n.e.s.	— —	— —	260 ...	7 ...	87 ...
719.9		... 1	112 16	94 40	68 14	— —
72	**Electrical Machinery, Apparatus and Appliances**	222 ...	1,111 ...	2,293 ...	217 ...	149 ...
722.1	Electric power machinery	189 138	409 306	86 21	40 15	—
722.2	Electrical apparatus for making and breaking or for protecting electrical circuits (switchgear, etc.)	14 1	41 4	61 4	15 1	10 1
723	**Equipment for Distributing Electricity**	— —	259 170	15 1	26 45	— —
724.9	Telecommunications equipment, n.e.s.	1 1	48 ...	728 18	84 1	— —
724.91	Electrical line telegraphic, apparatus	— —	— —	216 9	84 1	— —
726	**Electric Apparatus for Medical Purposes and Radiological Apparatus**	1 ...	1 ...	116 5	1 ...	— —

Top line — value in thousand dollars
Bottom line — quantity in metric tons

Brit	Den	Norw	Swed	Austr	Switz	Japan	Fin	Total
—	—	—	—	—	—	1	—	207
—	—	—	—	—	—	...	—	...
186	24	—	33	—	61	6,655	—	8,073
60	6	—	4	—	12	...	—	...
100	17	—	—	—	15	598	—	1,623
31	5	—	—	—	3	...	—	...
146	—	—	130	—	—	444	—	1,473
81	—	—	27	—	—	...	—	...
22	1	—	1,038	—	86	1,933	—	3,492
6	...	—	60	—	5	...	—	...
135	—	—	—	—	—	29	—	876
55	—	—	—	—	—	...	—	...
18	—	—	1,677	—	3	6,706	—	11,309
7	—	—	668	—	...	3,640	—	...
121	—	—	—	—	54	476	—	1,005
58	—	—	—	—	8	...	—	...
122	1	—	6	—	26	2,369	—	2,798
42	...	—	1	—	1	...	—	...
1,602	448	18	56	—	219	5,081	—	11,416
...	...	...	...	—	...	...	—	...
4	—	—	4	—	9	204	—	945
1	—	—	1	—	1	...	—	...
93	—	—	12	—	18	233	—	497
10	—	—	...	—	2	...	—	...
66	—	—	—	—	—	958	—	1,324
44	—	—	—	—	—	491	—	...
436	1	—	6	—	—	83	—	1,386
...	...	—	...	—	—	...	—	...
20	—	—	6	—	—	10	—	336
...	—	—	...	—	—	...	—	...
4	42	—	23	—	16	413	—	617
...	1	—	1	—	...	...	—	...

II. Import of Machinery and Transport Equipment   — 17 —

1969 (4)

SITC Nos.	Description	Belg/Lux	France	W.Germ	Italy	Neth
729.1	Batteries and accumulators	— —	3 ...	... 1	— —	— —
729.4	Automotive electrical equipment	— —	65 14	27 6	16 3	— —
729.5	Electrical measuring and controlling instruments and apparatus	16 ...	264 4	738 40	23 ...	15 ...
729.92	Electric furnaces, equipments for electric welding and cutting	— —	3 1	214 34	— —	— —
73	**Transport Equipment**	1 ...	5,887 ...	290 ...	755 ...	— —
731	**Railway Vehicles**	... 1	1 ...	131 3,215	— —	— —
732	**Road Motor Vehicles**	1 1	5,770 3,141	155 45	755 225	— —
732.1	Passenger motor cars (other than buses or special vehicles), whether or not assembled	1 1	14 8	29 15	47 27	— —
732.3	Lorries and trucks (including ambulances, etc.), whether or not assembled	— —	4,882 2,895	12 8	2 2	— —
732.4	Special purpose lorries, trucks and vans, whether or not assembled	— —	— —	— —	— —	— —
732.8	Bodies, chassis, frames and other parts of motorcycles (not including rubber tyres, engines, chassis with engines mounted, electrical parts)	— —	874 238	114 22	706 196	— —
733.3	Trailers and other vehicles, not motorized, and their parts	— —	— —	— —	— —	— —
734.1	Airplane, gliders and kites; rotochutes	— —	— —	— —	— —	— —

Top line — value in thousand dollars
Bottom line — quantity in metric tons

Brit	Den	Norw	Swed	Austr	Switz	Japan	Fin	Total
2	—	—	—	—	3	128	—	136
...	—	—	—	—	...	...	—	...
5	—	—	—	—	—	241	—	354
...	—	—	—	—	—	...	—	...
669	405	18	7	—	136	1,873	—	4,164
...	7	...	...	—	3	...	—	...
—	—	—	4	—	31	101	—	353
—	—	—	...	—	4	...	—	...
1,496	1	647	816	—	3	8,998	—	18,894
...	...	...	...	—	...	...	—	...
76	—	—	—	—	—	4,732	—	4,940
8	—	—	—	—	—	...	—	...
1,134	1	55	667	—	—	4,213	—	12,751
...	1	...	225	—	—	...	—	...
162	1	—	2	—	—	10	—	266
71	1	—	1	—	—	(N) 8	—	...
76	—	—	157	—	—	1,209	—	6,338
65	—	—	83	—	—	(N)415	—	...
—	—	—	—	—	—	179	—	179
—	—	—	—	—	—	(N) 10	—	...
890	—	—	508	—	—	2,815	—	5,907
243	—	—	141	—	—	...	—	...
—	—	66	149	—	—	—	—	215
—	—	...	136	—	—	—	—	...
277	—	—	—	—	—	—	—	277
...	—	—	—	—	—	—	—	...

II. Import of Machinery and Transport Equipment – 18 –

1969 (5)

SITC Nos.	Description	Belg/Lux	France	W.Germ	Italy	Neth
734.9	Airships, balloons and parts of aircraft, airships and balloons (not including rubber tyres, engines or electrical parts)	— —	116 2	3 ...	— —	— —
735.3	Ships and boats, other than warships, tugs, special ships and ships for breaking up	— —	— —	— —	— —	— —
86	**Professional, Scientific and Controlling Instruments; Photographic and Optical Goods, Watches and Clocks**	19 ...	530 ...	3,545 ...	124 ...	23 ...
861	**Scientific, Medical, Optical, Measuring and Controlling Instruments and Apparatus**	3 ...	239 10	3,522 199	50 5	16 1
861.3	Binoculars, microscopes and other optical instruments	— —	52 3	2,004 110	— —	— —
861.4	Photographic cameras (other than cinematographic) and flash-light apparatus	— —	— —	19 ...	— —	1 ...
861.9	Measuring, controlling and scientific instruments, n.e.s.	3 ...	76 3	1,336 84	36 4	2 ...
862.4	Photographic film, plates and paper	10 1	1 ...	8 2	71 16	— —
864.1	Watches, watch movements and cases	— —	275 2	— —	2 ...	7 ...
864.2	Clocks, clock movements and parts	6 ...	6 ...	13 3	— —	— —

Top line — value in thousand dollars
Bottom line — quantity in metric tons

Brit	Den	Norw	Swed	Austr	Switz	Japan	Fin	Total
—	—	—	—	—	—	—	—	119
—	—	—	—	—	—	—	—	...
—	—	526	—	—	—	—	—	526
—	—	...	—	—	—	—	—	...
2,217	3	—	180	—	7,114	4,064	—	17,819
...	...	—	...	—	...	...	—	...
1,059	3	—	180	—	2,766	3,646	—	11,484
...	...	—	5	—	103	...	—	...
46	—	—	5	—	28	746	—	2,881
...	—	—	...	—	1	...	—	...
—	—	—	2	—	—	242	—	264
—	—	—	...	—	—	...	—	...
965	2	—	151	—	2,689	2,175	—	7,435
...	...	—	4	—	101	...	—	...
1,080	—	—	—	—	—	174	—	1,344
...	—	—	—	—	—	...	—	...
7	—	—	—	—	4,000	240	—	4,531
...	—	—	—	—	...	...	—	...
49	—	—	—	—	348	4	—	426
...	—	—	—	—	...	...	—	...

III. IMPORT OF CHEMICALS – 1 –

1967 (1)

SITC Nos.	Description	Belg/Lux	France	W.Germ	Italy	Neth
5	**Chemicals**	10,109 ...	16,852 ...	37,144 ...	27,490 ...	10,443 ...
51	**Chemical Elements and Compounds**	3,616 ...	6,577 ...	14,232 ...	8,547 ...	6,577 ...
512	**Organic Chemicals**	2,828 ...	5,706 60,133	13,373 30,413	7,874 70,268	6,538 54,449
512.1	Hydrocarbons and their halogenated, sulphonated, nitrated or nitrosated derivatives	— —	1,202 3,335	748 4,320	1,840 5,112	148 1,342
512.2	Alcohols, phenols, phenol-alcohols, glycerin	— —	114 642	1,716 5,055	882 3,502	451 501
512.4	Aldehyde-, ketone- and quinone-function compounds	— —	— —	— —	452 1,262	— —
512.5	Acids and their halogenated sulphonated, nitrated or nitrosated derivatives	235 608	786 1,949	2,013 5,546	1,241 3,164	2,373 6,333
512.6	Inorganic esters, their salts and derivatives	— —	— —	3,369 3,445	— —	— —
512.7	Nitrogen-function compounds	2,553 41,598	2,930 53,286	1,788 8,931	3,356 57,128	3,406 45,954
512.8	Organo-inorganic and hetero-cyclic compounds	— —	670 921	2,301 1,613	104 101	129 114
512.9	Other organic chemicals	— —	— —	— —	— —	— —
513	**Inorganic Chemicals; Elements, Oxides and Halogen Salts**	— —	171 618	166 933	— —	— —
513.2	Chemical elements, n.e.s.	— —	— —	147 900	— —	— —

Top line — value in thousand dollars
Bottom line — quantity in metric tons

Brit	Den	Norw	Swed	Austr	Switz	Japan	Canada	Total
10,867	2,166	1,374	1,239	3,933	2,078	98,658	223	222,576
...	...	...	...	...	...	...	...	...
6,504	2,122	—	1,017	104	408	47,607	222	97,533
...	...	—	...	...	...	...	...	...
5,490	2,122	—	998	101	403	34,256	—	79,689
...	4,010	—	...	305	...	...	—	219,578
—	—	—	—	—	—	2,743	—	6,681
—	—	—	—	—	—	25,059	—	39,168
898	—	—	235	—	103	1,824	—	6,223
...	—	—	749	—	...	...	—	10,449
333	—	—	—	—	—	511	—	1,296
...	—	—	—	—	—	2,336	—	3,598
1,382	1,507	—	762	—	—	1,252	—	11,551
...	3,802	—	2,038	—	—	3,609	—	27,049
218	—	—	—	—	—	284	—	3,871
...	—	—	—	—	—	230	—	3,675
835	—	—	—	—	—	26,372	—	41,240
...	—	—	—	—	—	424,970	—	631,867
1,786	592	—	—	—	183	1,107	—	6,872
...	147	—	—	—	53	2,664	—	5,613
—	—	—	—	—	—	120	—	120
—	—	—	—	—	—	190	—	190
160	—	—	—	—	—	2,089	—	2,586
...	—	—	—	—	—	6,155	—	7,706
120	—	—	—	—	—	807	—	1,074
...	—	—	—	—	—	1,591	—	2,491

III. Import of Chemicals – 2 –

1967 (2)

SITC Nos.	Description	Belg/Lux	France	W.Germ	Italy	Neth
513.5	Metallic oxides, principally used in paints	— —	169 598	— —	— —	— —
513.6	Other inorganic bases and metallic oxides	— —	— —	— —	— —	— —
514	**Other Inorganic Chemicals**	787 1,792	657 2,293	693 2,229	589 2,142	— —
514.1	Metallic salts and peroxy-salts of inorganic acids	— —	— —	— —	168 701	— —
514.2	Other metallic salts and peroxysalts of inorganic acids (I)	— —	454 1,330	— —	— —	— —
514.3	Other metallic salts and peroxysalts of inorganic acids (II)	625 1,509	114 670	258 543	421 1,441	— —
515	**Radioactive and Associated Materials**	— —	— —	— —	— —	— —
521	**Mineral Tar and Crude Chemicals from Coal, Petroleum and Natural Gas**	— —	– —	267 662	— —	— —
521.4	Oil and other products of the distillation of coal tar	— —	— —	267 662	— —	— —
53	**Dyeing, Tanning and Colouring Materials**	— —	390 ...	2,268 ...	239 ...	— —
531	**Synthetic Organic Dye-Stuffs, Natural Indigo and Colour Lakes**	— —	390 66	1,997 401	159 26	— —
533	**Pigments, Paints, Varnishes and Related Materials**	— —	— —	263 70	— —	— —
533.1	Colouring materials, n.e.s.	— —	— —	— —	— —	— —

Top line — value in thousand dollars
Bottom line — quantity in metric tons

Brit	Den	Norw	Swed	Austr	Switz	Japan	Canada	Total
—	—	—	—	—	—	1,047	—	1,216
—	—	—	—	—	—	3,160	—	3,758
—	—	—	—	—	—	233	—	233
—	—	—	—	—	—	1,402	—	1,402
853	—	—	—	—	—	11,262	—	14,841
...	—	—	—	—	—	325,793	—	334,249
285	—	—	—	—	—	9,972	—	10,425
...	—	—	—	—	—	320,565	—	321,266
397	—	—	—	—	—	568	—	1,419
...	—	—	—	—	—	2,272	—	3,602
164	—	—	—	—	—	650	—	2,232
...	—	—	—	—	—	2,520	—	6,683
—	—	—	—	—	—	—	222	222
—	—	—	—	—	—	—	—	...
117	—	—	—	—	—	—	—	384
...	—	—	—	—	—	—	—	662
117	—	—	—	—	—	—	—	384
...	—	—	—	—	—	—	—	662
1,025	—	—	—	—	1,266	873	—	6,061
...	—	—	—	—	...	...	—	...
849	—	—	—	—	1,147	491	—	5,033
273	—	—	—	—	214	234	—	1,214
173	—	—	—	—	119	374	—	929
...	—	—	—	—	...	60	—	130
120	—	—	—	—	119	—	—	239
407	—	—	—	—	...	—	—	407

SITC Nos.	Description	Belg/Lux	France	W.Germ	Italy	Neth
533.3	Prepared paints, enamels, lacquers, varnishes, artists' colours, siccatives (paint driers) and mastics	– –	– –	251 68	– –	– –
541	**Medicinal and Pharmaceutical Products**	– –	468 (k)13,500	675 14,900	– –	632 (k)20,674
541.4	Opium alkaloids, cocaine, caffein, quinine and other vegetable alkaloids, their salts and other derivatives	– –	419 (k)12,500	631 10,700	– –	– –
541.7	Medicaments	– –	– –	– –	– –	– –
55	**Essential Oils and Perfume Materials; Toilet, Polishing and Cleansing Preparations**	– –	– –	– –	– –	– –
554	**Soaps, Cleansing and Polishing Preparations**	– –	– –	– –	– –	– –
554.2	Surface-acting agents and washing preparations	– –	– –	– –	– –	– –
561	**Fertilizers, Manufactured**	5,689 188,645	8,178 353,246	13,617 470,050	14,617 508,433	– –
561.1	Nitrogenous fertilizers and nitrogenous fertilizer materials (other than natural), n.e.s.	5,689 188,645	8,037 350,846	13,614 470,000	14,367 498,072	2,404 78,074
561.9	Fertilizers, n.e.s.	– –	141 2,400	– –	250 10,360	– –
581	**Plastic Materials, Regenerated Cellulose and Artificial Resins**	797 607	989 4,157	1,398 1,175	3,016 13,262	– –
581.1	Products of condensation, polycondensation and poly-addition (e.g., phenoplasts, aminoplasts, alkyds, polyallyl esters and other unsaturated polyesters, silicones)	– –	168 40	1,067 631	– –	– –

Top line — value in thousand dollars
Bottom line — quantity in metric tons

Brit	Den	Norw	Swed	Austr	Switz	Japan	Canada	Total
–	–	–	–	–	–	336	–	587
–	–	–	–	–	–	32	–	100
533	–	–	–	–	296	128	–	2,732
...	–	–	–	–	7,037	...	–	56,111
299	–	–	–	–	221	–	–	1,570
...	–	–	–	–	(k) 397	–	–	23,497
234	–	–	–	–	–	–	–	234
...	–	–	–	–	–	–	–	...
–	–	–	–	–	–	1,722	–	1,722
–	–	–	–	–	–	...	–	...
–	–	–	–	–	–	1,708	–	1,708
–	–	–	–	–	–	3,155	–	3,155
–	–	–	–	–	–	1,680	–	1,680
–	–	–	–	–	–	3,120	–	3,120
1,669	–	1,284	–	–	–	32,349	–	77,403
61,615	–	31,101	–	–	–	(M)1,008	–	1,614,098
1,669	–	–	–	–	–	30,943	–	76,723
61,615	–	–	–	–	–	987,380	–	2,634,632
–	–	–	–	–	–	1,406	–	1,797
–	–	–	–	–	–	21,098	–	33,858
283	–	–	219	–	–	8,326	–	15,023
539	–	–	141	–	–	...	–	19,881
134	–	–	216	–	–	691	–	2,276
50	–	–	135	–	–	...	–	856

III.   Import of Chemicals – 4 –

1968 (4)

SITC Nos.	Description	Belg/Lux	France	W.Germ	Italy	Neth
581.2	Products of polymerisation and copolymerisation (e.g., polyethylene, polystyrene, polyvinyl, etc. derivatives, coumarone-indene resins	– –	813 4,117	282 488	2,924 13,144	– –
581.3	Cellulose esters, cellulose ethers and other chemical derivatives of cellulose, regenerated cellulose and vulcanised fibre	797 607	– –	– –	– –	– –
599	**Chemical Materials and Products, N.E.S.**	– –	207 110	4,609 4,722	980 1,386	747 2,578
599.2	Insecticides, fungicides, disinfectants (including sheep and cattle dressing) and similar preparations	– –	– –	3,450 3,070	– –	460 2,122
599.7	Organic chemical products, n.e.s.	– –	– –	305 124	933 1,326	– –
599.9	Chemical products and preparations, n.e.s.	– –	151 39	849 1,527	– –	274 456

Top line — value in thousand dollars
Bottom line — quantity in metric tons

Brit	Den	Norw	Swed	Austr	Switz	Japan	Canada	Total
139	—	—	—	—	—	6,947	—	11,105
481	—	—	—	—	—	26,952	—	45,182
—	—	—	—	—	—	688	—	1,485
—	—	—	—	—	—	1,042	—	1,649
671	—	—	—	495	—	7,653	—	15,362
...	—	—	—	...	—	19,054	—	27,850
—	—	—	—	—	—	6,771	—	10,681
—	—	—	—	—	—	16,828	—	22,020
291	—	—	—	—	—	—	—	1,529
...	—	—	—	—	—	—	—	1,450
352	—	—	—	495	—	781	—	2,902
...	—	—	—	101	—	2,104	—	4,227

NOTES:
1) — represents none or figures less than one thousand dollars.
2) — represents those not listed in the original statistics.
3) — values in general are on F.O.B. basis for exports and C.I.F. basis for imports, with some exceptions.
4) — K represents kilograms; M represents 1000× the figures shown.

SOURCE: UN; *Commodity Trade Statistics*

III. Import of Chemicals – 5 –

1968 (1)

SITC Nos.	Description	Belg/Lux	France	W.Germ	Italy
5	**Chemicals**	10,992 ...	13,431 ...	36,011 ...	34,052 ...
51	**Chemical Elements and Compounds**	4,035 ...	7,753 ...	16,303 ...	18,898 ...
512	**Organic Chemicals**	3,163 ...	6,437 64,005	15,681 48,056	18,606 227,111
512.1	Hydrocarbons and their halogenated, sulphonated, nitrated or nitrosated derivatives	591 2,222	1,829 8,565	730 3,562	1,660 4,741
512.2	Alcohols, phenols, phenol-alcohols, glycerin	— —	316 825	3,196 12,645	329 1,958
512.3	Ethers, epoxides and acetals	— —	— —	— —	— —
512.4	Aldehyde-, ketone-, and quinone-function compounds	— —	319 486	— —	— —
512.5	Acids and their halogenated, sulphonated, nitrated or nitrosated derivatives	220 631	596 1,616	1,093 4,091	5,247 15,100
512.6	Inorganic esters, their salts and derivatives	— —	— —	2,254 2,459	— —
512.7	Nitrogen-function compounds	2,350 42,766	2,729 51,885	4,145 21,659	11,132 204,790
512.8	Organo-inorganic and hetero-cyclic compounds	— —	647 617	467 311	169 204
512.9	Other organic chemicals	— —	— —	— —	— —
513	**Inorganic Chemicals; Elements, Oxides and Halogen Salts**	— —	616 2,417	— —	— —
513.2	Chemical elements, n.e.s.	— —	— —	— —	— —
513.3	Inorganic acids and oxygen compounds of non-metals of metalloids	— —	— —	— —	— —

Top line — value in thousand dollars
Bottom line — quantity in metric tons

Neth	Brit	Den	Norw	Swed	Austr	Switz	Japan	Total
25,847	8,445	1,241	561	1,521	1,857	3,120	111,716	248,794
...	...	...	...	...	...	...	...	...
14,157	5,474	1,188	155	1,359	372	279	68,750	138,723
...	...	...	...	...	...	...	...	...
14,080	4,996	1,188	—	1,357	372	279	52,754	118,913
220,835	—	2,940	—	...	1,313	...	...	564,260
—	—	—	—	—	—	—	2,226	7,036
—	—	—	—	—	—	—	20,143	39,233
—	923	—	—	—	—	—	2,103	6,867
—	...	—	—	—	—	—	...	15,428
—	—	—	—	—	—	—	300	300
—	—	—	—	—	—	—	522	522
—	370	—	—	—	—	—	409	1,098
—	...	—	—	—	—	—	1,947	2,433
1,580	1,259	894	—	1,258	—	—	3,947	16,122
4,904	...	2,832	—	3,519	—	—	15,284	47,977
—	—	—	—	—	—	—	—	2,254
—	—	—	—	—	—	—	—	2,459
11,947	602	—	—	—	—	—	41,467	74,372
215,378	...	—	—	—	—	—	655,921	1,192,399
388	1,774	251	—	—	—	140	1,991	5,827
298	...	58	—	—	—	20	4,501	6,009
—	—	—	—	—	—	—	242	242
—	—	—	—	—	—	—	295	295
—	—	—	—	—	—	—	2,630	3,296
—	—	—	—	—	—	—	7,539	9,956
—	—	—	—	—	—	—	1,249	1,249
—	—	—	—	—	—	—	3,045	3,045
—	—	—	—	—	—	—	102	102
—	—	—	—	—	—	—	564	564

III. Import of Chemicals — 6 —

1968 (2)

SITC Nos.	Description	Belg/Lux	France	W.Germ	Italy
513.5	Metallic oxides, principally used in paints	— —	666 2,416	— —	— —
514	**Other Inorganic Chemicals**	872 ...	626 1,802	567 1,397	271 1,177
514.1	Metallic salts and peroxysalts of inorganic acids	— —	— —	— —	— —
514.2	Other metallic salts and peroxysalts of inorganic acids (I)	489 1,501	589 1,630	185 602	— —
514.3	Other metallic salts and peroxysalts of inorganic acids (II)	384 1,065	— —	352 650	268 1,140
514.9	Inorganic chemical products, n.e.s.	— —	— —	— —	— —
521	**Mineral Tar and Crude Chemicals from Coal, Petroleum and Natural Gas**	— —	— —	— —	— —
521.4	Oil and other products of the distillation of coal tar	— —	— —	— —	— —
53	**Dyeing, Tanning and Colouring Materials**	— —	1,480 ...	4,204 —	178 ...
531	**Synthetic Organic Dye-Stuffs, Natural Indigo and Colour Lakes**	— —	1,479 279	3,937 803	157 21
533	**Pigments, Paints, Varnishes and Related Materials**	— —	— —	167 138	— —
533.1	Colouring materials, n.e.s.	— —	— —	— —	— —
533.3	Prepared paints, enamels, lacquers, varnishes, artists' colours, siccatives (paint driers) and mastics	— —	— —	165 138	— —
541	**Medical and Pharmaceutical Products**	— —	270 12,100	310 ...	106 4,935

Top line — value in thousand dollars
Bottom line — quantity in metric tons

Neth	Brit	Den	Norw	Swed	Austr	Switz	Japan	Total
—	—	—	—	—	—	—	1,257	1,923
—	—	—	—	—	—	—	3,842	6,258
—	381	—	—	—	—	—	13,366	16,083
—	...	—	—	—	—	—	345,181	349,557
—	273	—	—	—	—	—	10,794	11,067
—	...	—	—	—	—	—	335,499	335,499
—	—	—	—	—	—	—	2,093	3,356
—	—	—	—	—	—	—	7,193	10,926
—	—	—	—	—	—	—	279	1,283
—	—	—	—	—	—	—	1,114	3,969
—	—	—	—	—	—	—	200	200
—	—	—	—	—	—	—	1,375	1,375
—	159	—	—	—	—	—	—	159
—	...	—	—	—	—	—	—	...
—	159	—	—	—	—	—	—	159
—	...	—	—	—	—	—	—	...
—	221	—	—	—	—	2,346	1,141	9,570
—	...	—	—	—	—	...	...	...
—	199	—	—	—	—	2,325	385	8,482
—	39	—	—	—	—	375	127	1,644
—	—	—	—	—	—	—	439	606
—	—	—	—	—	—	—	72	210
—	—	—	—	—	—	—	101	101
—	—	—	—	—	—	—	35	35
—	—	—	—	—	—	—	333	498
—	—	—	—	—	—	—	34	172
390	446	—	—	—	—	371	—	1,893
17,381	...	—	—	—	—	10,770	—	45,186

III. Import of Chemicals — 7 —

1968 (3)

SITC Nos.	Description	Belg/Lux	France	W.Germ	Italy
541.4	Opium alkaloids, cocaine, caffein, quinine and other vegetable alkaloids, their salts and other derivatives	— —	203 11,500	238 10,100	— —
541.7	Medicaments	— —	— —	— —	— —
551	**Essential Oils and Perfume Materials; Toilet, Polishing and Cleansing Preparations**	— —	108 ...	— —	— —
554	**Soaps, Cleansing and Polishing Preparations**	— —	— —	— —	— —
554.2	Surface-acting agents and washing preparations	— —	— —	— —	— —
561	**Fertilizers, Manufactured**	6,745 240,812	3,462 149,554	6,994 280,365	10,222 390,646
561.1	Nitrogenous fertilizers and nitrogenous fertilizer materials (other than natural), n.e.s.	6,047 230,812	3,002 139,136	6,994 280,365	9,950 381,246
561.3	Potassic fertilizers and potassic fertilizer materials (other than crude natural potassic salts)	— —	— —	— —	176 5,000
561.9	Fertilizers, n.e.s.	698 10,000	460 10,419	— —	— —
581	**Plastic Materials, Regenerated Cellulose and Artificial Resins**	173 34	348 803	3,212 13,008	3,991 21,453
581.1	Products of condensation, poly-condensation and polyaddition (e.g., phenoplasts, aminoplasts, alkyds, polyallyl esters and other unsaturated polyesters, silicones)	— —	209 47	1,293 979	— —
581.2	Products of polymerisation and copolymerisation (e.g., polystyrene, polyvinyl, polyethylene, etc. derivatives, coumarone-indene resins)	— —	138 756	1,897 12,010	3,983 21,450

Top line — value in thousand dollars
Bottom line — quantity in metric tons

Neth	Brit	Den	Norw	Swed	Austr	Switz	Japan	Total
—	138	—	—	—	—	310	—	889
—	...	—	—	—	—	10,770	—	22,021
—	292	—	—	—	—	—	—	292
—	...	—	—	—	—	—	...	...
—	—	—	—	—	—	—	1,512	1,620
—	—	—	—	—	—	—	...	...
—	—	—	—	—	—	—	1,512	1,512
—	—	—	—	—	—	—	3,675	3,675
—	—	—	—	—	—	—	1,512	1,512
—	—	—	—	—	—	—	3,675	3,675
—	1,067	—	—	—	—	—	24,783	53,273
—	43,273	—	—	—	—	—	774,297	1,878,947
—	1,067	—	—	—	—	—	24,783	51,843
—	43,273	—	—	—	—	—	774,297	1,849,129
—	—	—	—	—	—	—	—	176
—	—	—	—	—	—	—	—	5,000
—	—	—	—	—	—	—	—	1,158
—	—	—	—	—	—	—	—	20,419
—	—	—	—	154	—	—	9,776	17,654
—	—	—	—	107	—	—	...	35,455
—	—	—	—	154	—	—	796	2,452
—	—	—	—	107	—	—	...	1,133
—	—	—	—	—	—	—	8,080	14,098
—	—	—	—	—	—	—	33,984	68,200

III. Import of Chemicals – 8 –

1968 (4)

SITC Nos.	Description	Belg/Lux	France	W.Germ	Italy
581.3	Cellulose esters, cellulose ethers and other chemical derivatives of cellulose, regenerated cellulose and vulcanised fibre	142 71	— —	— —	— —
599	**Chemical Materials and Products, N.E.S.**	— —	— —	4,971 5,957	642 1,127
599.2	Insecticides, fungicides, disinfectants (including sheep and cattle dressing) and similar preparations	— —	— —	4,377 5,048	— —
599.6	Wood and resin-based chemical products	— —	— —	— —	— —
599.7	Organic chemical products, n.e.s.	— —	— —	119 63	642 1,126
599.9	Chemical products and preparations, n.e.s.	— —	— —	466 807	— —

1969 (1)

SITC Nos.		Belg/Lux	France	W.Germ	Italy	Neth
5	**Chemicals**	6,915 ...	6,445 ...	38,464 ...	31,574 ...	22,122 ...
51	**Chemical Elements and Compounds**	2,689 ...	4,571 ...	21,625 ...	20,052 ...	14,980 ...
512	**Organic Chemicals**	2,370 ...	3,915 25,874	20,556 132,576	19,633 288,371	14,980 257,624
512.1	Hydrocarbons and their halogenated, sulphonated, nitrated or nitrosated derivatives	273 2,725	822 3,871	2,021 19,939	2,104 8,021	159 299
512.2	Alcohols, phenols, phenol-alcohols, glycerine	— —	211 622	3,834 17,255	644 4,087	— —

Top line — value in thousand dollars
Bottom line — quantity in metric tons

Neth	Brit	Den	Norw	Swed	Austr	Switz	Japan	Total
–	–	–	–	–	–	–	899	1,041
–	–	–	–	–	–	–	1,452	1,523
–	1,006	–	345	–	–	–	5,995	12,959
–	...	–	2,017	–	–	–	14,996	24,097
–	–	–	–	–	–	–	4,658	9,035
–	–	–	–	–	–	–	10,079	15,127
–	–	–	323	–	–	–	–	323
–	–	–	1,850	–	–	–	–	1,850
–	200	–	–	–	–	–	159	1,120
–	...	–	–	–	–	–	215	1,404
–	781	–	–	–	–	–	1,178	3,672
–	...	–	–	–	–	–	4,702	5,509

Top line — value in thousand dollars
Bottom line — quantity in metric tons

Brit	Den	Norw	Swed	Austr	Switz	Japan	Canada	Total
9,276	548	2,490	193	166	2,059	122,394	–	242,646
...	...	...	...	...	...	...	–	...
5,720	540	–	–	–	165	84,392	–	154,734
...	...	–	–	–	...	...	–	...
3,524	540	–	–	–	165	68,606	–	134,289
...	1,440	–	–	–	28	...	–	705,913
–	–	–	–	–	–	5,283	–	10,662
–	–	–	–	–	–	46,202	–	81,057
334	–	–	–	–	–	3,637	–	8,660
...	–	–	–	–	–	...	–	21,964

III.   Import of Chemicals – 9 –
1969 (2)

SITC Nos.	Description	Belg/Lux	France	W.Germ	Italy	Neth
512.4	Aldehyde-, ketone- and quinone-function compounds	— —	134 210	133 107	125 1,010	— —
512.5	Acids and their halogenated, sulphonated, nitrated or nitrosated derivatives	— —	— —	829 3,684	1,248 4,725	509 2,003
512.6	Inorganic esters, their salts and derivatives	— —	— —	5,494 5,671	— —	— —
512.7	Nitrogen-function compounds	2,035 37,787	1,644 20,294	6,104 83,823	15,391 270,424	13,841 255,127
512.8	Organo-inorganic and hetero-cyclic compounds	— —	964 465	441 392	121 104	455 117
513	**Inorganic Chemicals; Elements, Oxides and Halogen Salts**	— —	239 912	243 888	— —	— —
513.4	Halogen and sulphur compounds of non-metals or of metalloids	— —	— —	229 880	— —	— —
513.5	Metalic oxides, principally used in paints	— —	237 906	— —	— —	— —
514	**Other Inorganic Chemicals**	319 1,001	441 ...	826 1,199	413 1,835	— —
514.1	Metallic salts and peroxy-salts of inorganic acids	— —	— —	— —	— —	— —
514.2	Other metallic salts and peroxy-salts of inorganic acids (I)	319 1,001	314 1,000	— —	— —	— —
514.3	Other metallic salts and peroxy-salts of inorganic acids (II)	— —	— —	706 906	407 1,760	— —
53	**Dyeing, Tanning and Colouring Materials**	— —	867 ...	4,967 ...	355 ...	— —
531	**Synthetic Organic Dye-Stuffs, Natural Indigo and Colour Lakes**	— —	867 168	4,945 948	216 28	— —

Top line — value in thousand dollars
Bottom line — quantity in metric tons

Brit	Den	Norw	Swed	Austr	Switz	Japan	Canada	Total
279	—	—	—	—	—	—	—	671
...	—	—	—	—	—	—	—	1,327
565	310	—	—	—	—	2,391	—	5,852
...	1,200	—	—	—	—	11,591	—	23,203
—	—	—	—	—	—	—	—	5,494
—	—	—	—	—	—	—	—	5,671
1,100	—	—	—	—	—	52,644	—	92,759
...	—	—	—	—	—	...	—	667,455
1,177	163	—	—	—	17	3,627	—	6,965
...	44	—	—	—	116	7,219	—	8,457
872	—	—	—	—	—	1,078	—	2,432
...	—	—	—	—	—	2,895	—	4,695
782	—	—	—	—	—	—	—	1,011
...	—	—	—	—	—	—	—	880
—	—	—	—	—	—	—	—	237
—	—	—	—	—	—	—	—	906
1,324	—	—	—	—	—	14,708	—	18,031
...	—	—	—	—	—	454,449	—	458,942
534	—	—	—	—	—	—	—	534
...	—	—	—	—	—	—	—	...
687	—	—	—	—	—	—	—	1,320
...	—	—	—	—	—	—	—	2,001
—	—	—	—	—	—	—	—	1,113
—	—	—	—	—	—	—	—	2,666
261	—	—	—	—	1,552	963	—	8,965
...	—	—	—	—	...	...	—	...
238	—	—	—	—	1,517	666	—	8,449
53	—	—	—	—	242	224	—	1,663

III. Import of Chemicals – 10 –

1969 (3)

SITC Nos.	Description	Belg/Lux	France	W.Germ	Italy	Neth
533	**Pigments, Paints, Varnishes and Related Materials**	— —	— —	— —	139 1	— —
533.3	Prepared paints, enamels, lacquers, varnishes, artists' colours, siccatives (paint driers) and mastics	— —	— —	— —	139 1	— —
541	**Medical and Pharmaceutical Products**	— —	— —	711 17,100	— —	170 7,337
541.4	Opium alkaloids, cocaine, caffein, quinine and other vegetable alkaloids, their salts and other derivatives	— —	— —	711 17,100	— —	— —
541.7	Medicaments	— —	— —	— —	— —	— —
561	**Fertilizers, Manufactured**	4,026 168,607	591 25,940	6,864 259,053	7,948 288,933	6,714 240,466
561.1	Nitrogenous fertilizers and nitrogenous fertilizer materials (other than natural), n.e.s.	4,026 168,607	591 25,940	6,757 257,003	7,948 288,933	6,714 240,466
561.3	Potassic fertilizers and potassic fertilizer materials (other than crude natural potassic salts)	— —	— —	107 2,000	— —	— —
581	**Plastic Materials, Regenerated Cellulose and Artificial Resins**	182 110	253 1,311	773 2,514	2,144 10,960	176 503
581.1	Products of condensation, polycondensation and poly-addition (e.g., phenoplasts, aminoplasts, alkyds, polyallyl esters and other unsaturated polyesters, silicones)	— —	— —	345 116	— —	— —
581.2	Products of polymerisation and copolymerisation (e.g., polyethylene, polystyrene, polyvinyl, etc. derivatives, coumarone-indene resins	— —	215 1,280	416 2,390	2,124 10,953	102 476

Top line — value in thousand dollars
Bottom line — quantity in metric tons

Brit	Den	Norw	Swed	Austr	Switz	Japan	Canada	Total
—	—	—	—	—	—	297	—	436
—	—	—	—	—	—	104	—	105
—	—	—	—	—	—	171	—	310
—	—	—	—	—	—	50	—	51
462	—	—	—	—	175	103	—	1,621
...	—	—	—	—	3,603	...	—	28,040
120	—	—	—	—	112	—	—	943
...	—	—	—	—	291	—	—	17,391
304	—	—	—	—	—	103	—	407
...	—	—	—	—	—	...	—	...
1,456	—	2,490	—	—	—	18,774	—	48,863
...	—	54,752	—	—	—	627,827	—	1,665,578
1,456	—	—	—	—	—	18,774	—	46,266
—	—	—	—	—	—	627,827	—	1,608,776
—	—	—	—	—	—	—	—	107
—	—	—	—	—	—	—	—	2,000
—	—	—	—	—	—	11,770	—	15,298
—	—	—	—	—	—	41,147	—	56,545
—	—	—	—	—	—	1,084	—	1,429
—	—	—	—	—	—	...	—	116
—	—	—	—	—	—	10,389	—	13,246
—	—	—	—	—	—	40,733	—	55,832

1969 (4)

SITC Nos.	Description	Belg/Lux	France	W.Germ	Italy	Neth
581.3	Cellulose esters, cellulose ethers and other chemical derivatives of cellulose, regenerated cellulose and vulcanised fibre	169 63	— —	— —	— —	— —
599	**Chemical Materials and Products, N.E.S.**	— —	— —	3,409 3,558	978 2,020	— —
599.2	Insecticides, fungicides, disinfectants (including sheep and cattle dressing) and similar preparations	— —	— —	3,271 3,296	— —	— —
599.7	Organic chemical products, n.e.s.	— —	— —	— —	746 1,110	— —
599.9	Chemical products and preparations, n.e.s.	— —	— —	131 250	205 900	— —

Top line — value in thousand dollars
Bottom line — quantity in metric tons

Brit	Den	Norw	Swed	Austr	Switz	Japan	Canada	Total
—	—	—	—	—	—	297	—	466
—	—	—	—	—	—	414	—	477
1,266	—	—	—	—	—	1,789	—	7,442
...	—	—	—	—	—	4,246	—	9,824
—	—	—	—	—	—	1,789	—	5,060
—	—	—	—	—	—	4,246	—	7,542
549	—	—	—	—	—	—	—	1,295
...	—	—	—	—	—	—	—	1,110
716	—	—	—	—	—	—	—	1,052
...	—	—	—	—	—	—	—	1,150